# The Confidence Project

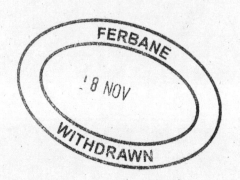

To Stephen, Judy and Steve – for helping me to build
a rock-solid foundation for my confident life.

# The Confidence Project

*Your plan for personal growth,
happiness and success*

## DR ROB YEUNG

JOHN
MURRAY
LEARNING

First published in Great Britain in 2017 by John Murray Learning.
An Hachette UK company.
Previously published as *Confidence 2.0*
Copyright © Rob Yeung 2017, 2019
*British Library Cataloguing in Publication Data:* a catalogue record for this title is available
from the British Library.
*Library of Congress Catalog Card Number:* on file.
ISBN: 978 1473 63417 6
eISBN: 978 1473 63419 0
1
The publisher has used its best endeavours to ensure that any website addresses referred to
in this book are correct and active at the time of going to press. However, the publisher and
the author have no responsibility for the websites and can make no guarantee that a site
will remain live or that the content will remain relevant, decent or appropriate.
The publisher has made every effort to mark as such all words which it believes to be
trademarks. The publisher should also like to make it clear that the presence of a word in
the book, whether marked or unmarked, in no way affects its legal status as a trademark.
Every reasonable effort has been made by the publisher to trace the copyright holders
of material in this book. Any errors or omissions should be notified in writing to the
publisher, who will endeavour to rectify the situation for any reprints and future editions.
Typeset by Cenveo® Publisher Services.
Printed and bound in Great Britain by Clays Ltd, Elcograf S.p.A.
John Murray Learning policy is to use papers that are natural, renewable and recyclable
products and made from wood grown in sustainable forests. The logging and manufacturing
processes are expected to conform to the environmental regulations of the country of origin.
Carmelite House
50 Victoria Embankment
London EC4Y 0DZ
www.hodder.co.uk

# Contents

# About the author

Psychologist Rob Yeung, PhD, is a bestselling author, thinker and adviser. His internationally bestselling books include *How to Stand Out: Proven Tactics for Getting Noticed* (Capstone) and *E is for Exceptional: The New Science of Success* (Pan Books).

He is an in-demand broadcaster and commentator and appears on major television shows globally including on the BBC, CNN and CNBC. He has written for newspapers and been quoted in publications including the *Financial Times*, *Daily Telegraph*, *Guardian* and *Wall Street Journal*.

Dr Yeung is also a keynote speaker who has spoken at conferences and corporate events all over the world. He is frequently asked to speak at conferences and runs workshops on topics such as the psychology of motivation, leadership, influence and persuasion, sales success, confidence, change and high achievement.

He has advised organizations ranging from large multinational corporations to smaller start-ups. And, when he can find the time to do so, he also coaches individuals and lectures to university and business school students.

www.robyeung.com
www.twitter.com/robyeung
www.facebook.com/drrobyeung

# Introduction

'You can't teach talent. You can't put in what God
left out – but you can teach confidence.'

*Gloria Naylor*

Welcome to *The Confidence Project*, a book that I hope will provide a useful new way of looking at the topic of confidence. Most of all, however, this book is about you, your confidence and what it can help you to do. So allow me to begin by asking you a question.

On a scale of 1 to 10, how confident would you say you are? Let's suppose that a 1 means you're filled with anxiety, worry and self-doubt over just about everything – both at work and in your personal life. You shy away from colleagues as well as people in social settings. You are troubled by much in life and find the world a very threatening place.

On the other hand, a 10 would mean that you feel completely confident in every area of your life. You are not only supremely at ease but quite certain that you can conquer all of life's challenges. You feel totally secure in your personal relationships and friendships. You know that you are brilliant at your job, too.

So where would you put yourself? Before we move on, can I suggest that you do give this a go and assign a number, a rating, to your confidence? In all likelihood, you are neither a 1 nor a 10. Clearly, exceptionally low confidence isn't a good thing: it would make everything in life quite difficult – speaking up at work, meeting new friends, dating, going for job interviews and generally having peace of mind.

But neither is extremely high confidence desirable. Now, you may imagine that more self-belief is a good thing. You may have picked up this book because you wanted to boost your confidence. And yes, *some* self-confidence is a good thing. But I'll show you that too much confidence can be as harmful as too little. In fact, a high level of fearlessness can occasionally be such a bad thing that I call it the curse of confidence. So this book is not only aimed at people who want to be bolder: it's also a warning and a set of recommendations for those who feel they are plenty confident as well.

Coming back to that 1–10 scale, I'll argue that the optimal amount of self-belief would put you only at a score of around 6 or 7 out of 10. No, really. You may find that surprisingly low – of course, I'll explain this fully later in the book. But that's already good news if you feel a little too timid. You don't need to aim to get to a 9 or 10 out of 10.

In our very first chapter, I'll show you that having too much confidence could in fact be problematic and self-defeating. And it's actually the people with only moderate levels of self-belief who do best.

## Understanding what really helps confidence

There are plenty of books around on the topic of confidence. However, I wanted to write a really easy-to-follow book to help everyone with their confidence. So that's both about supporting people who need greater confidence as well as advising individuals who perhaps need to steer clear of the little-recognized dangers of too much confidence.

But allow me to give you some context by explaining how I decided what to include in *The Confidence Project* – and what to leave out. To do so, here's a little thought experiment for you to consider.

Imagine for a moment that you get introduced to a friend of a friend – he's called Jack – who tells you about an experience he had to help him to feel more buoyant. He booked a session with a Mrs Dorothy Dreher, who was a neuro-dynamic confidence counsellor, apparently.

When he arrived at her office, he had been expecting someone in her fifties, but Mrs Dreher was probably in her mid-thirties. Dark hair pulled back into a ponytail. White blouse, dark skirt. Hint of an Eastern European accent.

Over the course of an hour, she helped him to achieve a deep state of relaxation. She played a CD of relaxing sounds: fat raindrops hitting wooden decking, bamboo wind chimes knocking together gently. She asked him to slow his breathing until he was nearly asleep.

Throughout the session, Mrs Dreher also asked Jack to tap the inside of his left wrist with his right index finger. Apparently, that was the neuro-dynamic bit: a technique of embedding the feeling of relaxed confidence into the deepest parts of his brain. With another four sessions, she said, it would reprogramme his brain to make that sense of confidence the new normal.

Yes, it was expensive, he tells you. But he has already paid for his next few sessions and can't wait to see the results.

So here's the question: would you give it a go? Would you pick up the telephone to book a session with Mrs Dreher?

Personally, I would want to know a lot more about this mysterious technique. Because we have no way of knowing purely from the recollections of a friend whether the treatment is genuinely helpful or merely an expensive waste of time.

Obviously, Jack felt that he benefited from it. But perhaps you're genuinely smarter and less naive. You're not the kind of person to fall for any old nonsense. And, of course, you don't want to be ripped off or to invest time in a method that's a dud.

Or, assuming that this so-called neuro-dynamic method does work – do you really need to visit Mrs Dreher and pay her eye-wateringly expensive fees? Could you get the same benefit from listening to a soundtrack of relaxing rain and chime sounds at home while occasionally tapping the inside of your wrist? Actually, is the tapping even necessary? Might it even be the case that simply listening to the relaxing sounds alone is enough to augment your confidence?

Unfortunately, we simply cannot know the answers to any of these questions. The testimony of a single – albeit utterly enthusiastic – individual just isn't enough.

The only way to find out would be to put the neuro-dynamic technique under proper scrutiny: to test its alleged benefits in a scientific experiment known as a randomized controlled trial (often abbreviated to RCT by researchers).

In RCT experiments, there are two main principles. The first is simply the need to test out the technique on sufficient numbers of people. Research scientists usually recruit dozens or even hundreds of folks into their studies rather than testing new methods out on only a single individual like Jack. Even a handful of people isn't enough. That way, they can tell whether a psychological technique works for *most* people.

Then, to figure out whether the tapping was truly an integral part of the technique, we would need to compare the tapping method against a plausible alternative. So we might instruct a group of people in the tapping over, say, the course of an hour. And we would invite a similar number of other folks to relax: to sit and listen to relaxing sounds for the same length of time.

If we thought that tapping should produce the more powerful boost to confidence, then the people in that group would be said to be in the experimental group. The people performing the plausible alternative would be in a control group – so-called because we're trying to control the experiment to rule out alternative explanations. And this is the second principle of scientific inquiry: the need for a control group.

Finally, we would ask our experimental participants to complete questionnaires measuring how they actually felt. Only by comparing the benefits that people reported in each group could we conclude what effects the neuro-dynamic technique actually had. Did it help people? Was it a waste of time? Or, even worse, did it actually harm people and make them feel less confident?

Of course, neuro-dynamic confidence counselling doesn't exist. It's something I made up. But the point is that this book is packed only with stuff that has been tested and shown to work.

## Harnessing the proven psychology of confidence

I work as a psychologist and I feel really passionately about the need for systematically tested advice. Because, without proper evidence for what works, we're all vulnerable to being taken advantage of.

> Without proper evidence for what works, we're all vulnerable to being taken advantage of.

We know there are people in all manner of trades and professions who are happy to make their living by ripping off or outright conning people. Everyone knows a horror story of an electrician or plumber, builder or decorator who charged a fortune but delivered massively substandard work. We hear of financial advisers and unscrupulous bankers who push financial products on to hapless customers who don't really understand what they've bought.

When it comes to our physical health, there are dodgy so-called nutrition experts prescribing expensive but ineffective diets for people struggling with troublesome medical conditions. And companies as well as individuals are selling alleged anti-ageing treatments that are either worthless or even harmful.

The same goes for our psychological health and well-being. Unfortunately, there are life coaches, motivational speakers, gurus and other advisers who are equally bad when it comes to boosting your confidence. Many of these advisers may be well intentioned. They may genuinely believe that their advice works.

But what if it doesn't? What if they're not just conning themselves – but the general public as well?

I want to protect you by offering you only proven methods to build your confidence, because that was the way I was trained when I did my two degrees in psychology. I completed an undergraduate degree in psychology at the University of Bristol and then a PhD, a doctorate in psychology at King's College London. And over the course of those six years of study, the one thing that was drilled, drilled, drilled into me was the importance of data-based evidence. No matter how much we sometimes may wish for something to work, we have to have proof that it works.

Now, as a practising psychologist, I try as far as possible to recommend techniques and interventions that have been backed by science. Whether I'm coaching an individual, running a workshop or speaking to a huge crowd at a conference, I don't just tell them what they should be doing. I explain why, too.

And that's what I aim to do with this book on confidence. Rather than merely telling you what you should be doing, I shall explain the experimental set-ups that researchers use in their studies. In this way, furnished with that extra background and the reasons why you should be using these techniques, you won't be taking only *my* word that these are effective interventions. You'll be reading about the evidence and judging for yourself that these work. By doing so, I hope that you'll feel more inspired to work the techniques into your own confidence project and stick with them.

Too often, so-called experts who tout solutions for low (or overly high) confidence do so based on opinion. But the solutions within this book are not based on the mere opinions of either myself or any other individuals; they are based on proven psychological research, which allows us to measure quite categorically what helps people with their confidence.

This book is filled with leading-edge advice. But I called this book *The Confidence Project* because I see it as a practical, helpful guide on how much confidence you need and how to make the most of yourself.

So remember, as we continue through the book, that these are not merely techniques that I have dreamed up. There is scientific knowledge underpinning every piece of advice.

But this isn't going to be a dry treatise about confidence. It's intended to be an intensely practical book for anyone interested in how to reprogramme thoughts, feelings and behaviours. You'll learn how to apply new psychological principles and use techniques to upgrade either your life or the lives of those around you.

And, as we explore the psychology of confidence, we shall see that there is genuine cause to be optimistic. You *can* be more confident.

---

There is genuinely cause to be optimistic. You *can* be more confident.

---

## *Navigating through* The Confidence Project

If you feel that either you or someone close to you does *not* need more confidence, you'll find advice on this special situation in Chapter 1. But, for the most part, this book is about feeling more confident, behaving more confidently and ultimately crafting a more confident life.

That can take many forms. Perhaps you crave more confidence when giving presentations or going for job interviews. Maybe you want to stand up for yourself more – whether that's with colleagues at work or domineering members of the family or friends. You may wish to network more assuredly at professional gatherings or make a better impression at social events, parties and on dates. Perhaps you're a dancer, a musician, an entertainer, an athlete who needs to perform at your very best during auditions or overcome your nerves in sporting arenas.

Or maybe you're hoping to change the trajectory of your life. You may feel that you're stuck in a difficult situation and have a pressing need to get out – or you got out but want help in moving on fully. Perhaps you would love to start up a business or embark on some new venture. Maybe you want to get better at handling criticism and rejection. Or you wish you could feel less fearful so that you can live your life more fully. Whatever your circumstances, I hope to provide you with advice that has been shown to make a difference.

To these ends, I'll be covering both speedy techniques as well as more deeply effective strategies. I've structured the book into four parts and a conclusion as follows:

- **Part I: Understanding the consequences and complications of confidence.** In this first part of the book, I'll do away with some outdated ideas about confidence. Yes, experts used to think not so long ago that high self-confidence was always desirable, but modern psychology punctures such claims. I already mentioned that too much self-belief may harm rather than help us – so why is that? And what can we do to avoid such pitfalls? Another myth: that folks who behave confidently in public must also feel confident privately. In actuality, we'll see that some people who act boldly may secretly be tormented by insecurity and self-doubt. That's because there's a big difference between *feeling* confident and *behaving* confidently. Confident feelings and confident behaviour are separate things. I call them inward-emotional confidence versus outward-social confidence. Maybe you want assistance only with one or the other sort – or both. So in the two chapters that make up Part I, I'll upgrade your understanding on the nature of modern-day confidence.

- **Part II: Increasing your inward-emotional confidence.** I mentioned the difference between feeling confident and behaving more confidently and this part tackles the feeling bit of the equation. Countless people agonize over past mistakes, failures, criticisms or rejections and relive them over and over again in their minds. Others worry about their present circumstances. And still others can't help but fret about what might go wrong in the days, months or years to come. 'What if I lose my job?' 'What if my partner leaves me and I'm left with nothing?' 'What if the audience laughs at me?' So many people are troubled by feelings of anxiety, distressing mental images or negative thoughts. But there is good news: there are plenty of simple but proven techniques that can help you to tackle bothersome feelings (Chapter 3), images (Chapter 4) and thoughts (Chapter 5).

- **Part III: Enhancing your outward-social confidence.** Part III will focus on the skills, strategies and simple rules that we can all apply when we want to broadcast confidence so that other people see us at our best. These chapters will cover scenarios such as giving speeches and presentations, standing out during job interviews or auditions, asserting ourselves and engaging in conversations whether with friends or potential romantic partners. I'll also include research-backed guidance on both dating and maintaining fulfilling, long-term relationships. Some of these tactics involve changes to our body language, our use of eye contact, our posture. Other techniques are more psychological in nature but have still been shown to give folks demonstrable boosts to their credibility, their likeability, their impact.

- **Part IV: Cultivating lifelong confidence.** I've already mentioned that true, deep, lasting confidence doesn't come about immediately. And, in this part of the book, I'll delve into several of the more involved methods that have been shown to bring about profound, literally life-changing levels of confidence. We'll discuss problem-solving strategies for tackling life's most difficult obstacles and opportunities. We'll look at how deep-rooted ways of thinking about yourself and the world can either support or stall your attempts to feel stronger. And we shall explore how you can set effective goals and achieve the kind of life that will genuinely contribute to your well-being and peace of mind.

- **Conclusions: Onwards, upwards and over to you.** By the time you've read the four main parts of this book, we will have discussed several dozen different techniques, exercises, tactics and rules for changing not only how you see yourself but also how you behave. It would be overwhelming to try to do everything at once and I suggest that you need to be more strategic, choosy and careful about how you spend your time. So I'll end the book by giving you some practical advice on how to pull it all together into a personal plan that will deliver results week after week, and month after month.

## Over to you

I hope that *The Confidence Project* isn't a book that you read. Well, of course I hope you read it. But I don't want you to *just* read it and then set it aside. I fervently hope that you will apply what you learn, that you will put pen to paper or fingers on keyboard to make a few notes or do the occasional exercise. I hope you will not only try the techniques once or twice but practise them enough that they become familiar and genuinely helpful.

Throughout the book, then, I will include boxes like this one to summarize exactly what you need to do in order to upgrade your confidence. My suggestion is to take your time with the book. Over the weeks and months to come, I sincerely hope that you will return frequently to the boxes scattered across these pages in furtherance of your confidence project.

There is also a glossary at the end of the book with a handy reminder of all the terminology that we cover.

## *Taking a modern look at confidence*

Whether you're reading this book to aid yourself or someone else in your life, I'm certain that you will come across genuinely new insights into the true nature of confidence. Actually, psychologists don't really even use the word 'confidence'. Different researchers refer to various specific, technical concepts such as self-efficacy, self-esteem, optimism, resilience, coping and psychological well-being. But you won't have to worry about any of those. My job is to wade into the morass of jargon to pick out what will actually enable you to feel stronger and get real results.

As we travel together from one chapter to the next, we'll look at techniques drawn from fields including sport psychology, cognitive behavioural therapy and neuroscience. We will review time-honoured approaches such as mindfulness and using your body language to best effect. And we'll investigate newer confidence-upgrading techniques such as imagery rescripting, cognitive defusion and hemispheric activation, too.

We will also examine some of the controversies in the field of confidence-building research. For instance, you may have heard of something that has been called the power pose. The original claim was that assuming a commanding posture – standing tall with your feet apart and your hands on your hips – actually boosts the dominance hormone testosterone and reduces levels of the stress hormone cortisol. However, recent research has disputed this. So what's going on? What helps your confidence – and what doesn't?

We'll debunk myths along the way as well. An example: it is often assumed that extraverts are always confident while introverts are always anxious and self-doubting. But we shall discover the truth is that many extraverts don't actually feel terribly confident. At the same time, introverts can feel absolutely secure and happy within themselves.

> Many extraverts don't actually feel terribly confident. At the same time, introverts can feel absolutely secure and happy within themselves.

By the time we get to the end of *The Confidence Project*, you'll be able to separate the facts from the hype. And you'll be equipped to begin a personal project that will genuinely make a difference to either your life or the lives of those around you – no matter how much (or how little) confidence you have.

Anyway, enough of the preamble; it's time to get started by exploring why you may not need as much self-belief as you think you do. In fact, I'll show you in our first chapter that too much confidence may actually be quite debilitating.

# PART I

# Understanding the consequences and complications of confidence

# 1

# Beating the curse of confidence

'Well, I think we tried very hard not to
be overconfident, because when you get
overconfident, that's when something snaps up
and bites you.'

*Neil Armstrong*

Imagine you're flicking through the TV channels and you come across a talent show. Maybe it's *The X Factor* or *Britain's Got Talent*. It could be *The Voice*, *American Idol* or any one of the many copycat shows. A thin, young man perhaps in his mid-twenties steps in front of the judges. He has a smattering of acne across his cheeks. He boldly, loudly announces, 'Hello, my name's Paul.'

He takes a deep breath and exhales slowly, his lips pursed. He opens his mouth to sing and out comes a horrendous, tuneless wail. It truly is awful, but the judges allow him to sing his whole audition piece. The judges are fighting not to laugh but can't help smirking or even giggling a little.

When Paul finishes, the judges tell him gently that he has no talent, that he really can't sing. But the would-be pop star gets angry. He disagrees. He snaps at the judges that he is hugely gifted – that they simply can't recognize true talent. He says he's going to get a record deal and sell more records than Michael Jackson or the Beatles. And, with a snarl on his face, he storms out, shouting something sufficiently offensive at the judges that the producers have to bleep it out.

I'm sure you're familiar with these kinds of auditions: where people really, really can't sing but believe that they can. And it's not just in English-speaking countries like the UK, the USA and Australia where you see such car-crash auditions. These TV formats are so supremely successful that there's hardly a country in the world that doesn't have one on its screens. In France, they have *La France a un incroyable talent* while the Arab world has *Arabs Got Talent*. Colombia has *El Factor X* and Lithuania *X Faktorius*. China has *Chinese Idol* while Poland's version is simply called *Idol*.

The filmed humiliation of these so-bad-they're-good contestants is enjoyed by all sorts of people worldwide. And perhaps one of the reasons such shows command enormous viewing audiences is because they allow folks at home to see what confidence looks like. And there's nothing that viewers love more than when that self-confidence puts on an ugly show.

How dreadful must it be to believe totally and truly that you're great at something and destined for success – when precisely the opposite is true? The combination of utterly high self-confidence and excruciatingly low competence makes these auditions shockingly watchable.

But we mostly watch these deluded contestants safe in the knowledge that such a degree of wrongheaded self-belief could never apply to us. Ha – aren't they stupid? That could never happen to us, right?

Wrong.

Here's the bad news: a staggeringly large proportion of people are actually rather overconfident in their abilities. Yes, there are *plenty* of folks who overestimate themselves – they're simply far too fearless. And even if you feel you're lacking in self-belief, you may be surprised to hear that you may still be overconfident in at least some parts of your life.

> Even if you feel you're lacking in self-belief, you may be surprised to hear that you may still be overconfident in at least some parts of your life.

## *Considering your own ability levels*

How would you rate your various skills and abilities? Compared to the rest of the people in the country, how would you rate yourself as a communicator, a team player, an organizer, a friend?

But perhaps those are overly complex talents. Your definition of being a good communicator or team player may differ from mine. So let's simplify things by looking at one, much more narrowly defined, skill: compared to the rest of humanity, how good would you say you are at logical reasoning?

To give you an idea of what I mean by logical reasoning, here's an example question: 'Everyone who is kind is compassionate, and someone who has experienced adversity is always kind. Eleanor is compassionate, so she has experienced adversity. Is the statement about Eleanor true or false?'

I'll put the answer to the question in the notes at the end of the book.[1] But suppose for a moment that I persuade you to take a timed test with 20 of these questions. The example about Eleanor is a relatively easy one to start with. Imagine that subsequent questions get evermore difficult until your head is practically hurting from the effort of figuring them out.

Immediately after the test, I ask you to rate your performance as compared with other people of your age and education level. But I'd like you to rate yourself in a very particular way: I want you to allocate yourself to a percentile. For example, if you put yourself at the 80th percentile, you would be saying that you think you're better than 80 per cent of people of your age and education level. Putting it another way, you reckon you're in the top 20 per cent of the pack. Or, if you put yourself at the 35th percentile, you're better than only 35 per cent of people. So nearly two-thirds of people are better than you.

So go on. Just for fun, make a mental note of your percentile figure.

Now this series of steps is pretty much what two psychology researchers did in an eye-opening experiment on the dark side of confidence. Justin Kruger and David Dunning at world-famous Cornell University recruited several dozen undergraduates to take a 20-question logical reasoning test. Immediately afterwards, the investigators asked all the participants in the experiment to rate their own logical reasoning ability by way of a percentile ranking.[2]

The crusading scientists' first observation was that participants on average placed themselves at the 66th percentile. Mathematically, we would expect for half of the participants to be better than average and half to be worse than average, with an average rating at the 50th percentile. So the researchers could already see that more people were overestimating their ability than underestimating it.

But Kruger and Dunning made a more momentous discovery. The most incompetent logical reasoners (who on average had scored at the 12th percentile) believed that they had scored at the 68th percentile. In other words, these weak performers who were worse than nearly 9 in 10 people actually thought that they were better than nearly 7 in 10 people. These participants didn't think that they were just a little better than they actually were – they were massively, hugely, overwhelmingly overconfident about their logical reasoning skills.

## Appreciating the true scale of overconfidence

Logical reasoning is a somewhat obscure intellectual skill. So let's look at a more relevant, interpersonal one. People who feel that they lack confidence often wish they could be more assertive. Would you say that you're under-assertive (i.e. you don't speak up enough), over-assertive (i.e. you are sometimes a little too pushy) or appropriately assertive?

Exploring the precise issue of people's assertiveness skills, Columbia University research collaborators Daniel Ames and Abbie Wazlawek recruited 169 pairs of business students to engage in a negotiation skills test. One person in each pair was instructed to act as the seller of a product and the other person the buyer. After 20 minutes of haggling over a deal, all the participants were asked to rate both their own levels of assertiveness as well as those of their counterparts.

Analysing the results, the researchers immediately spotted a fairly major discrepancy between how participants were perceived by their opposite numbers and how they saw themselves. Sixty-seven per cent of those who were rated as under-assertive by their counterparts thought that they had been appropriate or even over-assertive. And 64 per cent of those who were rated as over-assertive by their counterparts believed that they had been appropriate or even under-assertive.

In both cases, then, approximately two-thirds of people got it incorrect. Individuals who actually needed to speak up more believed that they were either just assertive enough or even too pushy. But, more notably, people who were perceived as too pushy generally thought they either had got it right or were not assertive enough.

In other words, there were considerable numbers of people who believed that they were too quiet and meek but were judged by others to have been too talkative or even aggressive. Or, to phrase it slightly differently yet again, even people who feel less than entirely confident may actually be seen by others as overconfident.

> Even people who feel less than entirely confident may actually be seen by others as overconfident.

So yes. Even if you feel rather tentative, there's still a chance that the rest of the world will think otherwise.

We could look at more individual studies demonstrating that so many people are overconfident, but we don't need to. In 2014 social psychologist Ethan Zell at the University of North Carolina at

Greensboro and his collaborator Zlatan Krizan at Iowa State University published a definitive review of the research on overconfidence. They summarized the results of several thousand original studies looking at people's estimations of diverse abilities such as academic aptitude, raw intelligence, language skills, memory capacity, medical competence and even sporting prowess. Sadly, the researchers concluded that 'people have only moderate insight into their abilities'.[3]

*Moderate* isn't exactly great, is it?

But that's what the facts tell us. Remember that this is a conclusion based not on just one or two studies but several *thousand*. *Most* people – young and old, male and female, and from all walks of life – get it wrong.

OK. Perhaps you're convinced that *many* people are overconfident in some way. No doubt you can bring to mind examples of colleagues, perhaps even family members or friends, who think they're better than they actually are. But do you continue to think of yourself as more self-aware, more acutely attuned to your personal weaknesses, flaws and failings? So it's still *other* people that are overconfident, but not you?

To convince you that you – yes, *even you* – probably fall prey to bouts of overconfidence about at least *some* of your traits, skills or abilities, I'll tell you about one more study. In this experiment, Stanford University psychologists Emily Pronin, Daniel Lin and Lee Ross asked 91 Stanford students to rate themselves on six personality dimensions relative to other Stanford students. Three of these personality traits were positive (dependability, consideration for others and objectivity) while three were negative (snobbery, selfishness and deceptiveness).

After the students rated themselves, they were told to read a paragraph about the human tendency to be overconfident:

> Studies have shown that on the whole, people show a 'better than average' effect when assessing themselves relative to other members within a group. That is, 70–80 per cent of individuals consistently rate themselves 'better than average' on qualities that they perceive as positive, and conversely, evaluate themselves as having 'less than average' amounts of characteristics they believe are negative.

After being taught about their likely levels of overconfidence, the participants were given the chance to revise their self-judgements.

But even this piece of knowledge didn't make a difference: 87 per cent of the participants still believed that they were better than average on the six characteristics.[4]

Eighty-seven per cent! That's nearly nine in ten people. Or pretty much everybody, really.

Permit me to spell out the implications. People in this carefully constructed investigation were specifically taught about their likely overconfidence. But the overwhelming majority of them *still* believed that they were above average. So, even though you have read about this very same piece of research, the chances are that you, too, probably still believe that you're better than you actually are in at least *some* areas of your life.

## Comprehending the costs of high self-confidence

OK, I hope I've demonstrated that most people inadvertently overestimate themselves. So that means that a lot of folks – including you and me – are at least a little overconfident. So what? Should that really concern anybody?

A forty-something friend called Georgina is currently dating. She got married at the age of 20 but it lasted only a few years. And through her twenties and thirties she had a handful of fairly serious relationships, some of them lasting months and a few lasting a year or two. She didn't date at all for quite a few years. But several years ago she gamely plunged into the world of online dating.

Georgina gets plenty of interest: she has a ready smile, startling blue eyes fringed with long lashes and, with her unlined face, could pass for someone five or more years younger. Terribly, though, she seems locked into an unhappy pattern: men are initially very keen, but they end the nascent relationship after weeks or only a handful of months.

It's a shame, because she is vivacious, chatty, well read and media savvy: as capable of debating politics in the Middle East as the latest Taylor Swift video. She is socially adventurous, too: she loves dining at just-opened restaurants, discovering cool cocktail bars and kicking her high heels off on the dance floor.

If you met her, you'd say that she was confident. Georgina would agree that she's confident as well. But that's possibly the root of her relationship conundrum. She may be *too* confident.

Yes, she is vivacious and well informed. But she often talks too much. She can dominate conversations or be overly vigorous in voicing opinions. And her thrill-seeking streak means that she has a low boredom threshold. She thinks it's dull to visit the same venue twice and hates the idea of 'quiet nights in'.

I once tried to share my observations with her: that she could talk less and listen more. That she could compromise occasionally when choosing entertainments and activities. But my counsel was batted aside. She told me that she *knows* she's fantastic company. She's convinced that she is a great partner so she's unwilling to do anything differently.

Or consider someone I've encountered called Thomas, a lawyer by training. A silver-haired 52-year-old with nearly three decades of experience, he graduated from a top university and has worked for some of the most prestigious law firms around.

He is intelligent, charming and persuasive – he makes a superb first impression with clients, for example. And, in pursuit of his goals, he is dogged, tenacious and willing to work unspeakably long hours.

Regrettably, he has had to change jobs many times. He has been fired three times in his career and quit in frustration several more times. Each time, he has blamed circumstances or other people: a general downturn in the economy, the ineptitude of his boss, the stupidity of his clients and so on. But he has a reputation among his friends – both those who know him from legal circles as well as people who know him through other avenues – for being prickly, quick to judge and hot-tempered. He can be enthusiastic one day but angry or sarcastic the next. As you can imagine, none of this endears him to his workmates.

The worst thing for Thomas, sadly, is that he does not see his own flaws. He is confident that he is a proficient lawyer and that any firm would be lucky to have him. Perhaps he justifies his behaviour to an extent as the natural result of his being a tough and uncompromising leader. But the result is still the same: while he makes electrifying early impressions with both clients and co-workers, he doesn't learn.

He keeps making the same mistakes. He has had to move on from one job to the next so many times – and he will likely have to do so again and again in the future.

Of course, such individual cases may be idiosyncratic and unrepresentative of most people. But more rigorous studies also point to a similar conclusion: that overly high self-confidence may be harmful rather than helpful. Enter Randall Colvin, a scientist at Northeastern University who has been at the forefront of research into overconfidence for over two decades. He and his band of behavioural scientists began a provocative study by persuading over a hundred undergraduates to undergo three stages of evaluation in their laboratory.

> Overly high self-confidence may be harmful rather than helpful.

First, the participants filled in a battery of questionnaires, rating themselves on a number of personality and social characteristics. Second, each participant was rated by two of his or her peers – friends or family members – on the same characteristics.

Professor Colvin and his crew combined the self-ratings and peer ratings to calculate the extent to which participants had been overconfident about themselves. For example, if a participant said that he was 'very popular' but his two peers said that he was only 'moderately popular', that indicated a degree of overconfidence. On the other hand, if a participant said that he was 'quite popular' but his peers reported that he was either 'quite popular' or even 'very popular', that would imply a level of self-awareness or even modesty.

The third stage in the evaluation was to video-record all the participants for five minutes debating a tricky topic with someone they had never met before. Moments before hitting the record button on the video camera, the experimenter read out the following instructions:

> The next part calls for you to have a little debate. Specifically, the topic we have people debate is the use of capital punishment, because most people can come up with at least some arguments on both sides of that issue.

After collecting hours and hours of footage, the researchers asked a panel of independent observers to watch the videos and rate each of the participants on how they came across. Finally, Colvin's team were able to compare participants' tendency to overestimate themselves with the ratings that they were given by the independent observers.

Male participants who rated themselves more highly than they were rated by their peers 'were observed to speak quickly, to interrupt their [conversational] partner, to brag, and to express hostility'. In contrast, men who had not been overconfident about themselves 'were found to exhibit social skills, to express sympathy and liking toward their partner, and to be liked by their partner'.

Female participants who were overly bold about themselves were also rated by the independent observers more poorly. These women were 'described as seeking reassurance from their partner, as acting in an irritable fashion, and as exhibiting an awkward interpersonal style'. On the other hand, women who did not overestimate themselves 'were observed to exhibit social skills, to enjoy the interaction with their partner, to like and be liked by their partner, and appear to be relaxed and comfortable'.[5]

The implication is that people who overestimate their skills and attributes may be seen as possessing poorer social skills than those individuals who are more realistic or even modest about themselves. Overconfidence can be a bad thing.

> People who overestimate their skills and attributes may be seen as possessing poorer social skills than those individuals who are more realistic or even modest about themselves.

Why? Well, think about synonyms and associated words for overconfidence: arrogance, conceitedness, self-importance, ego, superiority, self-delusion, smugness, even narcissism. And such was the level of overconfidence in these participants that it was detectable by strangers watching them in only a five-minute video.

## *Understanding the reasons behind overconfidence*

What happens to overconfident people over time? As they age, do they become more mature and self-aware? As the years pass, do they perhaps learn to rein in their worst impulses?

In order to answer such questions, Randall Colvin and his entourage ran a follow-up study in which they tracked 101 young adults over a five-year period. Think about that for a moment. Five years is a long time. Imagine starting a project but having to wait not just one or two but a whole five years to finish it. That's rare in psychological studies, so the campaigning researchers should be commended for that alone.

As before, Colvin's team evaluated men and women at the start of the project; they assessed the participants again after five years had passed. On analysing the results, the researchers found that both men and women who overestimated themselves at the start of the investigation became *increasingly* hostile, defensive and even 'guileful and deceitful'. Far from being an issue that went away as people got older, it seemed that the problem of their overconfidence ballooned.

Why? Why on earth would anyone behave in such a manner?

Because it's a form of psychological self-protection, concluded Colvin and his compatriots. For such individuals, it's a way of artificially buoying their self-esteem and enabling themselves to feel good.

People with a healthy sense of self-esteem base their estimations on their real accomplishments, their actual relationships and the fact that they genuinely possess certain skills and traits. But overconfident people elevate their self-esteem unhealthily by deceiving themselves that they are better than they actually are: burying their heads in the sand rather than acknowledging what's really going on around them.

However, this inflated level of self-esteem is fragile. It's not based on reality. So overconfident individuals may try to defend it by engaging in what psychologists call downward social comparisons – or what ordinary people might call put-downs and insults. By knocking others, such individuals hope to lift themselves up. Overly bold individuals also tend to take less responsibility for their mistakes or harmful actions; they are more likely to blame bad luck or other people than themselves.

Unsurprisingly, Colvin and his colleagues warned that such behaviour might maintain self-esteem 'but at a continual and cumulative cost of alienating one's friends and discouraging new acquaintances'. After all, who wants to be friends with individuals who put down or blame others and who stridently believe they are better than they actually are? Not me. And probably not you, either.

> Who wants to be friends with individuals who put down or blame others and who stridently believe they are better than they actually are?

Appallingly, more people seem to have unhealthily inflated self-esteem than healthy high self-esteem. Or at least that's the conclusion reached by Roy Baumeister, a professor of psychology at Florida State University and one of the most prolific research psychologists of all time. In a now-famous 2003 paper, he and his colleagues published a major review of the several thousand research studies that had looked at the benefits of high self-esteem.

Their verdict: high self-esteem was far from a good thing. In fact, they warned that people who are possessed of high self-esteem tend to 'regard themselves as having an impressive range of superior social skills, but ... these skills are not readily discerned or confirmed by others'.[6]

Ouch. In other words, just because someone thinks that he or she is the life and soul of the party doesn't mean that others agree.

Furthermore, the psychologists wrote: 'We have not found evidence that boosting self-esteem ... causes benefits.' Indeed, they concluded that efforts to elevate self-esteem in either adults or children were simply not defensible.

The write-up by Baumeister and his associates was so stunningly damning that most reputable psychologists have since stopped talking about high self-esteem as a worthwhile goal. It's almost a shame, as there are plenty of tricks that can be used to augment your self-esteem. For example, you can remind yourself of your achievements. You can make lists of reasons why you're better than the people around you. Or you can seek compliments and praise from other people. But remember that high self-esteem is perhaps best thought of as a form of self-trickery, an unwarranted set of beliefs that may end up alienating others.

> High self-esteem is perhaps best thought of as a form of self-trickery, an unwarranted set of beliefs that may end up alienating others.

## Moving focus away from 1.0 self-esteem to 2.0 confidence

Be careful when you come across writers or advisers who want to help you with your self-esteem. It is true that working on your self-esteem may allow you to feel more self-assured. But this is a rather old-fashioned and not entirely healthy form of confidence that is no longer championed by most psychologists. Remember that Baumeister's critique was published way back in 2003. And evidence suggests that people with high self-esteem can end up engaging in questionable tactics, such as putting others down or ignoring problems in order to defend their self-worth.

So we won't be looking again at self-esteem. As we discuss boosting confidence in the rest of this book, we shall instead discuss more modern methods of fostering freedom from *inappropriate* worry and *unhelpful* levels of anxiety and other negative emotions. We will never aim to be entirely free from self-doubt, because reflection and self-questioning are entirely healthy – they help us to ensure that we really are on track to getting good results in the real world.

We will also look at developing something that psychologists call your self-efficacy – your belief in your ability to conquer genuine challenges – which has been shown countless times to boost people's ultimate performance in all sorts of tasks. So even though I'd like us to move away from the 1.0 concept of self-esteem, I promise that we will still discuss many 2.0 ways to assist you to feel more positive and achieve your goals in life.

## *Harnessing the objectivity of others*

We've talked about overconfidence in social settings. But what about at work? Does it matter if a person's self-perceptions differ from the perceptions of their co-workers?

Before I answer such questions, could I ask you quickly to rate your agreement or disagreement with four short statements, please? For each statement, choose a rating from one of the following:

1 = Strongly disagree
2 = Slightly disagree
3 = Neither disagree nor agree
4 = Slightly agree
5 = Strongly agree

Here are the statements:

- I think of myself as someone who is a reliable worker.
- I think of myself as someone who does a thorough job.
- I think of myself as someone who perseveres until a task is completed.
- I think of myself as someone who makes plans and follows through with them.

The set of statements measure a personality dimension that psychologists typically call Conscientiousness, which indicates the extent to which a person is thorough, careful and disciplined. Someone who scores highly on Conscientiousness tends to be organized and dependable. Someone who scores lower may prefer things to be less structured and to live their lives more impulsively.

Many dozens of studies have found that young people who are higher on Conscientiousness tend to do better in their academic studies. So schoolchildren and university students who are more thorough and disciplined tend to get better grades.[7] Hardly surprising, right?

Scores of other studies have probed how this personality trait predicts performance at work as judged by people's bosses or colleagues. Typically, these studies also find that people who are higher on Conscientiousness tend to be more successful at work. Again, it's hardly shocking news to hear that people who are organized and meticulous tend to do better at work.

But here's the thing. Individuals' performance is only weakly predicted by their judgements of their own personalities. The biggest predictor of both academic and job performance is *other* people's judgements of individuals' personalities.

If you look back at those questions, you may be able to see why. *Most* people would say that they are 'reliable workers' – even some who are arguably a bit lazy. A lot of people would describe themselves as 'thorough' or the kinds of people who persevere with tasks – even though their co-workers or friends or family might laughingly disagree.[8]

Data sleuths Brian Connelly of the University of Toronto and Deniz Ones of the University of Minnesota wrote arguably the definitive paper on the predictive power of self-ratings (i.e. the judgements that we make of ourselves) versus other ratings (i.e. the judgements that other people – our friends, family, bosses and colleagues – make of us). Looking at the many hundreds of studies on the topic, they conducted a massive statistical analysis to see which of the two proved the better predictor of actual career success. In the final paragraphs of their report, they observed that 'traits predicted academic achievement and job performance considerably better when ratings came from others than when they came from the self'.[9]

In other words, the people around us typically know us better than we know ourselves. We are not accurate at identifying our own strengths and shortcomings at work. And when it comes to predicting how well we might do in our studies or at work, our personal judgements are pretty much worthless.

> When it comes to predicting how well we might do in our studies or at work, our personal judgements are pretty much worthless.

You can see how it could hurt people's livelihoods. Someone with high self-esteem may *believe* that she's a superstar singer, dancer or competitive athlete. So she might waste time and money pursuing that career even when the best coaching in the world might only make her mediocre. A would-be entrepreneur who *believes* in himself could pour money into his business venture despite not having the skills, experience, contacts or motivation to prosper.

Even without believing that they're great, people are still at risk of overconfidence. Suppose someone thinks she's a little worse than average at analysing data or giving presentations. But if in reality she's *far* worse than average, that's still a form of overconfidence. She could end up becoming complacent because she thinks she's good enough. She could subconsciously avoid or outright ignore good advice from knowledgeable people that might puncture her illusions.

## *Steering a path between overconfidence and lack of self-belief*

Now I'm not saying that you are overconfident about *everything* in your life. You may have fairly decent insight into what you're good and not good at. But the chances are there will be *something* – some skill, some domain of knowledge, some trait – that you overestimate.

Here's where it can get a bit seemingly contradictory, though. Yes, we've been talking about overconfidence. But the big statistical analysis by Connelly and Ones didn't just find that *everybody* overestimates themselves. It concluded only that people rarely had entirely accurate pictures about themselves. Yes, some people overestimate themselves. But some people underestimate themselves, too. And that can be equally damaging. People who could genuinely become good entertainers or entrepreneurs, chefs or chief executives, might otherwise fail to pursue their callings.

There's an incredibly important lesson here for all of us, then, no matter how much – or how little – confidence we may have in ourselves and our abilities. Even though it sounds unlikely, we have to trust the evidence. If there's only one thing to take from this chapter, it's that other people tend to be more accurate in their evaluations of us than we are about ourselves.

> Other people tend to be more accurate in their evaluations of us than we are about ourselves.

So don't rely on your own opinions. You can only know which skills you are overestimating and which ones you are actually underestimating by seeking the judgement of the people around you.

But it's crucial here to seek the opinions only of *knowledgeable* people who can give you constructive criticism. Don't fall into the same trap as those TV talent show wannabes. They probably get told all the time by family and friends that they are exceptional singers. But I would contend that they shouldn't be asking friends and family for advice unless they're in the music industry and can provide them with genuinely useful comments.

I'm not trying to put you off your dreams. If you aspire to be an entertainer or an athlete or a business owner or a manager or anything else, go for it. But to afford yourself the very best chance of succeeding, seek feedback from people who are genuinely knowledgeable about what you want to do, who have legitimate experience in your field of interest and deep insights to offer. You need to speak to people who have a track record of success and the ability to point out and correct flaws. Don't just rely on the opinions of your best mates or the people who love you.

## Seeking out genuinely helpful feedback

Getting opinions and advice from other people can be an immensely useful exercise. You will almost certainly be enlightened about weaknesses that you need to work on. At the same time, you may be pleasantly surprised to find that you're significantly better at some other skills than you thought – and that may mean that you just don't have to worry about those parts of yourself.

In addition, I'm sure that you can think of some people around you – either in your personal or professional life – who could arguably do with a dose of reality. So why not encourage them to read this chapter?

In my experience, here are three tips that will enable you to get good-quality feedback:

## 1. Give people permission to give you negative feedback.

If I were to ask my close friends how I am as a friend, the chances are that they would gush about my positive attributes. But if I really want to learn how I could be a better friend, I would need to make it abundantly clear that I'm looking for constructive criticism about what I could do better. Think about how you phrase your request to spur your friends, family, colleagues, customers or whoever to impart the truth about what you could change.

## 2. If you can, seek anonymous, written feedback.

An experiment by Australian academics Carla Jeffries and Matthew Hornsey looked at ways of getting better-quality feedback. When participants were asked to critique a written essay and told that they would need to deliver the feedback face-to-face to the person who wrote the essay, they tended to give trite, positive feedback about the essay. It was only when they were allowed to appraise the essays and deliver their comments anonymously that they gave more negative but constructively critical feedback.[10]

Of course, it involves more work on your part to ask people for anonymous comments – you may have to appeal to a friend or co-worker to collect evaluations for you. Or you could email people and ask them to send you anonymous letters with their comments in the post. But if you can't do that, then at least plead for written feedback in the first instance. People are more likely to tell you bad news about you when they can think of a way to phrase it in writing than if you are standing there glowering at them.

## 3. Thank everybody and be gracious.

Criticism hurts. You won't enjoy hearing it. And you may want to justify yourself or explain certain mitigating circumstances.

But I strongly suggest that you don't. Because anything you say could easily come across as defensive. Instead, just thank the person who gave you the feedback. Tell them that you appreciate their candidness. And then go home to think about what you've been told.

One last point about feedback: the best way to think of criticism is that it is a gift. Whenever I lecture business school students or run seminars for executives on how to get ahead in their careers, I always reiterate this point. Constructive criticism benefits you more than the person giving it to you. You may learn to avoid making the same error again. You may discover how to make better use of your time or how to address your shortcomings. You get the chance to change your ways and set yourself up for future success.

So always, always, always treat criticism as a gift. And respond accordingly. Be utterly thankful – as much as if someone had bestowed upon you a big box covered in shiny wrapping paper and finished off with ribbons. Or it may just reduce the chance that you ever receive the gift again.

## *Understanding the value of middling confidence*

Allow me to finish this chapter by returning to the very first idea I pitched to you at the beginning of the book. You may remember that I asked you to rate your overall levels of self-confidence on a scale of 1 to 10. And I said that the optimal amount would put you at a score of around 6 but no more than 7 out of 10. I hope that you now appreciate why: superior self-belief is rarely matched by equally superior skill.

Allow me to summarize the argument graphically. Figure 1.1 shows a diagram that I presented at a recent conference on the dangers of overconfidence in leaders and, indeed, employees of all disciplines.

As you can see, I argue that people with only moderate levels of confidence do best. Statisticians would call the graph an inverted-U, but I habitually describe it more as a hill. So people who feel very

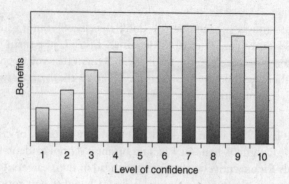

FIGURE 1.1 The dangers of overconfidence

timid could do with climbing up the hill. But, once you get to the top, you don't want to go down the other side, either.

The research we've covered in this chapter is unreservedly clear on this: past a certain point, more confidence is definitely not a good thing. Feeling too self-assured does not lead to better results. We've seen that people who are overconfident may actually suffer as a result of their overly high self-estimations. They are often *less* good at making friends in the long term. They may interrupt others and be perceived as bragging. They get slated for being defensive and lacking insight into their own behaviour. They may push themselves into situations that they simply don't have the skills or experience to succeed at.

> Feeling too self-assured does not lead to better results.

So take heart if you score lower on self-confidence – because you really don't want to be too high on it. I say this over and over again in workshops and conference presentations to lawyers, accountants, managers, entrepreneurs, executives and even charity workers: it may be more dangerous to be too confident than not confident enough.

In fact, the modern 2.0 way of thinking about confidence suggests that a degree of self-doubt may be a good thing. And, to prove it, we'll look at just one example of when it may be helpful. Several years ago, a group of researchers posed a thought-provoking and important question: how does the confidence level of psychotherapists affect the mental health of their clients? Or, phrasing it slightly differently, do more self-assured therapists actually get better results?

The instigator of the project was Helene Nissen-Lie, a psychological scientist at the University of Oslo. Under her direction, her team began by surveying the confidence levels of 70 psychotherapists. The therapists were asked to report how often they felt that they were 'lacking in confidence that you might have a beneficial effect on a patient' and 'afraid that you are doing more harm than good in treating a client', for example.

Then, over the next two years, the psychological detectives monitored 255 clients who had been treated by the 70 therapists. These clients completed detailed questionnaires on their mental health and reported on the extent to which they were still experiencing psychological distress.

When Nissen-Lie and her colleagues finally analysed the results of their two-year project, they found that the therapists' self-doubt about their professional skills was a strong predictor of clients' improvements in mental health: the more doubt and self-questioning therapists experienced, the more their clients tended to get better. Or, putting it another way, the more confident therapists felt, the worse their clients ultimately fared.[11]

In that study, it was clear that therapists who were too bold about their abilities tended to be less successful in treating their clients. Remember that unjustifiably high self-belief is merely a form of trickery – it deludes the individual and possibly cons those around them, too. So it's likely that people of *any* occupation who are overly confident about themselves tend to be less successful, full stop.

A bit of worry can keep you learning and growing. A little nervousness about how you might perform at work or come across at a social event may give you the jolt you need to prepare thoroughly and stay focused. Indeed, countless actors and entertainers say that it's the fear of looking stupid that helps them concentrate and deliver show-stopping performances. Athletes often say that they find their nervousness energizing.

A smidgeon of worry will keep you open-minded to advice and new ideas. You will seek out constructive criticism and be eager to learn from your mistakes. You may not quite believe it, but the surprising truth is that feeling less than entirely confident may actually be a brilliant motivator, a driving force that will make you better in the future.

> Feeling less than entirely confident may actually be a brilliant motivator, a driving force that will make you better in the future.

You would be shocked at how many of the most successful people I work with – business owners, salespeople, chief executives, music producers, entertainers, sportspeople, doctors and so on – score themselves as only a 4 or 5 out of 10 for overall self-confidence. Despite often prospering in their respective fields, they still worry that they're not as good as they could be. But that genuinely is a good thing: it keeps them working hard and looking for ways to be even better.

Of course, I'm not saying that you should simply put up with having lower confidence. No, there's still a lot you can do to make the best of what you have.

But, if you want more confidence, what do you mean by that exactly? Do you want to feel less anxious and worry less? Or do you want to be able to project your confidence so that others sit up and take notice? The two are not the same thing. So let's explore in the next chapter the type – or types – of confidence you might actually need.

## Onwards and upwards

- Consider that more confidence is not always better. People with too much self-belief often have unjustified, unrealistic notions about themselves – they are often deluding themselves. They may waste time and effort pursuing goals for which they aren't really suited. Perhaps worst of all, unwarranted overconfidence can be a real turn-off to others.

- Understand that most human beings are overconfident in at least some ways. So the vast majority of people overestimate at least *some* of their skills and qualities. You may feel unassertive and quite tentative about much in life, but there's a chance that there are still a few areas of your life in which you may think you're better than you really are.

- To dodge the curse of confidence, ask for negative feedback – constructive criticism about your faults and failings. Only by having a realistic picture of your strengths and weak spots can you decide what you genuinely need to upgrade.

- Finally, consider that you may have less far distance to go than you might originally have thought. If you score yourself as having quite low overall confidence, bear in mind that the optimal level of confidence would probably put you as a 6 or at most a 7 out of 10. Remember, remember, remember that people who score much higher may merely be deceiving themselves about their true skills.

# 2

# Disentangling the complexity of confidence

'There's a difference between wanting to appear confident and actually feeling confident. I think there have been many times when I've overcompensated for how nervous or out of place I feel.'

*James Corden*

Allow me to tell you about two individuals. While you're reading about them, keep asking yourself: who would you say is the more confident of the two?

Let's start with Cassandra, a doctor specializing in cardiology, the branch of medicine that deals with keeping the heart alive and healthy. A lithe late-40-something, she is a consultant physician, one of the senior doctors at her hospital who must make literally life-or-death decisions about the many hundreds of people who find their way into her care each year.

She is also a tireless fundraiser, hosting events for the hospital at which she entertains and wins over wealthy donors. She is articulate and good company – someone who can both talk and listen with apparent ease.

She lives in a converted farmhouse with acres of land and its own stables. Married for nearly 20 years and with three smart children, she appears to have it all. But that's purely how it appears on the surface.

For she has always been a worrier. She is often prone to immense bouts of self-doubt. She beats herself up about things she may have said or done incorrectly – both at work and in front of friends and family. She frets about her own attractiveness, too, and she finds herself craving compliments about her looks.

Her husband is handsome and successful in his own right. However, she has started an affair – with a man she met at the hospital gym. But in that tumultuously rollercoaster relationship, she veers from feeling madly in love to being reduced to tears when they argue. He occasionally belittles her and has laughingly called her 'haggard' and 'past it'. As a result, she has become more insecure about her appearance and physical attractiveness. Her preoccupation is such that she reckons she is on the verge of developing an eating disorder. She recognizes the irony that being a doctor allows her to see it coming but not remedy it.

Next, we have Rohan, an intense, 28-year-old data engineering manager at a mobile app development business. By any definition of the term, he is pretty much a genius, a computer-science mastermind with deep experience of SQL, ETL, Java and other technical topics that mean nothing to most human beings on the planet.

It's a demanding technical challenge but he finds his work immensely satisfying. He happily spends a dozen hours a day squinting at a computer screen: the time simply whizzes by. And, even on weekends when he should be relaxing, he often finds himself picking up his laptop to unravel the many knotty problems that seem to beg for his attention.

But Rohan wants to be more socially confident. At work, he boldly supervises and instructs a team of three data scientists. But outside work, he finds himself listening, smiling and nodding rather than contributing. Even with small groups of close friends, he tends to go along with what they want rather than speaking up. He tends to drink more alcohol than he ever sets out to do, simply because it gives him something to do. He says that his friends would probably describe him as 'nice' but 'quiet' while he would prefer to be thought of as 'charming' or 'entertaining'.

He is single and would like to meet someone but doesn't really know how. He doesn't feel at all comfortable with the idea of going to bars or clubs and talking to complete strangers. Even when he gets introduced to an attractive woman in less pressurized social settings, he finds himself tongue-tied and immensely aware of the uncomfortable silences in the conversation. And he worries how people see him: he knows he comes across as socially awkward and that just makes him even quieter and more closed-off.

So there we have our two contenders. Who would you say is the more confident?

## Contrasting internal versus external confidence

Out of the two, I'm not sure who I'd pick. And, if you were to ask a handful of your friends to pick the more confident of the two, I'm willing to bet that they wouldn't all agree either.

On the surface, Cassandra appears carefree and gregarious: she is articulate, charming, delightful company. In contrast, Rohan would likely be seen by most people as less confident – at least socially – because of his timidity around others. But is Cassandra really deep-down confident? No. Her insecurities have pushed her into an extramarital relationship, which may be harming her psychological well-being even further.

At the beginning of the book, I encouraged you to rate your confidence on a scale of 1 to 10. But I hope that you can see that any single rating can only ever be an oversimplification. And that's why confidence is complicated – because confidence is not one thing. It's not a single quality that you either do or don't have.

> Confidence is not one thing. It's not a single quality that you either do or don't have.

Many behavioural scientists distinguish between two facets of personality, two types or dimensions of confidence. When I'm explaining the distinction to clients during a workshop or seminar, I usually show them the two-by-two grid in Figure 2.1.

As you can see, I distinguish between inward-emotional confidence and outward-social confidence. Broadly speaking, the two are separate or uncorrelated. It's possible for people to be high on one but low on the other. But it's also possible for people to be high on both or low on both. Let's look at each in turn.

- **Inward-emotional confidence** is a measure of how people see themselves and their own self-worth. Moreover, it measures people's beliefs in their ability to deal with life's problems and challenges. Other researchers have called it emotional adjustment or emotional stability; I use the word 'inward' because this is how self-assured we *feel* in our private, innermost thoughts. People who are high on inward-emotional confidence tend to feel secure about themselves; they believe that they have the skills to negotiate with the things that life might throw at them and they are resilient in the face of adversity. On the other hand, people who are lower on inward-emotional confidence tend to worry or feel afraid about things; they may agonize about past mistakes, their own failings or what could go wrong in the future, too.

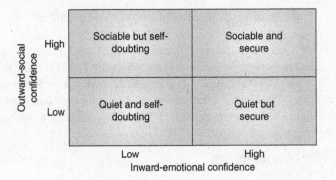

FIGURE 2.1 The two types of confidence

- **Outward-social confidence** is a measure of how gregarious or courageous people seem in social situations. Some scholars have used the terms 'interpersonal confidence' or even 'extraversion'; I use the word 'outward' because this is how outspoken or carefree we *appear* to the outside world. This is about the extent to which people behave in public or social situations rather than how they feel about themselves deep down. People who are high on outward-social confidence tend to be affable or even entertaining at parties or when dating. They are often charming and engaging in work situations, perhaps networking or meeting customers or giving speeches and presentations. Individuals who are lower on outward-social confidence tend to shy away from noisy, bustling social situations; they may appear quieter, more reserved or (inadvertently) even disinterested or aloof.

Putting the distinction as simply as possible, inward-emotional confidence is about how confident we feel privately. Outward-social confidence is about how much confidence we express or display publicly.

## *Evaluating your inward-emotional confidence*

Enough about these theoretical dimensions of confidence, though. Let's explore your situation now. How self-assured do you really feel?

To answer this question, I'm going to present you with a dozen statements. Please read each statement and indicate your level of agreement or disagreement with it. Use a 5-point scale to indicate your response as follows:

1 = Disagree strongly
2 = Disagree
3 = Neither disagree nor agree
4 = Agree
5 = Agree strongly

For each of the following statements, then, please choose a number from between 1 and 5. OK?

If you prefer, you can complete the questionnaire online by visiting my website: www.robyeung.com/confidencecheck

To get access to the questionnaire, you will need to enter the password for the page: #fearless#

To work out the total score for your inward-emotional confidence, begin by adding up the individual scores you gave yourself for statements 1, 3, 5, 7, 9 and 11. That should give you a sub-score of between 6 and 30.

Next, for the even-numbered statements 2, 4, 6, 8, 10 and 12, subtract the score you gave yourself each time from 6. For example, if you decided for any statement that you would award yourself a score of 2, then you would need to take 2 away from 6, which gives you 4 for that statement. Add up your reversed scores for these even-numbered statements to give you a further sub-score of between 6 and 30.

Finally, add up the two sub-scores to get an overall confidence score of between 12 and 60.

Sorry, I know the whole subtraction thing is a bit awkward. But remember: you can also take the test by visiting www.robyeung.com/confidencecheck. Don't forget to enter the password #fearless#.

| Statement | Your score |
|---|---|
| 1. I am confident I get the success I deserve in life. | |
| 2. Sometimes I feel depressed. | |
| 3. When I try, I generally succeed. | |
| 4. Sometimes, when I fail, I feel worthless. | |
| 5. I complete tasks successfully. | |
| 6. Sometimes I do not feel in control of my work. | |
| 7. Overall, I am satisfied with myself. | |
| 8. I am filled with doubts about my competence. | |
| 9. I determine what will happen in my life. | |
| 10. I do not feel in control of my success in my career. | |
| 11. I am capable of coping with most of my problems. | |
| 12. There are times when things look pretty bleak and hopeless to me. | |

## Comprehending your levels of inward-emotional confidence

The questionnaire you just completed was developed by a squad of researchers from three universities led by Timothy Judge, a highly distinguished psychologist who was then at the University of Florida. Now I'm sure that you've come across similar questionnaires in magazines or perhaps your regular Sunday newspaper. You may have completed tests as part of your personal development at work. And there are plenty of questionnaires online these days, too.

But I'll let you in on a little secret. Chances are that most of the questionnaires you have ever completed were total rubbish. They were almost certainly dreamed up – even some of the ones you completed at work – either by journalists without psychological training or even corporate fraudsters trying to pass off their work as something rigorous and useful. But, unless the questionnaire was validated by scientists, it's unlikely to predict people's behaviour or offer any true insight into people's psyches.

The good news is that this questionnaire by Judge and his partners is a far superior creation. The questionnaire has been tested on employees and managers at companies ranging from truck drivers and warehouse workers to salespeople in the pharmaceutical industry. In total, the questionnaire has been used in over a thousand published studies on tens of thousands of people in countries all over the world.

Earlier, I introduced the idea of inward-emotional confidence. And I'm sure that you can see how the questionnaire measures the extent to which you feel courageous within yourself. The very first statement in the questionnaire talks about feeling 'confident'. Other statements measure the opposite: 'worthless', 'doubts' and not feeling 'in control'. So, yes, it's a broad measure of your inward-emotional confidence, your ability to handle life's challenges and feel good about yourself.

In the original research validating the usefulness of the questionnaire, Judge and his associates found that people who scored more highly on this quick test of confidence tended to report not only higher levels of job satisfaction but also higher job performance. Higher scores were generally linked to reports of greater satisfaction with life as well.[1]

Later studies have further confirmed the predictive power of the questionnaire. For example, people who score more highly on the questionnaire tend to earn more than people who score lower. And individuals who score highly likewise tend to report less conflict between their work demands and family lives, too.

Judge and his colleagues did publish average scores for the assorted samples that they surveyed. But that was over a decade ago, and I wanted to corroborate their results independently. So I administered the questionnaire to several hundred people over the course of a few months in order to create the following data table, which represents a snapshot of people's confidence levels in our modern age. So how do your current levels of inward-emotional confidence compare against those of other people?

| Your score | Interpretation |
|---|---|
| 30 | Ninety per cent of people score higher than you on the measure of inward-emotional confidence. This implies that you may experience higher levels of self-doubt or even anxiety than most people. But that's OK: remember that large numbers of people worry and feel apprehensive yet achieve tremendous things in life. Take a look at Part II for rapid techniques for firing yourself up and Part IV for longer-term solutions that will have a more lasting impact on your life. |
| 33 | Seventy-five per cent of people score higher than you. You may experience more nervousness and worry than many people. However, this book is geared towards helping people exactly like you. Dip into Part II of this book for relatively speedy methods for upgrading how you feel. And, perhaps when you have more time, delve into Part IV for longer-term approaches for building true lifelong confidence. |
| 39 | You are exactly at the midpoint on the test, making you statistically average. Your feelings of confidence are not a major issue. But just because you are statistically average probably isn't enough for you. You probably have goals and ambitions to better yourself. So do read through the rest of this book to pick out the handful of interventions that may be most beneficial to you. |
| 47 | You score higher than 75 per cent of people on the measure of inward-emotional confidence. However, that does not mean that you are always free from self-doubt or misgivings. In the few high-pressure situations that you still find daunting, do consider applying some of the techniques from Part II to help you to manage your emotions and stay feeling strong. And be careful that you don't fall into the trap of overconfidence. |

| 49 | You score higher than 90 per cent of people in terms of your inward-emotional confidence. That suggests that you are fairly unflappable, calm or even audacious in the face of adversity. But remember the curse of confidence from Chapter 1? This may be the greatest danger for you. If you aspire to be truly successful in life, seek out plenty of constructive criticism from knowledgeable people who can help you to become even better. |
|----|------|

So now you have a brief measure of your inward-emotional confidence – the extent to which you feel able to negotiate the challenges that life may throw at you. People with lower scores tend to see themselves as having less ability to cope, persevere and succeed in life; they may lack the conviction that life will turn out well for them.

Remember, though, that higher scores on the inward-emotional confidence questionnaire aren't automatically desirable. A very high score indicates a higher level of belief in your ability to handle things. But is it simply a *belief* – like a form of delusion or self-deception – that is unmatched by reality? Or is it predicated on a genuine ability to deal with challenges and impasses in life? We can't know simply from a quick 12-statement questionnaire such as this.

> Higher scores on the inward-emotional confidence questionnaire aren't automatically desirable.

In a later research paper, Timothy Judge specifically warned that high scores on the questionnaire 'may cause individuals to ignore negative information, take unwarranted risks, or overestimate their abilities'.[2] In other words, more confidence may bleed into overconfidence, complacency or even arrogance and all of those other things that we discussed. So be careful. As I recommend in Chapter 1, the only way to check that you're not deluding yourself is to ask for candid criticism from knowledgeable and genuinely discerning people.

But enough about your inward-emotional confidence for now. How do you stack up when it comes to your behaviour in public or social situations?

## *Evaluating your outward-social confidence*

To measure your outward-social confidence, I'm going to ask you to ponder a different set of 12 statements shortly. As before, please read each statement and indicate your level of agreement or disagreement with it. Again, please use a 5-point scale to indicate your response. The scale is as follows:

1 = Disagree strongly
2 = Disagree
3 = Neither disagree nor agree
4 = Agree
5 = Agree strongly

If you prefer, you can also complete this questionnaire online by visiting the following link: www.robyeung.com/confidencecheck2

To access the questionnaire, you will need to enter the password #outgoing#

To work out your overall outward-social confidence score, begin by adding up the individual scores you gave yourself for the odd-numbered statements 1, 3, 5, 7, 9 and 11. This will give you a sub-total of between 6 and 30.

Next, for the even-numbered statements 2, 4, 6, 8, 10 and 12, subtract the score you gave yourself each time from 6. For instance, if you chose for any statement to give yourself a score of 1, then you would need to take 1 away from 6, which gives you 5 for that statement. Add up your reversed scores for these even-numbered statements to give you a further subtotal of between 6 and 30.

Finally, add up the two subtotals to get an overall score, which should be between 12 and 60. This is a measure of your outward-social confidence, the extent to which you can be poised and at your best when interacting with or being evaluated by other people.

To avoid all the hassle of reversing the scores and adding up sub-totals, do remember that you can also complete the questionnaire at www.robyeung.com/confidencecheck2. Be sure to enter the password #outgoing#.

These 12 statements are based on a questionnaire that was originally conceived by psychologists Sandra Baker, Nina Heinrichs, Hyo-Jim Kim and Stefan Hofmann from Boston University.[3] Their full social confidence test was considerably lengthier, but I have excerpted a smaller number of statements (and updated some of the

| Statement | Your score |
|---|---|
| 1. I feel very confident when meeting strangers. | |
| 2. I prefer to talk to people I know well. | |
| 3. I look forward to meeting new people at parties. | |
| 4. I dislike talking to people in authority. | |
| 5. I can express disagreement or disapproval with people I do not know well. | |
| 6. I prefer not to work or write while being observed by others. | |
| 7. I know I can perform at my very best when taking tests and exams. | |
| 8. I dislike eating or drinking with others in public. | |
| 9. I enjoy giving talks, acting or performing in front of an audience. | |
| 10. I feel uncomfortable being the centre of attention. | |
| 11. I am happy to complain or return goods to a store. | |
| 12. I find it difficult to resist persuasive or high-pressure salespeople. | |

language) to give you a snapshot of your outward-social confidence. The higher your score, the more you are likely to appear outspoken, audacious or even brash.

The scores in the following data table are again based on the scores gleaned from the many people that I've tested. How does your outward-social confidence compare against that of other people?

Clearly, your overall score and how it compares with other people's may give you an idea of the extent to which your outward-social confidence is an issue. But I would make the case that how

| Your score | Interpretation |
| --- | --- |
| 31 | Ninety per cent of people score higher than you on this measure of outward-social confidence. That suggests that projecting confidence in public situations may be quite challenging for you. To make the most of yourself in such situations, the advice in Part III of this book may be of particular interest to you. |
| 38 | Seventy-five per cent of people score higher than you. This implies that behaving boldly in social and/or professional situations may often be a challenge for you. Part III of this book is particularly aimed at helping people to boost their outward-social confidence. |
| 41 | You are exactly at the midpoint on the test, making you statistically average. In all likelihood, you may sometimes appear nervous but at other times confident (or even overconfident), too. That may sound like a contradiction. But consider that we humans are complex creatures: perhaps you appear more outspoken in certain situations and less so in others. |

| | |
|---|---|
| 44 | You score higher than 75 per cent of people on this test of outward-social confidence. Remember, though, that high levels of fearless behaviour are not always desirable. Just because you are able to socialize and perform in public doesn't mean that you should always do so; there may be times when it's better to hold back and be quieter. To ensure that you avoid the curse of confidence, you may wish to refer back to the advice given in Chapter 1. |
| 52 | You score higher than 90 per cent of people. Consider that having more outward-social confidence than nine out of ten people may not always be to your advantage. Remember the curse of confidence? If I were working with clients who had such high levels of outward-social confidence, I would emphatically recommend that they take a look back at Chapter 1 for advice on how to evade the pitfalls of behaviour that may inadvertently come across as overly cocky. |

you compare in the league table almost doesn't matter. Your score may turn out to be somewhat higher or lower than you imagined. Ultimately, *you* are the only person who can judge whether your outward-social confidence is something you want to work on. Even though you may already possess more of it than other people, you may decide that it's still something you really want to work on: you may want to be *even* stronger at it.

> *You* are the only person who can judge whether your outward-social confidence is something you want to work on.

## *The components of outward-social confidence*

The questionnaire we just encountered doesn't merely give us a measure of your outward-social confidence. The Boston University psychologists' major discovery in psychological tests of their questionnaire was that there were five factors within the questionnaire. We can think of each factor as an individual cluster of behaviours. In other words, there are five broad components to outward-social confidence. So, even though two people may have similar scores on the outward-social confidence questionnaire, they could behave quite differently in different social situations.

> There are five broad components to outward-social confidence.

For example, I have a friend who is a marvellous entertainer at social gatherings. I've known David for decades since we were both undergraduates, and even then I used to admire (and envy a little) his ability to tell stories and regale people with the strange or amusing things that happened to him.

But he has never been very good at complaining or standing up for himself. The last time we met up for dinner, David ordered a pan-fried duck breast for his main course but it was far too undercooked for him to eat. He insisted that it was fine. I encouraged him to say something to our waiter but he demurred. He proceeded to slice off and eat only tiny pieces of the duck breast – the very outermost layers that had been cooked properly. It was clear that he intended to leave the vast bulk of his dish uneaten, so I brought the matter up with the waiter who immediately agreed that the duck breast was disastrously undercooked. The waiter apologized, replaced the dish and even brought us complimentary coffees by way of restitution.

It used to amaze me that someone who was so brave in front of even strangers at parties was so fazed by the prospect of standing up for his rights. But the fact that there are five factors, or components, to outward-social confidence makes sense of this apparent contradiction. David is strong at one component of outward-social confidence but much less so at another. Outward-social confidence does not always translate from one situation to the next.

Another example from my university days was a fellow undergraduate on my psychology course, whom I'll call Marie. She was one of the few students who spoke up in answer to lecturers' questions. Most of the rest of the class – me included – were too alarmed by the potential shame of saying something stupid, but not her.

Devastatingly, she fell apart when it came to sitting our final written exams, which comprised a total of 15 hours of lengthy essay questions. Coming out of our exams, she knew that she hadn't done well. She said that her mind had gone blank. She had spent far too long on some questions and consequently had almost no time to answer others.

Despite the fact that she was probably one of the top handful of psychologists on our course when it came to knowledge of our subject, she got a final grade which put her in the bottom half. I felt bad for her because her poise in lectures wasn't matched by her performance when taking tests.

Many people who feel that they could do with more social courage are concerned about feeling embarrassed, humiliated or judged by others. But just as people have different amounts of inward-emotional versus outward-social confidence, it turns out that many people also have inconsistent – and sometimes seemingly contradictory – levels of confidence in distinct social situations, too.

So what are the five components of outward-social confidence?

- **Social interaction confidence.** Take a look back at the first five statements of the outward-social questionnaire above and you will get a picture of this first component. Social interaction confidence measures the extent to which people feel comfortable meeting new people, conversing with them and even dealing with conflict situations. This is the biggest chunk or component of outward-social confidence.
- **Nonverbal performance confidence.** Statements 6 and 7 measure nonverbal performance confidence, or the extent to which people feel that they can take tests and exams or do work while being watched by other people.

- **Ingestion confidence.** Statement 8 provides an indication of ingestion confidence. Many people have no trouble eating and drinking in public, even in front of complete strangers. However, a small proportion of people find this quite challenging and may try to avoid such situations.
- **Public performance confidence.** Statements 9 and 10 together indicate the extent to which people feel brave when speaking, presenting or otherwise performing in front of others. That may be in social settings, such as giving a speech in honour of a friend's birthday or at a wedding. That could be at work, for example when pitching to customers or giving an update to colleagues. It could be in sporting situations, auditions or competitions as well.
- **Assertiveness.** Finally, statements 11 and 12 measure the extent to which people feel confident in standing up for their rights. That could involve expressing a grievance, asking for an exchange or a refund for a purchase, or in saying 'no' to a salesperson who is a bit too persistent.

Remember that the researchers' analysis suggested that these represent five fairly separate components of outward-social confidence. In other words, you may be good or great at some but struggle at others.

Now, you may be thinking that it would be nice if you could compare your scores on each of the five components against those of other people. But that's not a good idea. Psychological scientists who specialize in the construction of psychometric tests tell us that tests with only a few questions rarely allow meaningful comparisons between individuals.

Another quibble: a short questionnaire like this cannot be expected to capture absolutely every situation in which people desire more outward-social confidence. For example, some people are anxious drivers who feel that their driving gets worse when they have passengers in the car with them. And certain people worry that they won't be able to keep their composure in very specific scenarios, such as on aeroplanes, in public toilets or when they feel stared at by onlookers.

However, the original questionnaire was based on statistical analysis, so it is likely to identify the five most frequently occurring categories of situation in which people feel that they need more outward-social confidence. It allows the majority of people to think about their relative strengths and limitations.

When I'm working with clients, I use this questionnaire not as a way of categorizing or labelling them as individuals with a certain fixed amount of outward-social confidence. No; I deploy it only as a device to stimulate their thinking about the situations in which they feel more able or challenged.

I encourage you to use the questionnaire in a similar way. Do any of those five components resonate with you? Or are there other, specific situations not mentioned in the questionnaire that bother you, too? Whichever is the case, having a think about your unique profile of gifts and gaps will help you to focus your efforts in the later chapters.

## Delving into the combinations of confidence

So there we have the two dimensions of confidence. Inward-emotional confidence is the extent to which you feel capable and free from inappropriate worry and trepidation. Outward-social confidence concerns the degree to which you are able to perform and be at your best in public situations.

It's worth partitioning the types of confidence because they illustrate that people can be fearless in different ways. Often, it's easy to believe that people who behave confidently must be confident – that partying, outgoing extraverts must feel confident inside, too. But conventional wisdom happens to be wrong, wrong, wrong. Specifically, some people can *appear* quite confident on the surface but secretly *feel* quite self-doubting. And other people can seem quite reserved but actually be totally content with themselves.

> Some people can appear quite confident on the surface but secretly feel quite self-doubting.

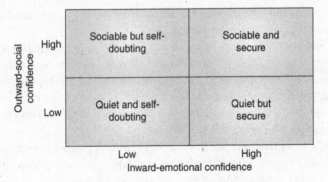

FIGURE 2.2 The two types of confidence revisited

You've already seen the grid in Figure 2.2. But I'll pop it here again as I think it's a good, visual way of depicting how the two types of confidence interact with each other.

Let's look at the top-left quadrant of the two-by-two grid: people who are sociable but self-doubting. A friend of mine named Damien fits this profile: he is high on outward-social confidence but low on inward-emotional confidence. His high outward-social confidence means that he's good at being the centre of attention, at putting on a show: he's talkative, has a lot of opinions about the world and tells a fair number of amusing stories and jokes, usually with accompanying hand gestures and facial expressions. Most people would say that he's clearly a raging extravert.

Damien always seems to have something to say, whether he's entertaining friends at a party or colleagues at work. In fact, there's an ongoing joke at work that he just doesn't shut up. In his spare time, he spends many of his evenings and weekends hanging out with friends. He goes dancing at nightclubs and likes nothing more than heading to cool, new bars. He talks with ease to both men and women and he often finds himself striking up conversations with complete strangers.

But, deep down, Damien is a worrier and far from carefree. His low inward-emotional confidence means that he beats himself up about mistakes he's made and things he's said. He frequently anticipates problems and catastrophes that might never arise. He worries about his appearance and attractiveness, too.

Sure, he seeks companionship and tends to be surrounded by people, but he wonders whether his friends really like him and why he doesn't have even more friends. He often feels hurt, let down or even angry with the people in his life as well. He doesn't share these insecurities with many people, but that doesn't stop these concerns from taking up a lot of his waking hours.

Contrast that with the bottom-right quadrant of the matrix: individuals who are quiet but secure. An ex-colleague named Jenny possesses this combination of low outward-social confidence but high inward-emotional confidence. Her low outward-social confidence means that she tends to be a listener rather than a talker. She doesn't like to draw attention to herself – she often speaks in a voice that is barely audible. And she is uncomfortable revealing too much about herself to people she feels she doesn't know well.

She prefers to spend time conversing with people either one-on-one in quiet cafés and restaurants or in small groups rather than in large groups or at parties. She frequently travels on her own to visit English stately homes. Even though she spends a significant proportion of her time by herself, she is far from lonely; in fact, she looks forward to time away from the melee of other people to go to the gym, read and try new recipes in the kitchen. Based on how she spends her time, most people would characterize her as an introvert.

While Jenny may seem modest or even bashful on the surface, she's comfortable in her own skin. Possessing high levels of inward-emotional confidence, she doesn't tend to dwell on past failures or fiascos. After all, what's done is done. She tends not to worry about the future, either. Why obsess about things that have yet to happen – or may never happen? And when things do go wrong in her life, she handles them matter-of-factly. She is relatively unruffled by adversity: she bounces back from life's occasional knocks quickly. Or, when friends cancel social engagements, she doesn't take things personally or overreact. Overall, she tends not to experience terrible lows or highs in her emotional life. As a result, she is calm, collected and imperturbable.

Now, I am not saying that everyone in those two quadrants is exactly like Damien and Jenny. These two individuals may not mirror your personal experience or even those of the people close to you. But they should serve to illustrate how people with those profiles of outward-social confidence versus inward-emotional confidence *tend* to think, feel and behave.

Publicly, Damien appears to be self-confident; privately, he is more self-doubting. He may behave like an extravert but below the surface he is tormented by fears and insecurities. In contrast, Jenny appears less confident in public, social situations. But, privately, she feels content and happy with herself. Yes, some could call her an introvert, but she's secure and happy within herself.

I don't think that the extravert versus introvert label is always helpful: for example, there are innumerable people who fall somewhere between the two. But I will comment on it one last time. Too many people believe that extraverts are just more generally confident than introverts. As a result, there's a danger that people who categorize themselves as introverts may end up limiting what they can do – they mistakenly resign themselves to the fact that they will never be able to feel confident. But I really hope that I have debunked this myth. The truth is that a fair number of extraverts can even appear brash on the outside but feel quite anguished on the inside. By the same token, many introverts may behave quietly but actually have rock-solid belief in themselves.

> Many introverts may behave quietly but actually have rock-solid belief in themselves.

Looking back at the two-by-two grid, there are of course two other permutations. People in the top-right quadrant are sociable and secure: they both behave boldly in social settings and feel secure about themselves. They seem to be blessed with the greatest combination of gifts. But, at the same time, they may be the most likely to be afflicted by the curse of overconfidence.

Sadly, people in the bottom-left quadrant may be both quiet and nagged by doubt: they shy away from social situations and feel uncertain about themselves. When they are with other people, they feel overlooked and may wish to be alone. But, when they spend time on their own, they may find themselves wondering why they aren't more outgoing and popular.

## *Your next step*

Before we finish this chapter, allow me to recap briefly. We've established that there tend to be two broad, main types or dimensions of confidence. On the one hand, we have inward-emotional confidence, which is a measure of the degree to which we *privately* feel calm and free from anxiety. On the other hand, we have outward-social confidence, which is the extent to which we *publicly* come across as outgoing and courageous to the people around us.

Here is a brief summary of the two:

| Outward-social confidence | Inward-emotional confidence |
| --- | --- |
| Relates to how people appear on the surface | Relates to how people feel deep down |
| Reflects public behaviour in social situations | Reflects private thoughts and feelings |
| If you score highly on this, others may see you as friendly or extraverted. | If you score highly on this, others may see you as calm or composed. |
| If your score is low on this, others may see you as quiet and reserved. | If your score is low on this, others may see you as anxious or tending to worry. |

The point of raising the distinction is that people may have different needs when it comes to boosting their confidence. Some people want to work on their private, inward-emotional confidence so that they can *feel* more self-assured. Others yearn to develop their public, outward-social confidence so that they can *appear* more engaging. Still others may want to work on both – or neither.

People may have different needs when it comes to boosting their confidence.

So what are your needs?

Do you want to soothe the worries, doubts and fears that run around privately in your own mind? Maybe you torment yourself over past blunders, failings and regrets. Or you spend too much time envisaging bad things that might happen in the future. Perhaps you often feel edgy, tense or afraid. If you want to feel less anxious and beat self-doubt, you will find plenty of practical advice in Part II: Increasing your inward-emotional confidence.

Or do you wish you could be more talkative, assertive and entertaining in public? Perhaps you want to make a determined impact at work, at job interviews or auditions, or socializing with friends. You may wish that you were more of a performer, the centre of attention, even an entertainer. You desire to be described as dynamic, charming or fun. If you want to make a better impression, then you will find Part III: Enhancing your outward-social confidence more useful.

The situation gets a little messy because we'll discover that a handful of the techniques that boost your inward-emotional confidence may occasionally also benefit your outward-social confidence. If you think about it, this makes sense. When you feel more in control of your inner emotions, you may end up behaving in a more emphatic fashion that is detectable to the people around you, too.

However, the opposite is rarely true: the tactics aimed at lifting your outward-social confidence seldom improve your inward-emotional confidence. But then we shouldn't expect that to happen. Outward-social confidence is all about putting on a show for the benefit of others. It's by definition about airbrushed appearances and impressing others rather than genuinely changing ourselves.

As we conclude Part I of the book, you now have a choice. Start with Part II to work on your inward-emotional confidence. Or jump ahead to Part III to enhance your outward-social confidence and make other people sit up and take notice of you. Where would *you* like to go next?

## *Onwards and upwards*

- Consider a great truth about confidence: people who appear unflappable outwardly may not feel anywhere near as brave inwardly. Be aware that there are two broad dimensions of confidence, which are largely unrelated. In other words, some people may have much higher levels of one than the other; other people may have high levels of both or neither.

- Remember that inward–emotional confidence is a measure of the extent to which we feel calm and secure versus anxious and worried. Higher scorers on inward–emotional confidence feel composed and sure of their ability to handle difficulties in life. Lower scorers tend to be more troubled by bothersome doubts or unpleasant feelings.

- Understand that outward–social confidence indicates the degree to which we appear outgoing or even entertaining in public. Individuals with higher scores on outward–social confidence tend to be perceived as talkative, charming performers. Individuals with lower scores tend to be seen as quieter and more reserved.

- Keep in mind that the techniques aimed at improving your inward–emotional confidence may sometimes additionally boost your outward–social confidence. However, the reverse is unlikely to be the case. So there may be an argument here for working more on your inward–emotional confidence as it may also ultimately benefit your outward–social confidence.

- Finally from this chapter, recall that different people can have quite dissimilar challenges when it comes to their outward–social confidence. For example, some people are good at meeting strangers at parties but may be less able to assert themselves. Others may be good at giving talks or presentations but feel panicky during tests and exams or when having to eat in front of others. The point is to understand your unique pattern of outward–social confidence strengths and weak spots.

# PART II
# Increasing your inward-emotional confidence

I often define confidence as the ability to deal with life's obstacles and opportunities in an effective manner – to be able to get on with things rather than be paralysed by fears and worries. Before we discuss how to feel stronger and more confident in the face of adversity, allow me to ask you three questions.

I'm going to present you with three pairs of life events. In each case, I'd like you to imagine which of the two you would find more traumatic. Or, if you're unfortunate to have experienced any of them, think back to which you actually found more harrowing.

So here's the first pairing: being fired from your job versus going through a divorce. I know: it's a tough one. Which would you personally find more gruelling? Being forced out of your job against your will (and losing both the respect of your colleagues as well as your livelihood) or suffering the breakdown of your marriage?

How about this twosome: gaining a new family member versus having one of your children leave home? So in one instance, your family grows; in the other situation, your home may seem that little bit emptier. Again, which would you find more difficult?

On to the third choice: trouble with your boss versus trouble with your in-laws. The first situation may mean pressure and strain in the office; the second, problems and stress at home.

Most people find such decisions quite daunting. But, in 1967, psychiatrists Thomas Holmes and Richard Rahe from the University of Washington School of Medicine published a scientific paper that presented a definitive list chronicling the stressfulness of different life events. The investigative duo asked hundreds of people to look at a list of 43 life events with a view to rating the amount of *social readjustment* that each might entail, that is, the amount, duration and intensity of change in one's life and habits as a result of each life event.[1]

The full list is a little long, but the one below shows the top 15 life events along with the amount of social readjustment that each was said to cause.

This social readjustment rating scale generated a monumental amount of interest among researchers, psychologists, medical doctors and other clinicians all over the world. Here, finally, was a way to measure incidents that might dent a person's psychological confidence and predict who might physically fall ill.

| Rank | Life event | Social readjustment points |
|------|-----------|----------------------------|
| 1. | Death of a spouse | 100 |
| 2. | Divorce | 73 |
| 3. | Marital separation | 65 |
| 4. | Jail term | 63 |
| 5. | Death of a close family member | 63 |
| 6. | Personal injury or illness | 53 |
| 7. | Marriage | 50 |
| 8. | Fired at work | 47 |
| 9. | Marital reconciliation | 45 |
| 10. | Retirement | 45 |
| 11. | Change in health of family member | 44 |
| 12. | Pregnancy | 40 |
| 13. | Sexual difficulties | 39 |
| 14. | Gain of new family member | 39 |
| 15. | Business readjustment | 39 |

Over the next couple of years, dozens of studies showed a statistical relationship between people's experience of the listed life events and their subsequent health. Essentially, the more social readjustment points people racked up, the more likely they were to fall ill.

However, these studies also unearthed a major problem. In one of his own studies, Richard Rahe, with new collaborators Jack Mahan and Ransom Arthur, assessed the number of social readjustment points (which by then had been renamed Life Change Units) experienced by 2,463 sailors aboard three US Navy cruisers. Reviewing the sailors' subsequent health records, the researchers found the expected statistical relationship between Life Change Units and ill health. But it was an exceedingly weak relationship.

Sailors who reported a very low number of Life Change Units (somewhere between 0 and 99 points) were ill 1.5 times a year on average. Sailors who reported exceptionally high Life Change Units (of between 800 to 899 points) were more likely to be ill, but only fractionally so: they experienced around 2.1 illnesses a year.[2]

Take a look back at the list of life events and you'll see that a range of 800 to 899 points would mean a fairly staggering number of major life events. Even experiencing all 15 of the life events in the above list only gets you 760 Life Change Units. So it's a somewhat disappointing result: even people who accumulated a whopping eight to nine *times* as many Life Change Units were only 40 per cent more likely to fall ill.

The initial promise of the social readjustment rating scale never really paid off. And it has pretty much been consigned to history as an interesting notion that simply did not work out.

What went wrong?

## Appreciating the meaning of meaning

In conceiving their social readjustment rating scale, Holmes and Rahe originally took their inspiration from the physical sciences. In the world of physics, things are much more clear-cut, absolute, black and white. The loudness of a sound can be measured precisely in decibels, the brightness of a light in lumens, force in newtons, power in watts, and so on. Likewise, the researchers wanted to create a scale that measured the absolute impact of assorted life events.

In their paper, Holmes and Rahe argued that each life event 'is either indicative of or requires a significant change in the life pattern of the individual. The emphasis is on change from the existing steady state and not on psychological meaning, emotion, or social desirability.' In other words, they saw each life event as having the same effect on all people.

But this emphasis on measuring the impact of life events irrespective of the meaning, emotion or desirability attached to events simply didn't work out – because two people can experience exactly the same situation but feel completely differently about it.

Let's take an example. The academics ranked 'divorce' as the second most life-altering event on their list. But even this could have entirely different repercussions on people's lives. Imagine for a moment that two guys, Tom and Frederick, both find out on the same day that their wives want divorces.

Tom's wife confesses that she has been having an extramarital affair and no longer loves him. It's a gigantic, unwelcome, damaging blow to his self-confidence. Tom feels crushed. He blames himself and worries that he will never find someone to care for again.

Frederick also hears from his wife that she has been having an affair. She tells him that she does not love him and that divorce is the only option. Again, it's unwelcome. Frederick feels initially flattened by the news. But he tells himself that it's his soon-to-be-ex-wife's fault: she should have communicated her needs to him more assertively. And he reminds himself that he found a wife once, so he should be able to do it again.

Tom and Frederick experience an identical shock, the same devastating situation. However, their interpretation of what it means for them is vastly different. So while Tom's self-belief may be severely diminished, Frederick's may only be slightly dented.

The research collaborators Holmes and Rahe had lofty goals: to look at the absolute impact of life events. But subsequent studies failed to support their hypotheses. So compelling was the evidence that Richard Rahe changed his mind completely; to his credit, he eventually came to agree that the occurrence of life events was a poor predictor of ill health.[3] How people view, interpret or appraise a life event is a far better predictor of health outcomes. In determining people's physical health, it turns out that meaning, emotion and social desirability don't just matter a bit – they matter hugely.

The same is true for people's psychological health, too. How people think about any life event – a major setback, a minor hassle, a magnificent opportunity – determines its effects on their mental well-being. It is our subjective appraisal of events – and *not* the events themselves – that harms or helps our inward-emotional confidence.

> It is our subjective appraisal of events – and *not* the events themselves – that harms or helps our inward-emotional confidence.

This fact should be a great cause for celebration. Because we can to an extent choose the meaning and significance we attach to life events and the things that happen to us. See a problem, wrong turn or hassle as negative and it will damage your well-being and confidence. Interpret the same situation in a more neutral way and it may have a more limited impact on your state of mind. Even better, if you can choose to see it as something positive, it could even buoy your confidence.

I cannot emphasize enough the importance of this one central fact. It is a key principle underlying many of the confidence-building techniques that we will encounter in not only this chapter but several others to come.

You do not have to be a passive victim of your circumstances. You can to an extent control how you will feel. Choose your own interpretation of a situation and you choose how it will affect your inward-emotional confidence.

> Choose your interpretation of a situation and you choose how it will affect your inward-emotional confidence.

## Learning to react to your reactions

What situations make you nervous? Countless people have mild to moderate fears about heights, snakes, spiders and blood. And, of course, many people shy away from having to speak in public, whether that's in a social setting, such as a wedding, or a work situation, such as delivering a formal business presentation.

What happens when you feel nervous? Perhaps your heart races or your throat feels dry. Your palms may feel sweaty or you may notice that you're breathing more quickly than usual. Psychologically, you may notice worrisome thoughts such as 'I'm no good at speaking in public' or 'I'm going to pass out' swirling around in your head.

CREATING A STORY OF A STRONGER YOU

Thankfully, though, research tells us that we can consciously choose healthier, less heartrending interpretations. I'll show you how by sharing with you a notable study by Harvard University researchers Jeremy Jamieson and Matthew Nock in collaboration with Wendy Berry Mendes at the University of California, San Francisco.

The research trio corralled 25 men and 25 women for an experiment looking at the effects of varying psychological techniques on the body's physical reaction to stress. These devious researchers began by deliberately inducing a state of anxiety in their participants by asking them to deliver a five-minute talk to two experimenters who were instructed to sit with crossed arms and furrowed brows. Imagine for a moment how nerve-wracking it must be to give a speech and have your audience shaking their heads, sighing and scowling!

There was more. The participants were made even more unsettled by being asked to engage in a mental arithmetic task: counting backwards from 996 in steps of seven. That's tough to do. And they had to do this for a further five agonizing minutes while the two experimenters sat there again sighing, shaking their heads and generally looking on critically.

But here comes the clever experimental bit of the study. Immediately before these two panic-inducing tasks, the participants were split into three groups. And each group was given a handful of sentences to read.

One group was taught a technique called reappraisal – a way of interpreting their feelings in a less distressing fashion. They read statements telling them that physiological arousal (i.e. elevated heart rate, faster breathing and all of the other physical symptoms of stress) is not harmful. In fact, the body's response to stress has evolved to help us successfully tackle challenges and ordeals; this physiological arousal is designed to help us cope better. The body's physical response is functional and adaptive.

A second group was instructed to ignore stressful situations. They read paragraphs saying that the best way to reduce nervousness is to ignore whatever is making us feel anxious. Simply look away. Turn our attention away from it.

The third group of participants acted as a control group. They were given no further instructions and ushered straight into the two anxiety-provoking tasks.

To measure the participants' levels of trepidation, Jamieson and colleagues didn't just ask people how they felt. They used an array of medical devices including an electrocardiograph, an impedance cardiograph and a blood pressure monitor to check how the participants' bodies reacted.

Comparing responses across the three groups, the researchers found that participants in the first group – who were taught reappraisal – fared best. These participants had a more favourable physiological response to the two anxiety-inducing tasks than participants in either of the other two groups.[4]

In other words, a purely mental tactic was able to calm their physical symptoms. The astonishing implication is that simply choosing a more positive interpretation about whatever situation you're in may help your body to respond in a healthier, less stressed fashion.

> Simply choosing a more positive interpretation about whatever situation you're in may help your body to respond in a healthier, less stressed fashion.

That alone should have you scrambling to incorporate reappraisal into your life. But there's even better news from a truly landmark study looking at the impact of reappraisal on people's exam performance.[5]

In the United States, most undergraduates who wish to study for a master's degree or doctorate need to take the Graduate Record Examination (GRE), which is a computerized test of verbal and numerical reasoning, critical thinking and analytical writing skills. It costs several hundred dollars to take and lasts three hours and 45 minutes. Given that an individual's score on the GRE could well determine not only where they study but also their future career prospects, it's an understandably daunting challenge for many people.

In this experimental inquiry, Jeremy Jamieson and a different crew of research partners asked a group of participants to take a practice GRE in his laboratory. He allocated participants to one of just two groups.

Just prior to the mock exam, the experimental group were taught the trick of reappraisal. To be specific, they read the following paragraph:

> People think that feeling anxious while taking a standardized test will make them do poorly on the test. However, recent research suggests that arousal doesn't hurt performance on these tests and can even help performance ... people who feel anxious during a test might actually do better. This means that you shouldn't feel concerned if you do feel anxious while taking today's GRE test. If you find yourself feeling anxious, simply remind yourself that your arousal could be helping you do well.

The control participants took the same exam, but without the benefit of the short paragraph above. So what happened? As expected, participants who read the reappraisal paragraph said that they worried less about feeling anxious. They reported feeling less unsure about themselves, too.

That's a decent result on its own, something that again recommends the application of reappraisal. More crucially, though, the reappraisal participants also did better in their practice exams. Their scores were significantly better.

But I described this as a landmark study, and the fact that participants did better in a mock exam still doesn't seem that much of a big deal. What makes this study so truly important is that the researchers then monitored the participants as they went on to take their actual GRE tests. Between one to three months later, all the participants were asked to return to the laboratory with their official test reports. Again, participants who had been taught reappraisal eventually received conspicuously better grades. So it wasn't only their laboratory exam performance that got better. Even several months later, their actual exam results improved too.

Now *that* to me is a truly worthwhile result – something seriously worth celebrating.

I suggested in Part I that people often differ in the extent to which they feel confident versus the extent to which they behave confidently. It transpires, then, that reappraisal doesn't just augment inward-emotional confidence by helping people to feel less timid. It can lift people's outward-social confidence (specifically the component of nonverbal performance confidence) – their ability to perform in the real world as well.

But what *most* impresses me about reappraisal is that it isn't a lengthy intervention. If you went for a psychotherapy session to reduce feelings of uneasiness or panic and improve your inward-emotional confidence, you might have to talk and receive guidance for perhaps 45 minutes to an hour or so. Your therapist might even recommend multiple sessions. But the reappraisal intervention used in the pair of studies by Jeremy Jamieson and his colleagues took participants only a few minutes to read.

It's a powerful lesson to remember. Reappraisal has not only been shown to reduce anxiety and boost confidence and performance. It is also something that can benefit you in minutes, if not seconds.

## Learning to reconceptualize your physical energy

What situations make you feel nervous, tense, jittery? What makes your heart pound and gets the worrying thoughts whizzing around in your head? Maybe it's something like taking an exam or test, or speaking, auditioning or otherwise being scrutinized in public. It might even be having to criticize a co-worker or having to approach strangers at a party.

Reappraisal is a technique drawn from the cognitive behavioural movement, which is currently the most popular school of psychological therapy. Based on the instructions that many groups of behavioural scientists have used, I have put together a paragraph that you can read whenever you're feeling jittery and want to subvert how you're feeling:

*Our bodies have evolved to react by becoming more physiologically aroused when we face stressful situations. This enhanced arousal is designed to aid our performance. So think about your arousal as functional and adaptive. Arousal can help to focus your attention. It may help you to concentrate and stay sharp, so don't feel concerned if you feel nervous during nerve-wracking situations. If you find yourself feeling nervous, remind yourself that your arousal can often be beneficial: it could be helping you to perform better.*

## *Looking for reasons to feel confident*

The previous technique was about reappraising the role of your physiological state, the adrenaline coursing through your veins. But there are actually a few distinct ways you can reconceptualize how you're feeling.

Consider a different investigation, engineered by Allison Troy, an up-and-coming researcher at the University of Denver. Troy and her associates set out to explore the power of reappraisal in blunting the effects of sadness by inviting 78 participants into their laboratory to watch a series of downbeat film clips.

The researchers split the participants into two groups. The first, experimental group was asked to reappraise throughout the viewing experience. The second, control group was instructed simply to watch the film clips but given no advice on how to protect themselves emotionally.

The researchers measured participants' levels of sadness in two ways. First, they asked the participants how sad they felt. Unsurprisingly, the group who were taught reappraisal reported feeling significantly less sad. Second, the researchers measured changes in skin conductance levels of the participants, which is commonly used as a more objective, physiological measure of emotional sadness. Again, the group who were taught about reappraisal had demonstrably better skin conductance levels.

The results are as we would have expected. But I mention this study because I wanted to show you the written instructions that Troy and her colleagues issued to the participants about reappraisal:

As you watch [the film clip], try to think about the situation you see in a more positive light. You can achieve this in several different ways. For example, try to imagine advice that you could give to the characters in the film clip to make them feel better. This could be advice that would help them think about the positive bearing this event could have on their lives. Or, think about the good things they might learn from this experience. Keep in mind that even though a situation may be painful in the moment, in the long run, it could make one's life better or have unexpected good outcomes.[6]

Remember that these written instructions helped participants to feel less miserable while watching the heartbreaking videos. In other words, within that paragraph is the essence of a slightly different strategy that you can apply when you need to feel better. I call this particular technique storytelling reappraisal.

## Telling a tale with your own happy ending

We can blunt the harmful emotional effects of a crazy situation by thinking about the good that just might come out of it. Whether you've been hit by bad news or difficulties at work or home, try to envisage how it might benefit you or change you for the better – even if that might be quite a way off in the future.

Whatever your situation, imagine that you are the author of your own story. You're halfway through the saga and the hero or heroine is experiencing a challenging situation or perhaps even truly horrendous circumstances. Of course, you are that hero or heroine. Now project yourself into the future to the end of the narrative, the happy ending. What are some of the positive consequences that might arise as a result of your current circumstances?

Think about your situation optimistically. You don't have to believe that these benefits will *definitely* occur – only that they are plausible or possible.

In telling yourself a more optimistic story, here are some questions to prompt your thinking:

- What might you eventually learn from the situation?
- Who else might later benefit from the situation or your actions – and in what way?
- How might you ultimately become a stronger or better person as a result of what has happened?
- How might this bring you closer to the people who are important to you?
- What opportunities might this lead to in the end?
- What other benefits or upside might there be?

Storytelling reappraisal is about changing how you see a situation. Whether you got fired from work or your partner has admitted to lying to you, you can't alter the past. What's happened has happened. Or if you're about to go into a job interview or perform at a piano recital, tell yourself that you are growing your skills and augmenting your confidence in public arenas. The best thing you can do now is to protect your mental well-being by choosing to tell yourself a more constructive tale, looking for the positives to whatever's happened or is still going on.

A client told me recently about a presentation that he had to give. He found himself being overcome by a feeling of dread as he counted the rows upon rows of people in the audience. He began thinking, 'There are over a hundred people out there!' And that made him worry that they might be bored by him or, even worse, surreptitiously be laughing at him.

But he remembered to apply storytelling reappraisal. So he told himself, 'Wow, there are over a hundred people waiting to learn from me. There could be people out there who will think back on this as having been good and useful.' And that simple mental trick was enough to quieten his more worrisome thoughts; it allowed him to get on with giving his talk.

## Understanding the biological underpinnings of storytelling

Now, you could make the case that reappraising a situation by revising the story you tell yourself is merely a mind game: it's not changing the actual situation itself. But neuroscientific studies tell us that it can still have a potent effect on us.

One of the parts of the brain that is most associated with anxiety and distress is called the amygdala. I often call the amygdala the brain's early-warning system or security alarm – there to detect threats around us in the same way a smoke detector or burglar alarm is there to signal the presence of danger.

Neuroscientific explorations using brain-imaging equipment consistently find that the amygdala gets very activated when people experience fear or other negative emotions. However, cutting-edge studies by scientists, such as Stanford University's Emily Drabant, have found that the simple act of rewriting the narrative about a situation tends to quell activity in the amygdala.[7]

So it's not purely an attempt to con yourself. Medical science demonstrates that telling yourself a different story is an activity that can genuinely quieten the more unruly parts of your brain.

> Telling yourself a different story is an activity that can genuinely quieten the more unruly parts of your brain.

Having said that, I don't want to imply that it's a miracle cure. It can *reduce* the distress you may be feeling. But it won't eliminate it entirely. Then again, remember that the complete absence of anxiety, fear and doubt definitely isn't always a good thing. A degree of self-distrust is healthy in that it can stop us from being overconfident or arrogant – as we discussed in Chapter 1.

In my coaching work, I frequently support people who find themselves suddenly out of a job. Often, they would like to look for new employment but find themselves struggling: their confidence may be seriously low after having been fired or otherwise forced out.

To help clients, I often explain storytelling reappraisal and then ask them questions such as 'What's a better story here?' or 'What's a more confidence-boosting narrative to tell yourself?' Notice that I don't ask 'What's a more *likely* story?'

Because you don't have to believe that the future will turn out that way. The requirement is only to think of *possible* happy endings rather than *probable* ones. The goal is simply to interrupt the unnerving thoughts that may have hold of your attention.

At the beginning of the year I worked with a client named Jessica, a demure quality control manager in her mid-fifties. Until six months before I met her she had been working at a large pharmaceutical company. In her final year or so working there she had felt more and more harassed and bullied by a new boss. Feeling acutely demoralized, she had finally quit in order to preserve her peace of mind.

She sought the counsel of lawyers in an attempt to win back some earnings from the company. Dreadfully, though, there had been too few corroborating witnesses and her argument was ultimately reduced to a situation of 'she said' versus 'he said'. She lost the case.

Most of our time in coaching sessions was spent on rewriting her CV and helping her to rehearse strong answers to likely interview questions. But I suggested that storytelling reappraisal might aid her in feeling more optimistic.

Over the course of several days she spent time jotting down notes about how her future might actually turn out brighter. For example, she might find work in a more worthwhile sector, such as health care. She could cast around for employment within a smaller company in which she could take a larger role. She might end up working with a bunch of friendly and genuinely supportive colleagues – something she had lacked at the pharmaceutical company. She might actually be able to negotiate a bigger salary. And so on.

Whenever Jessica found herself chewing the skin around her nails and worrying about the future, she made a conscious effort to stop the flow of bothersome thoughts by listing reasons why her career might turn out brilliantly. It only ever took around a minute to do, but she found that it did help her to feel more in control. And she found it a sufficiently useful tactic that she continued using it in her day-to-day life even well after she eventually found a new job.

When you're stuck in an uneasy situation, you may struggle to list the ways in which your future might turn out better. But clinicians, such as Tanja Zoellner at the Roseneck Hospital Centre for Psychosomatic Medicine in Germany and Andreas Maercker of the University of Zurich, have observed that even people who have suffered enormously harrowing circumstances – cancer, rape, the death of loved ones, personal bankruptcy – often report that they look at life more positively.[8]

And the very latest findings suggest that people who have experienced greater adversity in life may actually become more empathetic and compassionate towards others, too.[9] So consider that there can often be genuine, quantifiable benefits to be had from going through stressful situations.

> There can often be genuine, quantifiable benefits
> to be had from going through stressful situations.

## Seeing the upside to feeling down

Do you ever like to watch movies that make you feel scared? Maybe you enjoyed the suspenseful ghost story *The Sixth Sense* or supernatural shocker *The Exorcist*. Perhaps you prefer psychologically terrifying films such as *The Silence of the Lambs* or *Scream*. Or you may be a fan of gory horror movies such as those in the *Saw* series or monster movies such as the *Alien* franchise.

If you're shaking your head about those, then maybe you prefer films that make you cry. One of the most successful movies of all time, the Leonardo DiCaprio and Kate Winslet movie *Titanic*, has been known to wring tears from more than a few people. Romantic drama *The Notebook* and dog drama *Marley and Me* are often cited as tearjerkers by people I know. Or maybe you have a penchant for classic weepies such as *Terms of Endearment* or *Beaches*.

If you have ever enjoyed either category of film, then you have actually taken pleasure from experiencing negative emotions. It's possible to relish the feeling of fear – even though many people may find fear something unpleasant and paralysing in other circumstances. It's equally possible to revel in a bit of sorrow, too – again, despite the fact that most of us would rarely wish to experience sadness in the real world.

Anger is another negative emotion, yet another state of mind that is often described as undesirable. But I know more than a couple of friends and clients who love going to the gym to do classes with names like 'body combat' and 'boxercise'. Yes, they actively look forward to gritting their teeth, yelling and knocking the hell out of imaginary foes or punching bags.

Psychologists talk about two broad categories of emotions: positive emotions and negative emotions. The positive emotions include joy, pride, amusement and gratitude. The negative emotions include anger, fear, sadness and shame. And the traditional view is that we ought to pursue more positive emotions and ward off negative emotions whenever possible.

Clearly, that's too simplistic a notion. In fact, it may do us good to value discomforting emotions, because, weirdly, the latest evidence suggests that we should all learn to see the good that can come from bad moods.

> It may do us good to value discomforting emotions.

The most compelling data comes from an investigation conducted by a quartet of scientists led by Gloria Luong, an expert on emotions at Colorado State University and the Max Planck Institute for Human Development. The researchers recruited a group of 336 men and women into a provocative study probing the links between emotions and both physical and mental health.

The investigative team began by asking their participants to answer dozens of questions about both positive and negative emotions. For example: 'How often do you experience the feeling of nervousness as pleasant?' The participants were asked to rate their response on a 7-point scale from 1 ('almost never') to 7 ('almost always').

Questions about less positive emotions included: 'How often do you experience the feeling of nervousness as helpful?' and 'How often do you experience the feeling of nervousness as meaningful?' and finally 'How often do you experience the feeling of nervousness as appropriate?'

Next, Luong's team issued the participants with smartphones to be carried on their person continuously for a three-week period. At random intervals throughout the day each participant's phone would signal and require its owner to answer questions about his or her current experiences and moods.

For instance, the phone would ask, 'How do you currently feel physically?' and require an answer on a 7-point scale from −3 ('very bad') to +3 ('very good'). Other questions would ask them about problems or hassles they had experienced. And, on each occasion, participants rated the extent to which they were feeling each of six negative emotional states: angry, tired, downcast, disappointed, nervous and tense.

The 336 participants answered hundreds of questions over the three-week period, generating many thousands of pieces of data. So what did the researchers find? As you might expect, participants varied massively in how they felt. Sometimes, they had been socializing with friends or celebrating achievements and felt relaxed, exhilarated or joyful. At other times, they had just experienced missteps or difficulties and felt notably angry, disappointed or nervous.

But here's the important bit: the more people valued their negative emotions in general, the better their physical and psychological health. So when people in the laboratory had said that they occasionally found feelings such as nervousness or anger to be beneficial, they tended to experience better physical and psychological health outcomes.[10]

Of course, that result was based only on the participants' subjective reports about how they felt. Rather ingeniously, though, the researchers gathered more objective data about the participants as well: during the visit to the laboratory, the researchers also tested each participant's muscle strength. Again, the results of the study found that participants who placed more value and significance on their negative emotions tended to be physically stronger. So this, too, corroborated the other findings of the investigation.

## Taking a 2.0 view of negative emotions

The old-fashioned 1.0 view was that negative emotions were usually 'bad'. However, the pioneering study by Gloria Luong and her partners suggests that placing value on negative emotions tends to be associated with better physical and mental health outcomes. Visceral feelings such as anxiety or outright panic, anger and grief, sadness and even disgust all exist because they had evolutionary benefits for our ancestors. So have a think about – reappraise – how these downbeat emotions might be useful for you, too. Modify the story you tell yourself about the turbulent emotions and bad moods you experience. No longer are they a curse, but something occasionally to be appreciated.

Based on the pioneering work of Luong's team, here are four points to ponder:

1 Remember that negative emotions can sometimes be **pleasant**. It can be fun to feel scared. Occasionally, it can feel empowering to feel angry or vengeful. Some people enjoy wallowing in sadness in order to learn what it might mean for them.

2 Reflect on the fact that negative feelings can often be **useful**. For example, nervousness can make people work harder. When people know that they tend to get nervous before crucial presentations or big dates, they tend to do more preparation. Entertainers and athletes often find their nervousness energizing. Anger, too, can grant people the motivation they need to confront others who have let them down or otherwise caused them frustration.

3 Consider that discomforting emotions are often **appropriate**. If you were to experience the loss of a loved one or observe, for example, the suffering of starving children, it would be highly inappropriate to run around laughing and trying to make yourself happy. Experiencing grief or sadness in such situations would be a humane and completely fitting response. Or, if you need to deliver bad news, consider that coming across as sombre and concerned would be quite a reasonable expectation.

4 Finally, bear in mind that negative feelings can be **meaningful**. Jagged emotions can often act as a powerful signal to other people. For example, imagine you are raising money for a dog shelter that is running out of money and in danger of closing for good. You may well get a better response being serious and sad than being upbeat and enthusiastic. Or, if you have been caught doing something inappropriate, feelings of guilt or shame may convey to others that you recognize your wrongdoing and truly want to atone for it.

Luong and her associates pointed out four ways in which negative emotions could be beneficial. But, in my work with clients, I typically find myself emphasizing the usefulness and appropriateness of discomforting emotions the most.

In particular, I often compare psychological discomfort to physical perspiration. When we go to the gym and exercise, we sweat. We get tired. It feels uncomfortable. That's physical discomfort with the eventual aim of looking good or improving our physical health.

In a similar way, when we give a presentation or go to a party, we may feel nervous. And that is merely psychological discomfort in service of improving our prospects and eventual psychological well-being. That anxiety is natural and appropriate because it tells us that we are doing something important to us. And it reminds us that we should pay attention and give something our very best shot.

> Anxiety is natural and appropriate because it tells us that we are doing something important to us.

When clients feel guilty about lapses in judgement or false starts they've made, I encourage them to think of their guilt as a form of psychological prompt. It's a way to focus their attention on the fact that they should look for ways to change what's happened – or perhaps to be more careful in future. So, again, it's a negative emotion that can be both useful and appropriate.

## Learning to label

Not too long ago, the head office team at a major restaurant chain asked me to give a speech at a conference event for their restaurant managers. The topic: managing stress.

I'm sure you can appreciate how tough it could get running a restaurant. On a busy Friday night or Sunday lunchtime a restaurant could be crammed with customers. There could be a queue of customers waiting impatiently to be seated. The kitchen runs out of salmon. One of your waiters phones in sick. A waitress spills red wine on a customer. There are wailing toddlers at a couple of tables and other unruly children running around and getting in the way. One customer is complaining that her steak is overcooked; another is moaning that his vegetables aren't cooked enough.

So I was asked to furnish the restaurant managers with a couple of super-simple techniques that they could apply in a hurry. These had to be methods that they could use not in minutes but mere seconds.

We've seen in this chapter that you do not have to be at the mercy of your feelings. Simply reconceptualizing your physiological arousal as helpful can take the edge off whatever feelings are whirling around in your head. Imagining a more neutral or even positive interpretation of your circumstances may give you a lift. Counselling yourself that negative emotions can sometimes be a healthy and even useful reaction can help, too. But this next tactic, which also involves reframing the nature of your emotions, may be the speediest of them all.

Psychologists call it affect labelling, but 'affect' is just psychological wording for 'emotion'. The premise is actually very straightforward. To feel better, simply acknowledge the emotion that you are feeling by naming it.

> To feel better, simply acknowledge the emotion
> that you are feeling by naming it.

Suppose you're feeling panicky; you could say to yourself, 'I am feeling panicky.' If you're feeling angry, you might want to whisper to yourself, 'I am feeling angry.'

I know it sounds almost too simple. But recent neuroscientific trials tell us that it works. In fact, behavioural scientists led by Lisa Burklund at the University of California, Los Angeles found that it was categorically as effective as telling a different story about a situation through reappraisal. Not only did affect labelling reduce the amount of distress that people felt, it also dampened levels of activation in the amygdala, the hazard detection centre of the brain.[11]

## Naming negative emotions

The plain act of describing a visceral feeling may be enough to dampen it down. The next time you get hit by an uncomfortable emotion, embrace it, analyse it and give it a name. Simply say to yourself, 'I am experiencing a feeling of ...' and then give it a label.

I know some clients who add a little more to what they say, but this is their personal preference rather than something mandated by research. So clients sometimes label the emotion *and* reappraise, with statements such as 'I am experiencing a feeling of disappointment, but I know it won't last for ever' or 'I am currently experiencing feelings of frustration and sadness. However, I know that I can get over it.'

The goal here is not to trick yourself into feeling better. This is merely about using the rational parts to take back control from the more emotional parts of your brain, such as the amygdala.

This method is both quick and versatile. One of my clients likes to reappraise by providing herself with an additional, soothing message. She might say: 'I am feeling lonely. However, it's entirely natural to feel like this sometimes. I'm allowed to feel this way.'

Another client came up with a version that works for him. He begins by labelling the emotion, but then says to himself what he wants to do instead. For example, he might say, 'I am experiencing a feeling of embarrassment. However, I choose to carry on regardless.' Or, 'I am experiencing a feeling of annoyance. However, I am going to walk away and say nothing.'

Whether you run a busy restaurant or are facing some other demanding situation, consider giving affect labelling a go. It will only take a few seconds. And it may just help you to feel that little bit more confident and in control again.

I shall end this chapter with a brief mention of what is yet to come. Affect labelling is a way to reduce the power of negative *emotions*. There is a very similar technique that can reduce the power of negative *thoughts*. It's called cognitive defusion, but we'll talk about it properly later in Chapter 5.

## Onwards and upwards

- Remember: it is *not* true that adversity, life events and ordeals must damage our psychological well-being, our inward-emotional confidence. It is our perception, interpretation or appraisal of any situation that determines its impact on us.
- Even though we tend to appraise situations automatically, bear in mind that we can choose to reappraise them through conscious effort. And this process of reappraisal can blunt the psychological impact of problems and calamitous circumstances.
- Consider that one way to reappraise is to remind yourself that the physiological arousal you're feeling is adaptive, functional and designed to help you to perform better. When you feel nervous, simply tell yourself that your body is getting you geared up and alert so that you can concentrate on the task at hand.
- As an alternative, imagine that you are the hero or heroine of a story. Whatever screwed-up situation you're in, project yourself into the future and try to conceive some plausible benefit or positive consequence that may come out of it.
- As a wider point, recognize that bad moods – negative emotions – are not always bad. If you can reconceive of them as sometimes being appropriate, helpful, meaningful or even pleasant, you may make yourself feel better.
- If you're in a hurry, just name the emotion that you're feeling. Complete the sentence: 'I am experiencing a feeling of ...'

# 4

# Modifying your mental movies

'We suffer primarily not from our vices or our weaknesses, but from our illusions. We are haunted, not by reality, but by those images we have put in their place.'

*Daniel J. Boorstin*

Being a psychologist, I find that people tell me all sorts of things – and frequently with very little prompting. I often go to a local coffee shop for a change of scenery, to use the Wi-Fi and do some research and reading. One of the baristas, a friendly and effusive Italian woman in her early twenties called Valentina, told me about her intense phobia about snakes. She has never been in the physical presence of a snake. But even thinking about a snake makes her shiver. She gets a tingling across her scalp, her neck and down her back, which makes her intensely uncomfortable.

Widening her eyes, she said that one of the things that agitate her most is a recurring image: that she should wake up in the night to find that a gigantically long, thick snake has curled itself around her neck. She can picture its wetly glistening scales and black eyes. She imagines that it would feel cold and slimy, and that the snake would open its jaws wide to devour her head.

As she lives in England, the local snakes aren't terribly big. And I've never heard of anyone waking to find that a snake has infiltrated their bedroom – let alone a monstrously large snake. So it's not a very likely scenario at all. From a rational point of view, Valentina should feel assured that her dreaded mental movie will never play out. But it still worries her. Even though she knows that it's completely irrational and tremendously unlikely, she still feels frightened by it.

Some people see in their minds quite specific, frightening scenarios: of animals such as rats, dogs and spiders; of situations such as having job interviewers or audiences or guests at a party laughing at them. Such images can be quite vivid and terrifying to people. But there is hope. Because it turns out that we may be able to change such images – the mental movies we see in our minds – to overcome our fears and boost our confidence in all sorts of anxiety-inducing situations.

## Sending images away

In the interests of science and in order to unravel what can help us to feel more confident, psychologists often run experiments in which they deliberately make people feel worse. Let's recreate one of these now: suppose for a moment that you have bravely volunteered for one such investigation. You come into my laboratory and I ask you to sit down in front of a computer monitor.

I explain that I'm going to show you a series of images. Each image will appear on screen for a mere six seconds. And then I'll ask you to rate how negatively or positively you feel about it on a scale from very negative (−4) to very positive (+4).

The first photo comes up. It's a photograph of a young boy of maybe ten years of age who has had his leg amputated just above the knee. Maybe he suffered a disease or he was unlucky enough to have stepped on a land mine.

The second photograph is of a dead dog, a Labrador, in what looks to be a patch of grassland. The dog has been slit open from throat to belly. You can't help but wonder: was the poor dog tortured?

The next photograph is of a crying woman. Her face is twisted in agony and it's clear to see why. Her right hand is badly mangled. You can see that several large shards of glass are sticking out of her flesh. You can even make out parts of her wrist bone.

Not pleasant images, right?

But this is exactly the experimental protocol used by seasoned scholars Joshua Davis of Barnard College of Columbia University, James Gross of Stanford University and Kevin Ochsner of Columbia University. Unsurprisingly, the team found that most of the participants in their study reported feeling quite distressed about such images.

Here's the useful bit, though. The investigators split their participants into three groups and asked the participants in each to do one of three things. They instructed one group of participants to imagine that the scene was coming towards them and getting larger. They told a second group to envision the scene staying exactly where it was. And they asked the third group to conceive of the scene moving away into the distance and shrinking in size.

Guess which group felt the most distraught? Yes, you got it: the first group that imagined the scenes moving towards them and looming larger reported the most anguish: they rated the images most negatively.

So there's no prize for working out which group felt the least distressed: the third group that had been instructed to imagine the scenes receding away. Mentally pushing the images away from them and shrinking them helped to blunt the negative effects of those scenes.[1]

That's a brilliant result. Because this elegant study grants us a quick yet effective way for minimizing the discomfort associated with the unpleasant pictures and scenes that we may paint in our minds.

## Mentally resizing unpleasant imagery

Try the mental resizing trick the next time something is bothering you. You may be dwelling on something that happened in the past, such as playing over and over again a disgraceful mistake or a loss that still makes you sad. Perhaps you are feeling down about something in the here and now such as an ongoing argument at home or you're stuck in a traffic jam. Or you keep imagining something awful that just might happen in the future.

Whatever your circumstances, simply close your eyes (so long as it's safe to do so!) and imagine the scene in your head. Pretend that you have taken a photograph of the event or situation. Then send the upsetting scene away from you, backwards into space. As with anything that recedes into the distance, it will get smaller and smaller in your mind's eye. Keep pushing it away until it disappears entirely.

To finish off, some clients tell me that they find it useful to pause – to keep their eyes closed for a few seconds – before opening their eyes and returning to reality again.

I'll admit that, when someone first told me about this technique years ago, I thought it sounded like some pseudo-scientific gimmick. It was only when I had personally read several research papers on it that I became convinced enough about its effectiveness to endorse it to my own clients.

In an ideal world, this mental resizing technique would cancel out whatever negative emotions you're feeling. Unfortunately, that's an unrealistic goal. Mentally pushing away a disturbing scene can make a significant difference to how you feel. But it will likely only *reduce* your distress – not remove it entirely.

> Mentally pushing away a disturbing scene can make a significant difference to how you feel.

Still, I wish I had known about this when I was a kid. When I was about 13 or 14 years old, I begged and pleaded with my parents to let me watch a horror movie on TV called *The Omen*.

The film is decades old and has special effects that are pretty tame by today's standards. But, at the time, I was terrified. In particular, there was a scene where one of the characters got beheaded by a falling pane of glass. I don't know why it scared me so much. It just did. I didn't sleep well for about a week because I kept replaying that beheading scene in my mind. But perhaps if I had mentally shunted that image into the far, far distance away from me, I would have felt a bit better.

Oh, well. At least I hope that this technique will be of use to other scared children in the future.

## Visualizing a perfect performance

Mentally sending upsetting images and scenes away from you is a fairly simple skill. But if you are someone who likes the idea of playing around with the images in your head, you could try this next, more advanced visualization tactic for upgrading your self-belief.

American researchers Mike Knudstrup, Sharon Segrest and Amy Hurley define visualization as 'the internal re-creation within one's thoughts of what is, or could be, an external experience'.[2] It's not dissimilar from daydreaming, but with a specific purpose: an intention to control the way the scenes play out. Specifically, visualization is about generating an upcoming scenario in your mind and imagining how it would look to perform at your best.

> Visualization is about generating an upcoming scenario in your mind and imagining how it would look to perform at your best.

Psychologists have long known that many top athletes use visualization (also sometimes called mental rehearsal) to bolster their performance. All sorts of sports people utilize it, including golfers, tennis players, skiers, gymnasts, football players and figure skaters. More importantly, when American sport psychologist Daniel Landers conducted a comprehensive review of 60 separate studies involving visualization techniques, he concluded that mentally imagining performance was associated with quantifiable benefits.

Visualization can be particularly handy for athletes because they can't engage in physical training and practice 24 hours a day. Their bodies need rest. Even when they may be physically exhausted, mental visualization allows them to carry on training in their own imaginations.

Here's the question, though: can visualization aid people who aren't top-flight athletes?

Briefly, the answer is yes. However, there's a caveat: because it isn't simply a case of letting your mind wander and fantasizing that everything will go well. To reap the benefits of visualization, you have to do it in an ultra-structured and focused manner.

To illustrate how to make visualization work for you, let's look at a prominent study by the researchers Knudstrup, Segrest and Hurley. Lots of people hate or outright fear job interviews, so there have been lots of investigations into how people can feel more confident and perform at their best when being bombarded with interview questions.

Knudstrup and his associates enrolled 99 participants into their study and told them that they would all be participating in a mock interview for a job as a management trainee. To begin with, all the participants were given a booklet of typical interview questions and asked to write out answers to them. Questions included:

- 'Tell me about yourself.'
- 'What are your major strengths?'
- 'What is your greatest weakness?'
- 'What can you do for us?'
- 'What accomplishment gave you the greatest satisfaction?'

The researchers then divided their participants into two groups. One group of participants (the control group) was asked to sit quietly and to wait for an interviewer. The second group (the experimental group) was instructed to visualize an interviewer asking the ten questions that they had just answered in writing; they were told to envision the interview going well and concluding with a job offer from the interviewer.

Next, all of the participants were put through a gruelling interview and their performances rated by a crack team of four interviewers. Finally, the participants answered a handful of questions about their stress levels, for example rating the extent of their agreement with statements such as 'At this time I feel nervous.'

So, the results: the researchers found unmistakeable advantages for the visualization group. The participants who practised visualization reported feeling less nervous. They were rated more highly by the interviewers as well.

Obviously, that's a result that supports the benefits of visualization: it not only helped people to *feel* more self-assured (i.e. it lifted their inward-emotional confidence), it also enabled them to *perform* more boldly (i.e. it boosted the public performance component of their outward-social confidence), too. But before you disappear off into your own head to dream about how you want things to turn out, let's take a peek back at two vitally important details about the study.

Firstly, the visualization participants had done some actual preparation. They didn't just sit and conjure up images of an engaging and pleasant chat with an interviewer. They had already written down their responses to ten likely interview questions. In other words, they had done a fair amount of concrete groundwork ahead of visualizing how they wanted things to go.

Secondly, the visualization participants spent between ten and 20 minutes imagining how they would respond. This wasn't something they did in seconds or even a few minutes. Proper visualization isn't quick or easy; getting a result from it takes time.

---

Proper visualization isn't quick or easy; getting a result from it takes time.

---

## Mentally rehearsing your own success

I will summarize some instructions for how to get the most out of visualization shortly. Before I do that, there's just one more consideration.

Psychological scientists long ago figured out that there are two ways to visualize any activity.[3] Let's return to the scenario of a job interview again. One option would be to picture the scene from the viewpoint of, say, an observer or TV camera. So the camera would see both you and the interviewer in the scene. This viewpoint is known as the third-person perspective.

An alternative would be to adopt what's known as a first-person perspective, in which you imagine the scene through your own eyes. So you would see the interviewer sitting opposite you. And you might see your own hands or, if you were to use your imagination to glance down, you could see your own body and legs – but not your face.

Now, one of these viewpoints during mental rehearsal has been shown to be more effective at producing results. Care to gamble which?

For me, the proof that visualization is a rather amazing technique comes from a body of studies showing that it can actually improve muscle strength – without any physical exercise or even movement. An example is an experiment masterminded by Wan Yao, a professor of health and kinesiology at the University of Texas at San Antonio.

Yao's team recruited 18 volunteers and told them that they would be tested on their arm strength in six weeks' time. As in so many experiments, the participants were split into three distinct groups. One group was instructed to spend 15 minutes a day visualizing flexing their arms from a first-person perspective. A second group spent a similar length of time each day engaging in visualization from a third-person point of view. And the final group acted as a control – these participants were not taught to visualize at all.

Six weeks later, the participants who engaged in third-person perspective visualization were no stronger than the control participants who had spent six weeks doing no visualization at all. It was only the participants who imagined actually making the contractions from the more immersive first-person perspective who benefited.[4]

To me, the importance of perspective makes total sense. Earlier in this chapter, we looked at the mental resizing technique. There, we discovered that shoving a distressing scene away as if it were receding into the distance could help to reduce the turmoil it causes us. With visualization, we're trying to do the opposite. By bringing a mental scene so close to ourselves that we inhabit it and become the centre of it, we are trying to make it more likely that it will actually turn out that way.

In summary, visualization can work well, but only if you do it the right way. Before we move on to the next tactic, allow me to pull together some best-practice advice on how best to use visualization.

## Seeing success in your mind's eye

Perhaps you're a sportsperson or an athlete who wants to perform at your best. Maybe you're a dancer or an actor, a pianist or an entertainer who needs to conquer your nerves and showcase your talents. Or you need to mentally rehearse for a challenging situation such as a confrontation with a colleague, a job interview or a presentation. To get the most from visualization, here are several specific tips on making the most of the mental movies that you direct for yourself:

- **Prepare in actuality before you practise in your head.** You can't just picture a triumphant job interview if you haven't prepared your interview answers. You won't get the benefit from imagining a winning presentation if you haven't written your script and rehearsed it out loud. If you're going to play a musical piece at a competition or serve well in a game of tennis, you need to understand what you're supposed to be doing and practise, practise, practise it for real first. Visualization should be an additional or final stage of preparation – mental rehearsal does not replace all your other preparation.

- **Focus on the process rather than the outcome.** Imagine seeing yourself working through the process of speaking, playing or performing. Spend only a little time (if at all) on what it would look and feel like to achieve a successful outcome: having an interviewer offer you a job, getting a round of applause or holding the trophy aloft, for instance. Your mental rehearsal is about preparing you to perform to the best of your ability – it shouldn't be fantasizing about results that are not likely to be fully within your control.

- **See your situation from a first-person perspective.** Envisage how the situation would play out as seen through your own eyes rather than seeing the third-person or camera's eye view of you in the situation.
- **Spend enough time visualizing what you want.** Studies tend to ask subjects to spend many minutes visualizing. It's not something that takes just seconds or mere minutes. The benefits are likely to come from imagining in detail a whole event from start to finish.

Visualization should be an additional or final stage of preparation – mental rehearsal does not replace all your other preparation.

## Tackling your mental monsters

What's your biggest fear? Perhaps you're terrified of spiders, rats or some other animal. It might be heights, flying in a plane, the sight of blood or the dark. Or you want to conquer your fear of public speaking or being judged when meeting new people.

One way to get over a fear is to expose yourself to the feared stimulus, be it an animal, an object or a situation. For spiders or rats, or any animal, you need first to look at photographs and then videos of them; you ultimately need the opportunity to be in a room with and maybe even interact with the living animals. If you fear flying, you need to get close to planes and eventually be able to board one.

(This method is called *in vivo* exposure treatment and we'll encounter it again in Chapter 9.)

But there is an alternative – especially if you have a powerful imagination. So allow me to ask you specifically about your own greatest fear for a moment. Do you associate any particularly horrifying images with it?

Clinical psychologist and researcher Melissa Hunt has long been interested in the role of imagery in different phobias. In one experimental inquiry conducted by Hunt and her associates, she found that 78 per cent of people with phobias reported experiencing imagery of some kind in relation to their fear.[5]

Here are a handful of the scenarios that people pictured in their heads:

- 'I can feel myself falling off the edge of the cliff. I get a sickening feeling in my stomach just thinking about it. It's like I'm grabbing at the crumbling rock and I'm just falling and the air is whistling past me and the ground is rushing up and I know I'm going to die.'
- 'I imagine the dog running up to me and jumping up. I can feel its claws raking across my cheek and drawing blood. Then it would sink its teeth into my throat and rip out my oesophagus. I can see the blood splattering everywhere.'
- 'I can feel the rat sinking its teeth into my big toe. I would scream and shake my foot and try to fling it off, but it would hold on and I'd just be there with this huge evil rat biting my toe.'

Hunt and her team didn't merely collate a bunch of phobic people's stories, though. They also rated the amount of horrific imagery – the vividness and detail – present in each description. And they found that phobic individuals who reported more fear also tended to describe their imagery in more horrifying and vivid terms. Based on that research, Hunt and her various collaborators began to come up with a hypothesis. Given that people who fear a particular animal, object or situation can frequently describe their mental images in terrifying detail, could simply changing those images help them to feel more confident?

## *Turning the creepy into the merely curious*

Hunt and Co. worked up a method called imagery rescripting, which involves playing around with the images in your head. Great. But does it work?

Let's look at a study conducted by Hunt with a colleague, Miriam Fenton, who was also at the University of Pennsylvania. The research duo gathered together 52 participants who all wanted treatment for snake phobia.[6]

Immediately, the participants were divided into four groups. The first (the control) group spent 20 minutes learning a deep-breathing technique and then watched a 25-minute relaxation video. In other words, they didn't do anything that was expected to make a material difference to their confidence around snakes.

A second group spent 45 minutes in a room with a real, living, breathing, slithering snake. These rather shocked participants were given the chance to meet one of two snakes: either a four-foot-long, black, brown and tan python or a three-foot-long red, orange and light-brown corn snake. The participants were allowed plenty of time to acclimatize themselves to the mere presence of the snake in the room. And when they felt comfortable enough to do so, they were encouraged to inch closer to it.

The third group, the one that we're most interested in, were taught to rescript the imagery in their mental landscapes. To begin with, these participants were asked to think about and describe the frightening or warped imagery they had about snakes. For instance, many of the participants said that they could 'see' or 'feel' a snake biting them – perhaps on a hand or arm or, more horrifyingly, on their neck, face or even an eye.

The participants were then asked to rescript or alter the frightening images using either humorous or fantastical imagery. For instance, some participants who were scared of snake's teeth summoned up images of snakes with no teeth, as if they were old men. Or, to protect them from the teeth, they imagined themselves clothed in Kevlar body armour that would surely shatter a snake's teeth.

Other participants had particular fears about the gruesome pain that a snakebite might inflict on them. And these participants were taught to substitute their overblown fears with more realistic concerns, for example imagining that a bite from a small snake might be no more painful than an injection of a needle at the doctor's.

These imagery rescripting sessions lasted 45 minutes. Throughout, the goal was to revise the frightening images until they seemed nonsensical and no longer made the participants feel scared.

The fourth and final group spent time doing a mix of cognitive ('talking') therapy for 35 minutes combined with ten minutes of actually being in a room with a snake. Here, the researchers wanted to know if the mix of talking about their fears in conjunction with some real time with a snake would be the most powerful treatment of all.

After one of the four treatments, all the participants were introduced to one of the two snakes – either the python or the corn snake. They were given the chance to reach into a glass tank to touch the snake if they felt they could. And their anxiety levels were measured.

So what was the very best treatment?

First of all, the researchers found that the deep breathing and relaxation treatment did nothing. Not one of the participants felt comfortable enough to touch the snake.

However, all three of the other treatments were equally effective. Whether participants spent 45 minutes actually meeting a snake, mostly talking about a snake or changing their mental imagery about a snake, they all benefited the same amount. In just three-quarters of an hour, many of the participants got sufficiently comfortable that they were able to reach out and stroke the snake for real.

Now, one way of looking at the results of this study would be to say that exposure to an actual scary situation is a good way to get over it. But, for me, the takeaway is somewhat different. If you fear rats or spiders, for instance, it may be a bit time-consuming as well as expensive to buy or otherwise track one down. If you're petrified of job interviews or exams, you may not have that many actual opportunities for practice. So imagery rescripting can provide us with a practical, cost-effective method for boosting our confidence instead.

## Taking apart your mental monster

Do you have vivid and disturbing images about your fear? The images you see flashing through your mind may be quite improbable; they may not make sense at all. You're almost certainly not going to be eaten by a dog/spider/snake/rat. The chances of your being hurt in a plane crash are statistically miniscule. The worst that might happen in a job interview, audition or presentation is that you're somewhat embarrassed – you won't actually keel over and die.

Not everyone does have vibrantly negative images running through their heads (and, if that's the case, this technique may not be particularly useful for you). But if you are bothered by recurring, unsettling images, you could try to rescript them. Essentially, studies suggest that it can sometimes be the images in your mind that are causing you anxiety rather than actual objects, animals or situations. So, if you can take apart those frightening images, you may cope more easily with the real objects, animals or situations. Here's how:

1 Begin by identifying all of the mental imagery or scenes that you associate with the object, animal or situation that frightens you. You could try talking them through with someone or perhaps writing them down. Give yourself plenty of time to list everything – every last element or even sensation – that you don't like.

2 Try taking apart your mental images through humour and using nonsensical imagery. If your mind keeps dwelling on an animal's fangs, perhaps imagine that they're actually made of jelly. If you see in your mind's eye an audience jeering you off stage, picture that you're wearing a magical cloak that has rendered you completely invisible. There's no right answer here. What works for someone else may not work for you; it's about discovering whatever funny, silly or surreal images help you. The key is to keep imagining the new scenes until you have banished the old ones.

3 Also, try replacing unrealistic or distorted images with more realistic ones. So, if you keep imagining that your plane might explode in mid-air, try changing the picture: see your plane gliding uneventfully through the skies for hour after hour instead. Or, if you fancy that a job interviewer might laugh at you, see in your mind instead the interviewer more realistically sitting with a neutral or even mildly bored expression on his or her face.

Imagery rescripting isn't a quick fix. It's not something that you can do in mere seconds. Participants in research studies have typically spent 30 to 60 minutes modifying the images stuck in their heads. It requires a genuine investment of time. But I love that research has come up with a verified method for tackling the images that may haunt us. So, if you're someone who feels tormented by the horror movies in your skull, consider rescripting them and turning them into Disney family features or comedies instead.

## *Onwards and upwards*

- To reduce the distress associated with a situation or event, imagine it as a scene playing out in your mind. Then send the scene gradually away from you so it gets progressively smaller and smaller. This mental resizing trick won't completely stop you from feeling upset, but studies have shown that it can make a significant difference to how people feel.

- Remember that many competitive athletes and sports stars engage in mental rehearsal or visualization of how they would like to perform. To augment your confidence and performance, begin by preparing thoroughly: you need to have written and rehearsed a presentation or interview answers, for example. You must first know what good execution should look like. Only then should you rehearse in your mind's eye how you would like your performance to proceed. Make no mistake: use visualization only when you've trained and familiarized yourself with a skill in depth.

- As an alternative (or complementary approach), consider imagery rescripting. If you keep experiencing the same vivid, scary images, try using humour or fantasy to metamorphose them. Or work at replacing unrealistic, irrationally scary images with more plausible ones.

- Don't expect immediate results. When it comes to both visualization (which is about rehearsing how you would like things to turn out) and mental rescripting (which is about demolishing the bad scenes you see in your head), studies typically find that the benefits are only detectable after 20, 30, 40 or even more minutes. So take your time to do it properly.

Imagine for a minute that it's a Saturday evening and you've just left a party. You hadn't really wanted to go. You didn't think you would know many people there, but the host was a good friend who was keen for you to be there, so you made the effort. Unfortunately, you arrived only to find that your intuition had been correct: there was hardly anyone you knew there. You got chatting to someone you'd never met before – his name was Alan or Adam or something like that. And the conversation was incredibly awkward.

When you asked him a handful of polite questions, he gave rather short answers that sounded more like bullet points than full sentences. That made you nervous so, when he asked you any questions, you ended up answering in even shorter sentences. He also kept looking around the room rather than making eye contact, as if he was trying to find someone better to talk to. And the pauses got longer and longer until neither of you was speaking.

It was one of the most excruciating conversations you've ever had. It left you feeling both upset and embarrassed. But thinking about what happened, which of the following statements is most likely to describe your state of mind?

- 'I clearly wasn't saying the right things to make him more interested in me. It was my fault.'
- 'I'm not going to think about what happened. I'm really not going to think about it.'
- 'I didn't even want to go to that party. I must remember to turn down the next invitation to an event rather than feel compelled to go.'
- 'I suspect that he had poor social skills or his own hang-ups that prevented him from being a good conversationalist.'

Of course, the four options are an oversimplification. You may be thinking some combination of several of them – and maybe other things, too. But the larger point is this: the way that we think about both the world and ourselves goes a long way towards determining our confidence.

94

> The way we think about both the world and ourselves goes a long way towards determining our confidence.

Many people worry and beat themselves up about past events or what's going on at the moment. Others dread what the future might bring. Some squirm with worry about everything: the past, present and future. Such thinking patterns are often deeply ingrained and can be devastatingly damaging to our state of mind. However, we don't have to let that be the case.

Psychologists continue to develop new tools for cultivating healthier, more assured ways of thinking about both yourself and the world. For example, cognitive behavioural therapy (CBT) is one of the most high-profile methods, a set of strategies that has crossed over into the mainstream. But CBT is sometimes described as a second-wave treatment as there is now a third wave of even newer mental techniques.

Hold that thought, though. We're getting ahead of ourselves a little. So let's start by looking at one of those unhealthy, confidence-sapping modes of thinking first.

## Defusing mental bombs

No one enjoys being criticized. You probably wouldn't relish having someone tell you that you're crazy, boring, fat or useless. So it's ironic that many people who crave more confidence are often their own worst critics – far worse than the folks around them. When things go wrong or you're feeling inadequate, you may notice self-sabotaging thoughts popping into your mind such as:

- 'I am not good enough.'
- 'I'm so ignorant.'
- 'I'm not good looking enough.'
- 'I am terrible at presentations/spreadsheets/studying/ making decisions/etc.'

- 'I should not have done that.'
- 'I'm a bad person/friend/lover/parent/etc.'

> It's ironic that many people who crave more confidence are often their own worst critics.

Psychologists call these automatic negative thoughts. We don't want them in our heads. They just seem to happen – whether we want them to or not.

Unsurprisingly, such unbidden thoughts can ravage your self-confidence. Imagine trying to get on with a task while a colleague or a friend whispers hurtful, negative comments in your ear. That is essentially what you may be doing to yourself when you have such thoughts running around in your head. However, you don't need to allow them to run rampant. Research over the last decade or so has identified a technique for stamping out negative thoughts. It's called cognitive defusion. And, remarkably, it may take only seconds to apply.

When you have a thought or belief about yourself, it's easy for that thought to seem like a fact. You can get stuck on – or fused with – your thought. For example, if you have the thought 'I'm so useless', you may end up acting as if it is true. The thought may make you give up or stop trying, even though you might actually have succeeded if you had only persisted with it.

The idea behind cognitive defusion is to disconnect consciously – or 'de-fuse' – your thoughts from reality. Coming back to the thought 'I'm so useless', it can help to remind yourself that this is only a thought in your head. This is subjective judgement on your part rather than a proven, unarguable truth. It's not as if a panel of experts in the field of intelligence has tested you and concluded that you are quite categorically useless.

If you're thinking 'I can't do this', the thought itself may be damaging your ability to concentrate. If you only could counter the belief, you may be able to focus more readily and get a better result.

> The idea behind cognitive defusion is to disconnect consciously – or 'de-fuse' – your thoughts from reality.

To explain the origins of the technique, we need to go back in time to 1916, when a British psychologist by the name of Edward Titchener speculated that merely saying a word out loud repeatedly could rob the word of its literal meaning.[1]

Try it now if you like. Take any word that comes to mind. Watch the second hand on a clock. And just repeat the word aloud as many times as you can in 20 seconds. When people do it, they often find that they focus less on the meaning of the word and more on the sound of the word or maybe the movement of the muscles in their faces. However, Titchener's idea was never properly investigated, so no one knew for certain whether it could actually help to combat the power that negative thoughts have over us.

It took nearly a century before a young doctoral student at the University of Nevada, Reno, became sufficiently intrigued by Titchener's suggestion that he decided to test it. In one of the earliest studies on this method, Akihiko Masuda instructed experimental participants to reduce negative thoughts to a single word. For example, someone who might have been thinking 'I am a bad person' simply picked out the word 'bad'. Participants were then taught to repeat the word out loud for 30 seconds. Soon afterwards, the participants reported that they not only believed the thought less – they moreover felt less distressed.[2]

In a later study, Masuda and his colleagues asked different groups of participants to repeat the single word for varying lengths of time. They noticed that just three seconds of fast repetition was enough to reduce participants' level of anguish. And around 30 seconds of repetition was required before participants started to question the believability of the negative thought.[3]

The way I look at it, that's a magnificent result. Absolutely superb. As little as three seconds may be enough to make us feel better. That's incredibly fast. And even 30 seconds isn't a huge investment of time to decimate the power that discouraging thoughts can sometimes have over us.

So Titchener was right. And the idea of defusion has become central to a treatment method called acceptance and commitment therapy (ACT), one of the newer, so-called third wave of psychological procedures that has gained credibility in recent years. I mention it in passing only in case you're interested. Having said that, we don't really need to think about where defusion comes from. The important thing is that it works.

I admit that the notion of simply repeating a word again and again does smack of quackery. If you were to explain one-word cognitive defusion to most folks, you might find many of them were either mildly sceptical or completely incredulous. 'What? Say a word over and over and you'll feel better?'

Yes, it's a weird-sounding technique. But remember that it has been tested by investigators and the results subjected to laborious statistical analysis. The results were then sent to the editors of various scientific journals, who then asked panels of anonymous academics to critique the results of the studies. Only when the investigators were able to answer the academics' every criticism were the results allowed to be published.

Many hundreds of hours went into the original research and probably dozens more into the publication process. So we should take it on good authority that this odd little technique of repeating a word rapidly might genuinely help to take the sting out of negative beliefs.

## Applying one-word cognitive defusion

The next time you are plagued by a negative thought, try one-word defusion. Pick out the single word that is most upsetting you. There's no right or wrong answer here. For example, if you're having the thought 'I'm a stupid, lazy idiot', it may be that there are three candidates for the most damaging word. Some people may choose 'stupid'. Others may find 'lazy' more hurtful. Still others may find 'idiot' the most critical of the three.

Then repeat the word out loud to yourself as quickly as you can. If there are people nearby, it's OK to whisper it.

After just a few seconds, you may start to feel a bit silly. And that's a good sign. It shows that you're pushing the distress away and replacing it with something else: perhaps a warm sense of amusement that you're doing something faintly ridiculous. Or a dreamlike feeling as the word decays into meaninglessness.

But keep going. Don't stop yet. Keep going for a half-minute or so and you may come to realize that the thought has lost its hold over you.

## Identifying thoughts as thoughts

The basis of defusion is to remember that even the most terrible, most pernicious thought is only a thought – a point of view that you conjured up about yourself. It's about defusing or separating our subjective thoughts from objective reality.

Self-criticisms such as 'I'm hopeless' or 'I'm a failure' or 'I should give up' are only opinions that you may be telling yourself. They are *not* facts in the same way that 'the Empire State Building is 443 metres tall' or 'water boils at 100 °C' or 'pigs cannot fly' are verifiable truths.

The one-word repetition technique is one way to defuse thoughts from reality. But there is another way to combat negative beliefs. This next technique is also a type of defusion method. It just takes a different form.

A line-up of researchers headed by Hilary-Anne Healy at the National University of Ireland, Maynooth, taught participants to change their negative thoughts by adding the phrase 'I am having the thought that …' to them. For example, if someone was thinking, 'I am simply hopeless', he would turn it into the slightly longer phrase, 'I am having the thought that I am simply hopeless.' Or, if someone else was having the doubt 'I am too old for this', she might revise it as 'I am having the thought that I am too old for this.'

It's another simple tactic. But it worked. Again, when participants were trained to apply this technique, they rated their own negative thoughts as less believable. They also reported feeling better about themselves.[4]

Clearly, defusion has benefits for our inward-emotional confidence then. It helps us to feel less distressed and more positive about ourselves. But other research suggests that it may have an additional advantage: it may augment our performance at real-world tasks, too.

Research duo Nic Hooper of Middle East Technical University and Louise McHugh of University College Dublin are pretty much experts in the field of research on acceptance and commitment therapy. Several years ago they began an experiment by splitting 65 participants into three groups. One group was taught defusion. They were told:

> Notice each of your thoughts as they pop into your head. The thought may be 'this is too easy', 'I am very bad at this exercise' or 'I don't know what I'm thinking!' One by one, notice each thought that you have and let them just pass by your consciousness. It may even be helpful to alter the thought from 'this is too easy/I am very bad at this exercise' to 'right now, I am having the thought that this is too easy/I am having the thought that I am very bad at this exercise.'

Another of the three groups was taught to replace negative beliefs with positive ones:

> Any time bad thoughts come into your mind, immediately replace them with a good thought.

In other words, the first two groups were taught active mental strategies. A third and final group was given no further instruction and acted as a control group.

All the participants were then given a sheet of paper with a maze on it. Use the following example if you feel like trying to solve it (Figure 5.1). Begin about a third of the way up on the left-hand side. See if you can find your way to the exit on the right-hand side.

Anyway, back to the study. The research team simply asked all their participants to solve the maze as quickly as possible. Participants who were taught no mental techniques on average took 49.1 seconds to solve the maze. Participants who were taught to replace

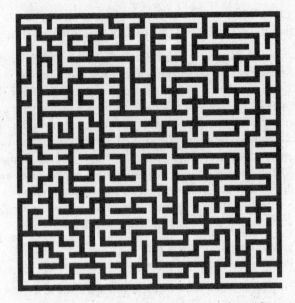

FIGURE 5.1 Can you find your way to the exit?

negative thoughts with positive ones were marginally slower at 52.5 seconds. But the defusion group, who were taught to identify their thoughts as thoughts, sped through their mazes in only 39.0 seconds.[5]

In other words, the study found that simply replacing negative thoughts with positive ones did not help participants at all. In contrast, learning to nudge their thoughts aside spurred the defusion participants to perform better at the mentally challenging task.

The broader implication is that defusing thoughts by labelling thoughts as thoughts may improve both inward-emotional confidence as well as the nonverbal performance component of outward-social confidence. I'm speculating here, but this technique may therefore even help us to raise our productivity when we're feeling frazzled or panicky at work. And that wouldn't be a bad result at all from simply noticing the negative thoughts in our heads and saying, 'I'm having the thought that …'

## Defusing negative thoughts by labelling them as thoughts

When you experience negative beliefs such as 'I can't do this' or 'I'm pathetic', it can be quite easy to believe that you really can't do a task or that you are genuinely pathetic. And that belief may not only make you feel bad. It may also hinder your performance or even stop you entirely from getting on with things.

Use defusion by reminding yourself that your thoughts – even the most self-critical and destabilizing ones – are *only* thoughts. So whenever you get an unhelpful thought popping into your head, don't try to ignore it. Neither should you endeavour to push it aside by telling yourself something overly positive. Just notice the thought and add a phrase such as:

- 'I am having the thought that …'
- 'Right now, I am experiencing a thought that …'

And that's it. That's all you have to do. You don't have to argue with your thought. You don't have to try to debunk it or otherwise dispute it. The mere act of recognizing that your thought is *only* a thought may help you to both feel better and perform better.

By the way, if you think this form of defusion sounds familiar, you'd be right. It bears a striking resemblance to the affect labelling method we encountered in Chapter 3. Affect labelling involved naming your feelings by using the phrase 'I am experiencing a feeling of …' In contrast, this defusion technique entails identifying your thoughts by using the phrase 'I am having the thought that …'

But what both have in common is that they encourage us to identify our feelings or thoughts for what they are. So our feelings are only fleeting emotions rather than a permanent state of affairs. Our thoughts are only personal points of view rather than objective reality.

> Our thoughts are only personal points of view rather than objective reality.

## *Avoiding the trap of overthinking*

One of my clients, named Brian, watches a lot of television. Like many people, the 45-year-old follows popular American shows such as *Game of Thrones* and *The Walking Dead*. He records every episode of British soaps *EastEnders* and *Hollyoaks* and tries to watch them the same evening so he can join in with conversations when his friends talk about the shows the next day at work. He also binge-watches shows; for example, he worked his way through all six seasons (121 episodes) of the sci-fi drama *Lost* in under a month. And that was while keeping up with all his regular TV shows, too.

But, forcing an unconvincing smile on his face, he admitted that the many hours of television that he watches may be more of a diversionary tactic than something he actively wants to do. He hates being alone with his thoughts. He doesn't just get a couple of automatic negative thoughts popping into his head. They seem to arrive in vast waves to the extent that he can find himself losing track of time.

In particular, Brian ends up replaying mistakes he has made. Those could be blunders or gaffes from the last few hours – something he said at work to a co-worker or a client, for example. Or, equally as easily, he finds himself bothered by events from months or even years ago: quarrels he had with family or friends, the reasons why he lost touch with various friends or painful break-ups with exes.

Alas, this tendency to recall miserable or painful events is all too common. Do any of the following statements describe how you ever feel?

- 'I tend to dwell on things that happened to me in the past.'
- 'I often replay in my mind how I acted in past situations.'
- 'I spend a lot of time thinking about my embarrassing or disappointing moments.'
- 'I often think back to past arguments or disagreements.'
- 'I find myself reflecting on events in my life that should no longer concern me.'

These statements are derived from a questionnaire created by seasoned researchers Paul Trapnell of Ohio State University at Mansfield and Jennifer Campbell of the University of British Columbia.[6] If you identify with any of them, you may be prone to something that psychologists call rumination, a tendency to think about yourself or past events from a negative point of view.

People who ruminate may criticize themselves for their shortcomings, faults or failings. They may think over and over again about past flops, injustices and regrets. And, in doing all of this, they often focus on themes of loss, disappointment, rejection or threat.

As you can imagine, this isn't going to be terribly good for your inward-emotional confidence. Thinking constantly about everything that's wrong with you or the world is only going to make you feel glum or angry, or both. In the long term, there's persuasive evidence that high levels of rumination may contribute to the development of conditions such as clinical depression, anxiety, substance abuse and eating disorders.[7]

> Thinking constantly about everything that's wrong with you or the world is only going to make you feel glum or angry, or both.

Clearly, a desirable ambition would be to avoid thinking negatively about yourself and everyone else. But that doesn't mean you should stop thinking about yourself or analysing events and other people's motivations. It simply means learning to take a more neutral rather than negative viewpoint when thinking about things.

Consider these five further statements, also based on questions from the test developed by Trapnell and Campbell:

- 'I enjoy analysing why I behave the way I do.'
- 'I like to think about the nature and meaning of things.'
- 'I enjoy exploring my inner self.'
- 'I am fascinated by my attitudes and feelings.'
- 'I often look at my life from a philosophical point of view.'

This second set of statements measures something that social scientists call reflection. They define reflection as thinking about ourselves or past events in a way that is motivated by curiosity or the simple desire to learn about ourselves. In other words, people who engage in reflection tend to revisit past experiences from a more balanced, objective point of view. For example, when thinking back on past mistakes, they may be as likely to ascribe them to bad luck or the faults of other people as their own failings. And, once they have analysed past situations, they tend not to dwell on them.

The point is that rumination and reflection are two entirely distinct modes of thinking. Trapnell and Campbell found that they were statistically separate. People could be high on one or the other – or both or neither. For instance, some people may be highly prone to rumination with hardly any reflection; others may have the opposite pattern of doing a lot of reflection but hardly any of the more self-critical and harmful rumination.

> Rumination and reflection are two entirely distinct modes of thinking.

Why does this matter? A later study instigated by Greg Siegle of the Western Psychiatric Institute and Clinic at the University of Pittsburgh School of Medicine found that the two styles of thinking had different psychological repercussions. People who ruminated were more likely to report symptoms of clinical depression, yet people who engaged in a lot of reflection did not.[8] In other words, it's fine to think about yourself and past events – so long as you do it from a neutral, analytical point of view.

## Beating rumination through deliberate distraction

Rumination is a style of thinking that is likely to damage your inward-emotional confidence. To spot and stamp out rumination, take a look back at the two sets of statements in the section above. When you find yourself thinking back on past situations or regrets, ask yourself which you are doing. Are you engaging in pessimistic rumination or more neutral reflection? If it's rumination, then find a way to stop. Tell yourself, 'I need to interrupt this unhelpful pattern of rumination.' Then go do something else – even if it's only for a few minutes.

Deliberate distraction is one of the most effective ways to break out of cycles of rumination. I call it *deliberate* distraction because this is about choosing to do something that you have decided on beforehand, rather than simply doing what's available or allowing your mind to wander.

So figure out what works for you. Watch television or a cat video on YouTube. Listen to upbeat music. Take a look at old photographs that make you smile. Phone a friend. Go for a run. Do 20 press-ups. Count the number of red cars that you can see on the street. Do something – *anything* – else. Do whatever helps you to break out of your self-destructive reverie and possible downward spiral.

When it comes to deliberately distracting activities, I'm a big fan of physical exercise. I qualified as a personal trainer at the age of 19. And physical exercise was my specialist field of interest when I started out as a young researcher. For example, I did a study with my then-doctoral research supervisor, Professor David Hemsley, looking at the mood-improving benefits of exercise. Cutting a long story short, we found that just 15 minutes of moderately challenging exercise boosted people's mood significantly more than an equivalent length of time spent resting quietly.[9]

But you may not even need to exercise terribly hard to get the psychological lift. Other research has found that merely walking for only ten to 15 minutes can enhance mood.[10] And the very latest research coming out of the University of Cambridge found that activity or movement of practically any sort – not even exercise – tended to be associated with greater levels of happiness.[11]

Some authorities believe that even gentle exercise may promote the release of endorphins – the so-called feel-good hormones – although others are not so convinced.[12] But it doesn't matter why exercise works as a method of boosting people's mood. The point is that it does. It works. And, of course, cycling, running, dancing or even a leisurely walk around the block is better for your heart and physical health than just listening to a favourite piece of music or watching a cat video.

But exercise is merely one tool for combating rumination. More broadly, the point here is that understanding the nature of rumination versus reflection is a good start to developing your lifelong confidence. It won't happen overnight, but with sustained vigilance on your part, you should get better at spotting cycles of rumination. And you can get better and better at liberating yourself from them, too.

> With sustained vigilance on your part, you should get better at spotting cycles of rumination.

## Confronting your worries

Rumination is a tendency to overthink problems, relive painful situations over and over again, and worry endlessly. But some people fall into a different thinking trap in their attempts to avoid ruminating.

To see whether this might apply to you, take a look at the following four statements. Do any of these seem to describe you?

- 'I sometimes have thoughts that I try to avoid.'
- 'There are some things that I try not to think about.'
- 'I often try to put my problems out of mind.'
- 'I sometimes have thoughts that I don't like to tell other people.'

A Harvard University psychologist by the name of Daniel Wegner spent 30 years investigating a phenomenon known as thought suppression: the mental tendency to try to evade, block out, ignore or otherwise push out unpleasant thoughts or images. The more you feel that those four statements describe you, the more you may be prone to thought suppression.

Wegner famously first documented this effect in a 1987 experiment using the so-called white bear paradigm. He and his colleagues sat men and women one at a time in front of an audio recorder and a small bell. The participants were then instructed *not* to think of a white bear for five minutes. However, each time they did think about a white bear, they were to ring the bell.

As you may have guessed, participants who were told *not* to think of a white bear were significantly more likely to think about the white bear than people who were not given the instruction.[13] In other words, trying to suppress a thought may backfire: it may actually cause us to think more frequently about a thought or image than if we allowed ourselves to engage with the thought in the first place.

Trying to avoid thinking about a white bear is fairly harmless. But play along and imagine that you're a smoker trying to quit cigarettes. Trying *not* to think about cigarettes may actually make more images and thoughts of smoking pop into your head. The same goes if you're trying to avoid unhealthy foods such as chocolates and cakes.

But it's not just thoughts and images of physical objects that people try to wall off. For instance, one of my clients told me early when we met that she felt ensnared in an unhappy marriage. She did not want to divorce her husband because of their young children. However, her long-time strategy had been to ignore the issue: endeavouring to block out thoughts of both her husband and her feelings of heartache.

Unfortunately, thought suppression may damage people's inward-emotional confidence and make them feel worse in the long term. For instance, when behaviour specialists Richard Wenzlaff and Danielle Bates monitored a group of depressed people over the course of many weeks, they found that the tendency to quash thoughts was associated with a worsening of depressive symptoms.[14] In other words, people who attempt to block out their true feelings may ultimately make themselves feel worse rather than better.

> People who attempt to block out their true feelings may ultimately make themselves feel worse rather than better.

Thought suppression may adversely affect our behaviour in public – our outward-social confidence, too. In an innovative investigation devised by Emily Butler of Stanford University, 84 women were brought into a laboratory to watch a short film and then discuss it. The film was a deliberately upsetting documentary showing graphic footage of the aftermath of the nuclear bombs dropped on Hiroshima and Nagasaki during the Second World War.

Half the women were told to behave normally during the discussion. The other half of the women were asked to suppress their emotions with the instruction: 'During the conversation, behave in such a way that your partner does not know you are feeling any emotions at all.'

After the discussions, all the participants were asked to answer questions such as 'To what extent do you like your partner?' and 'To what extent is your partner the type of person you could become close friends with?' The researchers immediately spotted a clear pattern in the results: participants who had been told to suppress their emotions were less liked than participants who had behaved normally.[15]

To me, suppression is almost a childlike strategy: it's like ignoring issues in the hope that they will go away. It's a form of pretence – almost self-delusion. If you're feeling sad that someone you love seems to have pulled away from you, simply trying not to think about it is unlikely to solve the issue. In fact, the more you try not to think about something, the more it may bubble up and magnify the intensity of those nasty thoughts and feelings.

## Changing the story you tell yourself

Trying to suppress thoughts may make us feel worse rather than better emotionally (damaging our inward-emotional confidence). And trying to pretend to feel a way that we don't may make us come across as less friendly and likeable (impairing our outward-social confidence), too.

To what extent do you tend to censor your thoughts or feelings? Bear in mind that these could be about past mistakes, quarrels or regrets. They could be about current situations as well as events that have yet to occur, such as an upcoming job interview or a tough conversation you need to have. Understanding what you tend to suppress will undoubtedly help you to spot such behaviour in the future. But here's the question: if suppression is harmful, what should we do instead?

Experimental studies suggest that reappraisal is a far more successful psychological strategy.[16] Consciously try to transform how you see a situation. If you need a reminder, I wrote about storytelling reappraisal in Chapter 3.

If you're experiencing a conflict with someone, don't try to push all thoughts of the situation or the person out of your mind. Allow yourself to think about it but tweak the narrative: imagine that your nemesis is a bitter, lonely person who deserves your pity rather than hatred. Or, if you're panicking about a presentation you need to give, turn your worries upside down: think of it as an opportunity to showcase to your audience how much you know about a topic.

I make no apology for covering storytelling reappraisal again, because research suggests that reappraising a situation by telling a better story about it is one of the most powerful techniques available to us. Rather than trying to push unpleasant thoughts and negative emotions out of our heads – only to have them return with heightened intensity – we can consciously put storytelling reappraisal to work in order to feel more in control.

> Research suggests that reappraising a situation by telling a better story about it is one of the most powerful techniques available to us.

The research on reappraisal reminded me of a conversation I once had with Kaitlyn, a thirty-something marketing director whom I have been coaching every couple of months for several years now. She has lofty aspirations and sees coaching as an investment in herself and her career.

Several months ago she started a new job. Almost immediately, she found that her boss, Eric, the chief executive, was incredibly capricious and critical of her. She felt very beaten down by almost every interaction with him. She had even started smoking again – despite having given up cigarettes for nearly two years. But it wasn't until we talked about it that she hit upon an epiphany: that she had to some extent been trying to ignore the issue. Rather than deal with it positively, she had been trying to focus on her work and pretending that her boss didn't really matter.

I asked her, 'Why do you think he's so negative?'

Frowning for several long moments, she eventually guessed that he was quite traditional in his views. He probably didn't understand a lot of the newer developments in marketing. Perhaps he felt threatened by her knowledge. So she made a note on her phone saying: 'Whenever Eric criticizes me, I should remember that he probably does it because he needs to feel important. He finds it necessary to attack other people to make himself feel better.'

Was it the truth? We can't know for certain. It was only Kaitlyn's best guess. But as a psychological tactic it was a small, positive way for her to defend herself and feel less beaten down.

## Onwards and upwards

- Understand that people who lack confidence are often their own worst critics. In reality, the automatic negative thoughts that reside in your head may be more damaging to your inward-emotional confidence than the comments that other people share with you.
- Consider using one of the defusion techniques to disarm negative thoughts. To apply the one-word defusion method, repeat out loud key words for around 30 seconds. Or remind yourself that your thoughts are only thoughts by using the phrase 'I am having the thought that ...'
- Remember that rumination – that pattern of excessive thinking about dilemmas, regrets or worries – may contribute to conditions such as clinical depression as well as anxiety, substance abuse and eating disorders. So learn to distinguish reflection from rumination. And when you do find yourself ruminating, try to rescue yourself by engaging for at least a little while in a deliberately distracting activity.
- Bear in mind that suppression is another common thinking trap. Trying to bury or avoid pernicious thoughts or feelings is only likely to backfire. A better tactic for dealing with such thoughts or emotions is to concoct a different story about what you're experiencing. Remember that you don't have to believe the story: the mere act of considering an alternative narrative may often be enough to lessen your torment.

# PART III
# Enhancing your outward-social confidence

Respect. In a word, that was what Priyanka – a woman in her late twenties – wanted from her colleagues when she first came to see me for guidance. She explained that she tended to seize up in group conversations. She was totally comfortable speaking to either a colleague or a client on a one-to-one basis. But when there were more than a few people in a conversation, she defaulted to listening, nodding along and asking only infrequent questions.

To make matters worse, she often found her colleagues talking over her. On the rare occasions she did venture a comment, her teammates had few qualms about interrupting her. It was as if nothing she said could possibly be of use or interest.

The thing is: she has the brain of a rocket scientist. Working as an asset manager, she works with complex financial products such as CDOs, CLOs, SIVs and stuff that the rest of humanity (me included) doesn't have a clue about. She felt confident in her knowledge, intellect and technical abilities. She was certain that she knew as much about her field of expertise as any of her peers and even some of the managers above her. Yet her frustration was flagrantly clear: what could she do to get her colleagues to take her more seriously?

We're nearly halfway through the book, so allow me to restate where we are on our journey. I distinguish between inward-emotional confidence and outward-social confidence. Inward-emotional confidence is a measure of how fearless we feel, while outward-social confidence is how much we display or broadcast our swagger to those around us.

Do you ever wish that you could be seen as more interesting, persuasive, charismatic or fun? Perhaps, like Priyanka, you have a pressing need to be noticed in your professional life – by co-workers, customers, employers or investors even. Or maybe you're seeking to make a splash in your personal life with friends or a potential lover. If any of that sounds appealing, then you may want to work on your outward-social confidence, which is the focus of this chapter and indeed all the chapters in Part III.

I've already mentioned that there is potentially an argument for working more on your inward-emotional confidence than your outward-social confidence. We have seen that several techniques aimed at buoying people's inward-emotional confidence also boost their outward-social confidence. For example, we discovered in Chapter 3 that reappraising panic as a helpful bodily response allows people not just to feel more confident but to get better exam results, too. And we learned in Chapter 4 that visualization enables people both to feel more self-assured and to perform better during job interviews.

Critics may also make the case that aiming only to appear – rather than *be* – more confident is bogus or hollow. That it's mere bluff and swagger, style rather than substance. Such detractors may sneer and say that it would surely be a better idea to work on feeling genuinely stronger. And, to a large extent, I would agree with that view. In a perfect world, feeling content within ourselves should be enough – we shouldn't have to care what other people think of us.

Unfortunately, we live in the real world. Interviewers offer jobs to candidates who appear direct and outspoken – they can't tell who actually feels, deep down, emotionally confident. Audiences give standing ovations to actors who shine with swashbuckling confidence on stage rather than actors who feel sure of themselves but give forgettable performances. Clients and customers often choose to work with entrepreneurs and businesspeople who talk with certainty about what they can deliver rather than with their more timid and insecure counterparts.

The unvarnished truth is that we often need to project our personality, perform in public and behave in ways that make the rest of the world take notice. Yes, working on your outward-social confidence is mainly about appearances, about impressing others. But let me be clear: this isn't about creating some fake persona or pretending to be better than you are. No, this is only about helping you to display a level of confidence that matches the skills you legitimately have. Especially when you get only one shot at winning people over, this is about enabling you to perform at your genuine best.

> We often need to project our personality, perform in public and behave in ways that make the rest of the world take notice.

## *Deciding to adopt a bolder outlook*

It turns out that simply changing your mindset, your attitude and your focus can make a difference to how you come across. And, in working with Priyanka, I could simply have told her how to do this. I could have taught her a psychological intervention designed to boost her credibility. But I didn't do that – at least not at first.

Instead, I told her about a fascinating study done by two academics based in New York. I explained that the experiment had been written up in the *Journal of Personality and Social Psychology*, one of the most respected journals in the social sciences. A series of studies was carried out by a pair of academic stars: Gavin Kilduff of New York University and Adam Galinsky of Columbia University.[1] In total, the researchers conducted three experiments. And I'm willing to bet that you'll find something here that you can use to get noticed.

In their first experiment, Kilduff and Galinsky gathered together a group of just three women. This trio of participants was asked to spend 20 minutes debating how they would go about starting up a small business. Prior to going into the discussion, though, each of the three individuals was given a different instruction. One woman was asked to spend a few minutes writing at least two paragraphs about her aspirations and the ambitions that she hoped to achieve in life. A second woman was told to spend a few minutes writing about the duties and obligations that she had to fulfil in her life. The third woman was invited to describe her journey to the laboratory that day.

Immediately after the debate, each member of the group was required to rate the extent to which she 'respected and admired' each of the other women in the group. Each individual was also asked to score the degree to which each of her peers 'had influence over task decisions'. These two scores were then combined to compute a status score for each individual, that is, the extent to which each person was perceived as influential and deserving of respect.

The researchers repeated the experiment a further 18 times with different groups of three. Each time, all the participants were of the same sex, that is, the groups consisted either entirely of women or entirely of men.

So what did the researchers find? Which of the three interventions helped people to attain the most status?

Let's look back at the various sets of instructions and see if we can work out the answer. Clearly, the individuals within each group who wrote about their morning's journey to the laboratory had completed a control, neutral intervention. I'm sure you deduced that writing about your commute shouldn't be expected to benefit how you come across to others.

But which of the other two interventions do you think boosted people's status and outward-social confidence the most? Would reflecting on your aspirations and ambitions be better for you? Or thinking about your duties and obligations in life?

Before I reveal the answer, I should give you a little more context: the two interventions were designed to direct participants' attention to different aspects of their lives. A heavily researched theory in psychology claims that people can have one of two broad orientations in life. People with a so-called promotion focus tend to think about what they *want* to do in life; people with a prevention focus tend to dwell on what they *need* to do in life.

For example, I want to travel to Machu Picchu in Peru. I want to learn how to figure skate and do a double Salchow. I want to write a book that sells a million copies. Thinking about any of those is fun. On the other hand, I need to pay the mortgage. I need to fix the slow leak in our bathroom toilet at home. I need to back up the files on my computer. Not so fun.

As a result, the promotion focus tends to make people more fired up, eager and excited. They direct their attention to how they can grow and progress, how they can win and attain their cherished goals. They're willing to take risks to get what they want; they're willing to speak up and take a chance to get noticed.

On the other hand, the prevention focus tends to make people more cautious and careful. They tend to agonize over issues of safety and security and how not to lose what they've got. They tend to shy away from risks and take the prudent options instead; they try to avoid saying the wrong thing that might make them look stupid.

Coming back to the experiment, the individuals in each group of three who wrote about their aspirations and ambitions effectively had their minds shifted towards more of a promotion focus. The individuals who were instructed to describe their duties and obligations were nudged into more of a prevention focus. And, of course, it was the individuals with the promotion focus who were rated as deserving of the most respect. They received ratings of 82 per cent from their peers on the test of status. The participants with the prevention focus fared no better (or worse) than those who had written about their travels that day and received status ratings of only 72 per cent.

The individuals who wrote about their aspirations and ambitions were, moreover, rated as having acted more assertively and having taken more of the initiative in the group discussions, too. In other words, they stood out. They won the admiration that so many people desire.

Thinking about what we *have* to do clearly does nothing for us. However, thinking about what we *want* to achieve in life seems to boost our status and outward-social confidence.

> Thinking about what we *want* to achieve in life seems to boost our status and outward-social confidence.

Now, I can imagine some people feeling disappointed about the fact that it only lifted status ratings from 72 per cent to 82 per cent. But consider for a moment if someone offered you a 10 per cent pay rise. Or if you were taking an important exam and you knew that you could improve your mark from 72 out of 100 to 82 out of 100. And for only a few minutes' work. Wouldn't that be well worth doing?

## Completing an aspirations and ambitions review

The next time you wish to make a good first impression, spend a few minutes writing about your aspirations and ambitions. You only need to write a couple of paragraphs. But the crucial bit is to ensure that you focus on what you truly *want* to do as opposed to what you feel you *have* to or *need* to do.

Adopt the right outlook and you may help yourself to come across as more proactive, assertive and deserving of respect. So which of your personal and professional goals might be pleasant, enjoyable or fun? What do you hope to do one day? What would you love to achieve in life?

## Seeking strength from happiness and power

If you should ever apply for a job working for a large organization, you may be asked to get involved in a group discussion. It's not uncommon for employers to run assessment days – so-called assessment centres – in which a whole bunch of candidates are brought in to be evaluated at the same time.

See how you get on with this one if you like. Imagine that you're in a room with two other people. An assessor explains that the three of you are the only survivors of a plane crash. You don't know where you are, but the three of you suspect that you're within the Arctic Circle. It's freezing outside and all you can see is a snowy expanse all around.

After searching the plane, you and your fellow survivors find 12 objects. It's now your task to discuss among the three of you which of the items is the most and least important for ensuring your continual survival until you, with luck, get rescued.

The items are:

- a flashlight
- a butane (gas) lighter
- a one-litre bottle of vodka
- a hand axe
- 20 wooden matches in a plastic, waterproof container
- a bottle of water purification tablets, enough to purify 100 litres of water
- a magnetic compass
- three sleeping bags

- an empty flare gun
- two cartridges for a flare gun
- three pairs of snowshoes
- three thick blankets made of some synthetic material, perhaps polyester.

To be more specific, you need to rank the items from 1 to 12, with 1 for the most important item and 12 the least. I know it's a bit of an artificial task: why wouldn't you keep them all? But go with it and accept the task at face value for the purposes of the group discussion. You have 20 minutes in which to do it. Good luck.

If you are invited to attend an employer's assessment day, you may want to practise a group discussion such as this. Get together with a couple of friends and see how easily you can come to an agreement on a ranked list of the 12 items.

But coming back to the topic of outward-social confidence, why should you care? Because the research duo Kilduff and Galinsky again asked groups of three to spend 20 minutes debating a similar list of Arctic survival items. Just before the exercise, each person in each group was once again given a specific psychological task. One individual spent a few minutes writing about a time he or she felt excited and happy. A second individual wrote about a time he or she felt dejected and down. And the final person in each group wrote about a recent trip to a grocery store.

Immediately after the group discussion, each individual again rated the status and assertiveness of the other participants. Clearly, as I'm sure you suspected, the participants who wrote about a happy occasion were rated as having the most status and standing. Those who felt either sad or neutral (i.e. the participants who wrote about a recent shopping trip) tended to be rated as conspicuously less assertive.

In other words, this experiment demonstrated that our emotional state can make a real difference to how we come across in social situations. How we feel can encourage us to focus on either prevention (of mistakes) or promotion (of ourselves). So you now have a different method for boosting your outward-social confidence and your ability to make an impact on others.

## Exploiting the power of positive reminiscence

Dwelling on times we felt rejected or dejected can knock us into the prevention frame of mind. And that could hold us back from speaking up or coming across well in group situations.

To enhance how you are seen by others, spend a few minutes reminding yourself of a time you felt excited and happy. That may sound like a fluffy or silly use of your time – but remember: the technique has been shown by academics to nudge you into more of a promotion frame of mind. If you want to shine in a meeting or you're heading out to a party, spend a couple of minutes writing a few paragraphs about a previous occasion when you felt joy.

You don't need to be overly analytical. You don't need to scrutinize why you felt happy in that situation. Just remind yourself of the happy details and allow yourself to savour your positive feelings again.

There's more. In a third experiment, the researchers again brought together groups of three to rate 12 items in the Arctic survival task. This time, one participant was asked to recall and describe a time when they had power over another person or persons. A second participant was asked to describe an occasion in which someone else had power over him or her. The third participant was asked to describe a recent trip to a grocery store.

As expected, the researchers uncovered a similar effect. When participants were asked to recall a time they felt powerful, they tended to be evaluated as possessing significantly more status than the other participants. They were measurably more proactive, having been rated as having acted assertively, taking the initiative and speaking with confidence.

So there we have three differing, but related, tactics. You could write about your ambitions and aspirations. Reflect in writing on a time you felt excitement or unbridled joy. Or commit your thoughts to paper about an occasion when you had at least a modicum of power over others. Put yourself into a promotion frame of mind and you may help yourself to speak up when you need to make a bolder impact.

> Put yourself into a promotion frame of mind and you may help yourself to speak up when you need to make a bolder impact.

## Writing power paragraphs

Writing about a time you felt powerful – when you had power or influence over others – is likely to put you into a promotion frame of mind. By focusing your attention on what could go well, you may feel more encouraged to speak up. I call this the power paragraphs technique. But remember that I didn't make it up by myself. It's backed by evidence. Spend a few minutes mulling over an occasion when you had power or influence over another person or persons.

I worked with a client recently who said that she did not manage any people. But it turned out that there were plenty of situations when she had power over others. She sometimes had to instruct less experienced colleagues at work. She also had younger nephews and nieces who often needed guidance or even outright telling-off.

I encourage clients to make a list of a handful of situations when this may have happened. Then, when they need to boost their outward-social confidence, they can pick one of the situations off their list and write about it for a few minutes.

But I don't want to raise your expectations unrealistically. Yes, all three techniques have been shown to work. But there are some caveats, some limitations.

For a start, the benefits of these interventions are likely to be fairly immediate and perhaps fleeting. So aim to use the techniques in the minutes – rather than hours – before you want to make your good impression. Apply them in the moments before you head into a team meeting. Or put yourself into the promotion frame of mind when you're sitting in reception and waiting to go into a job interview – not while you're still at home thinking about the journey to the interview. Personally, I think of these methods in much the same way as a breath mint. If you pop a mint in your mouth, it freshens your breath for the next few minutes, not hours.

Second, all three of these methods *on average* boosted participants' status. That means that the majority of participants got a benefit. A minority of participants may have experienced relatively little benefit or none at all.

So I suggest trying all three techniques to find the one that works best for you. You may find one or even two quite helpful, but feasibly the third leaves you cold. So don't just try one of the tactics on one occasion and then discard it when you feel that it didn't work for you. Try them all and see what you personally find most beneficial.

## Recalibrating your expectations

I love seeing my clients learn and grow – people like Harrison, a mechanical engineer in his mid-thirties. He wanted to make more of an impact socially. In even small groups chatting over lunch or at the pub, he used to find himself sitting and laughing along rather than contributing. He described himself as 'wallpaper'. When asked even common questions such as 'How was your weekend?' or 'What have you been up to lately?' he often ended up muttering, 'Nothing much.'

To remedy the situation, I encouraged Harrison to write a set of bullet points summarizing what he had done recently. It's not a deeply psychological strategy but a practical method that a lot of people find useful when they feel that they aren't terribly good at conversing spontaneously – and I'll explain it a little more in the next chapter. Essentially, before each social encounter, he began recalling three or four things he had done recently. He spent a few minutes tapping a few notes on his phone, usually on the train journey en route to meeting up with friends. And doing so reminded him of things he could say, which helped him to feel more comfortable talking about himself – particularly when meeting up with his good friends.

But he still tended to shut down when meeting new people – at parties, at bars, on dates. He had such low expectations at times that he was hampering his own chances of making a decent impression. An example: a friend of his dragged him to a speed-dating event. Harrison felt that his friend was considerably better looking so assumed that all the women would be more interested in the friend than in him. So Harrison wasn't surprised when none of the women he picked expressed any interest in him.

When I heard about this, I suspected that this might be a case of a self-fulfilling prophecy. Harrison subconsciously expected to be rejected, so that probably led him to behave in a less friendly fashion. After all, why make an effort with people who are only going to snub you? In turn, the people around him – potential friends or dates – probably interpreted his unpromising behaviour as a lack of interest, and so they too behaved in a frosty, distant manner. And so his expectations were met. Through his own actions, he had fulfilled his own prophecy that he would be scorned.

A body of research substantiates that insecure people who expect rejection tend to behave in ways that serve only to confirm their expectations. In an attempt to protect themselves from rejection, self-doubting individuals tend to reveal less about themselves. They tend to express more disagreement, have a less positive tone of voice and possess a more negative general attitude than people who have more positive expectations.[2]

> Insecure people who expect rejection tend to behave in ways that serve only to confirm their expectations.

Clearly, having negative expectations leads to negative outcomes. Expect to be rejected and you make it more likely that you will.

## Adopting a friendly demeanour

If you're someone who tends to worry about meeting new people, beware of self-fulfilling prophecies. Whether you're looking to meet fresh faces at a party or make business connections at a networking event, assume that you will be rejected and it's likely that you will be.

So remind yourself to break the vicious cycle. Use the storytelling reappraisal technique we first discussed in Chapter 3 to think about possible positive consequences of whatever event you're about to attend. Think about how you might actually enjoy the conversations. Consider that you might actually get a positive result out of it all.

Another way to prepare would be to visualize how you would like things to unfold. For example, you may want to come across as smiling, warm and positive. As we saw in Chapter 4, though, remember that visualization is not the same as fantasizing. You first need to prepare what you might want to say before you can visualize how warm and affable you will come across when saying it.

### Performing at your best

Allow me to finish this chapter with an entirely unrelated mind trick. It's intended for quite different circumstances to what we've covered, but it is still aimed at allowing you to perform at your best.

In my mid-twenties I was working for a large American management consultancy. I was often giving 30-minute presentations to groups of up to a dozen or so managers. On one occasion I remember several managers trying to assert their dominance over me before I began: they pointed out that they had on average around 30 years of experience in their industry and that they had children my age. Yet it didn't faze me too badly. And, even though I sometimes felt nervous, I received reports that I came across reasonably well when speaking in public.

However, I had also started taking piano lessons at around the same time and was sitting piano exams. I only had to play three pieces lasting a grand total of maybe five minutes. I had practised the pieces literally hundreds and hundreds of times. There was just the one examiner, who was usually an encouraging, smiling individual. Yet I was ever so nervous. I remember my heart pounding in my chest. My mouth went completely dry. My fingers literally trembled. And I was always so relieved when I had finished.

I could give a lengthy presentation to a roomful of seasoned executives twice my age. So why did I feel apprehensive playing a handful of short piano pieces for a single kindly examiner?

I didn't realize it at the time, but now I can see that this yet again demonstrates the fragmentary nature of confidence. You may remember from Chapter 2 that I described five major components of outward-social confidence. Being able to give presentations falls under the component of public performance confidence, while performing well in a piano exam is part of nonverbal performance confidence.

Nonverbal performance encompasses all sorts of tests and exams. Of course, we've all taken exams at school or university. Many people go on to take professional exams later in life. And countless job hunters face psychometric tests as part of the interviewing process. But nonverbal performance can include physical challenges, sporting competitions and other pressured situations, too: driving tests, tennis matches, figure-skating competitions and musical performances.

Ever heard of a phenomenon called choking? Sports commentators often refer to it. Choking happens when someone overthinks during a high-pressure situation and suddenly turns in a rubbish performance. Strangely, though, the solution may be incredible simple.

> Choking happens when someone overthinks during a high-pressure situation and suddenly turns in a rubbish performance.

Let's look at the research: this time an elegant study led by Jürgen Beckmann of the Technical University of Munich in Germany. These sport scientists persuaded athletes in three different disciplines – football, tae kwon do and badminton – to perform a series of sporting challenges under intense scrutiny and pressure.

The football players had to score goals in a penalty shootout. The tae kwon do competitors kicked a hanging sandbag multiple times as rapidly and as accurately as possible. And the badminton players had to serve their shuttlecocks into a tiny area of their opponent's court.

Prior to each test, the athletes were asked to squeeze a soft ball in one hand for 30 seconds. Half of the athletes squeezed with the left hand; the other half used their right hand. The results: in all three experiments, athletes who squeezed the ball in the left hand tended to perform better than those who squeezed the ball in the right hand.[3]

Why?

For the answer, we need to delve briefly into neuroscience and how the different halves of the brain tend to get involved in various tasks. When we want to take conscious control of an activity, we tend to use the left hemisphere of our brains more. In contrast, when we allow our bodies to perform an automatic activity that we've practised many times before, we tend to use the right hemisphere more.

Squeezing a ball in the left hand tends to enhance activation in the right hemisphere, which helps our brains to perform in the more automatic, practised fashion. In contrast, squeezing a ball in the right hand activates the left hemisphere more, which encourages more conscious control and overthinking.

Essentially, when we have practised something enough times – a piece of music, a sporting manoeuvre, how to answer an exam question – all we want to do under test conditions is to perform as well as we practised. We want to fall back on our automatic, practised method of performing. We don't want to allow the left hemisphere of the brain to seize control, start worrying and endeavour to do things differently.

But the reasons matter less than the result. The point is that we have here an uncomplicated method for reducing people's tendency to choke under pressure – and this is perhaps the technique that I would most have wanted my 20-something-old self to have had back in those piano exams!

## Attenuating anxiety through hemispheric activation

The study by Beckmann's team illustrates a way for us to perform better – so long as we have already practised a skill to the point that it feels well rehearsed. To be clear: this is not a trick that will boost your performance in all situations. You already have to be absolutely familiar with what you're trying to do.

But the technique is incredibly simple. Find a soft ball and squeeze it for 30 seconds in your left hand. Actually, Beckmann and his colleagues later demonstrated that you don't even need a ball. Just making a fist and squeezing the fingers of your left hand together has the same effect.

I must mention that all the athletes in the study were specifically picked for having been right-handed. It would be a neat result if I could say that left-handed people should simply squeeze the right hand for the same benefit. But that may not be the case. As the relevant study hasn't been done, we unfortunately cannot say whether this technique works for left-handed folks.

## *Onwards and upwards*

- Recall that your outward-social confidence is a measure of how you are judged by *other* people. It is probably true that outward-social confidence mostly concerns the appearance of confidence – if you want to *feel* more self-assured, you should be working through Part II on your inward-emotional confidence. But that does not undermine the fact that we often need to make a good impression in public.

- Studies demonstrate that your state of mind can make a significant difference to how you are perceived by other people. Help yourself to promote yourself rather than prevent failure by recalling your aspirations and ambitions. Write about your hopes and dreams. What would you love to accomplish or experience in life?

- Consider two further alternatives that both encourage the promotion frame of mind: either write about a time when you felt unalloyed joy or excitement, or reflect upon an incident in which you had power or influence over another person or group of people.

- To make a warmer, stronger first impression in social situations, remind yourself not to make negative assumptions about other people. With self-fulfilling prophecy, if you expect others not to like you, you may end up behaving in a way that makes people dislike you. So be more open-minded. Remind yourself to smile and be warm – and others are much more likely to reciprocate.

- Finally, consider squeezing your left hand for 30 seconds when you need to perform in a high-pressure situation. So long as you're right-handed, this may help to reduce overthinking and boost your subsequent performance.

Not long ago I coached a 31-year-old woman named Olivia. She was working as a sales executive at an insurance company and was having a hard time of it. Every month she had a sales target. Of the seven months she had worked there, she had fallen short of her target four times. Her boss had even told her that her performance meant that she was in the bottom 25 per cent of the team.

It didn't help that the work was surprisingly solitary – soul-destroyingly so at times. Despite the fact that she was part of a notional sales team, Olivia spent most of her day on the telephone. Her colleagues didn't really socialize with one another. They tended to eat lunch at their desks, often surfing the web or playing games with their headphones on. And, at the end of the day, everybody disappeared off home pretty swiftly as well. Compounding the situation, Olivia had just moved to London. She was living in a shared flat with two people who were relative strangers. She didn't have friends in the city and she was finding it difficult to be away from her friends and family.

As she spoke, her voice quivered. I could see that she was fighting back tears. Despite the fact that we were sitting in an office only a few paces away from her colleagues, she eventually lost the battle and mascara-blackened tears started to tumble down her cheeks. I had to go to the bathroom to get some tissues for her to dry her eyes. She was lonely. She didn't ever use the word. But that was clearly how she felt.

We humans are innately social animals. On the simplest level, we enjoy or even need the companionship of others. Most of us feel more secure when we know that we have friends, family and confidants to whom we can turn. We customarily take more pleasure from activities done with friends rather than done alone. We appreciate being able to share jokes, ideas and intimacy with people who know, respect or love us.

Shockingly, surveys regularly show that people like Olivia are all too common. And that really matters because feeling socially isolated isn't only bad for us psychologically. Studies conducted in recent years have shown that loneliness actually changes us on a physical level: the DNA of lonely individuals differs from the DNA of more socially satisfied people. Specifically, lonely people have immune systems that are less active, making them more at risk of disease and illness.[1]

I find that result pretty extraordinary. It's something to pause and really think about. The fact that our genes can be affected by our level of social activity says to me that socializing is not merely something optional – a nice-to-have – but an unarguably important contributor to our health and well-being.

> Our genes can be affected by our level of social activity.

We encountered the five components of outward-social confidence back in Chapter 2. And you may recall that social interaction confidence is by far the biggest chunk of outward-social confidence. If this is a challenge for you, you're in good company.

Thankfully, social skill comes down more to nurture than nature. Your gregariousness when it comes to social interaction is not something that's fixed and unchangeable for the whole of your life. A good number of studies have shown that even relatively short training courses and interventions can have lasting benefits. In this chapter we'll look at what psychology can tell us about a playbook for better conversation and socializing.

## Giving people the opportunity to feel heard

I first started working with James, a forty-something accountant, a couple of years ago. He initially approached me because he wanted to make a stronger, more convincing impact in business meetings and when networking. After a couple of sessions, though, he quietly admitted that improving his confidence at work was conceivably more of a secondary priority. It had taken him a month to feel sufficiently comfortable, he told me, and his main interest in seeking coaching was because he wished he could be better at talking to women.

Sitting with his hands clasped in his lap, James revealed that he was intensely worried that he didn't have enough to talk about. He was concerned that most of his hobbies were either quite solitary or insufficiently exciting. He enjoyed reading biographies of famous historical figures. He listened to classical music and radio talk shows. He was very slowly teaching himself to play the guitar. He watched subtitled European dramas on TV.

But I had good news for him. True, we tend to notice people who manage to be the centre of attention in public – the kind of individuals who are able to regale onlookers with offbeat or outrageous stories. But talking incessantly really isn't the key to social success.

You don't believe me?

Before I tell you what research has to say on the matter, put yourself into a hypothetical situation for a minute. Imagine a psychological experimenter invites you into her laboratory. She explains that she will ask you to answer a variety of questions in exchange for small sums of money. And these questions will come in one of three formats:

- Self-questions – these questions will invite you to answer questions about your attitudes and opinions. For example: 'How much do you enjoy winter sports such as skiing?'
- Other questions – these questions will give you the chance to guess the attitudes and opinions of someone else. For example: 'How much does Tom Cruise enjoy winter sports such as skiing?'
- Factual questions – these questions will invite you to answer true/false questions. For example: 'Leonardo da Vinci painted the *Mona Lisa*. True or false?'

There will be 195 rounds of questions. And during each round you will be presented with two out of the three types of question. You will also be shown how much cash you would earn for choosing either question. For example, you may be given the choice between two questions: 'What do you think is your favourite food?' and 'What do you think is Beyoncé's favourite food?' Answering the first question may earn you, say, two pennies (or cents); choosing to answer the latter question may earn you four pennies (or cents).

Of course, this was an actual experiment – this time run by Harvard University psychologists Diana Tamir and Jason Mitchell. And they found that people mostly liked to talk about themselves – they mostly chose to answer self-questions.

That's not a massively shocking result. But remember that there were small cash prizes on offer for answering different questions. The researchers found that participants had such a strong proclivity for talking about themselves that they often chose the smaller financial pay-outs. On average, participants gave up 17 per cent of the money that they could have earned simply for the pleasure of talking about themselves.[2]

In other words, most people find it intrinsically gratifying to be allowed to express their thoughts and opinions. They find the buzz of speaking their minds so rewarding that they sometimes prefer it to real rewards of hard cash.

> Most people find it intrinsically gratifying to be allowed to express their thoughts and opinions.

So, if you want to make a good impression on other people, you don't need to talk about yourself. Simply give other people the opportunity to talk about themselves instead. That's splendid news for the millions of people who lack social confidence. Instantly, the pressure to entertain is gone – or, at least, greatly reduced. You can be a rewarding companion simply by encouraging others to self-disclose: to share their thoughts, opinions and ideas.

## Giving people the chance to feel good about themselves

Most people enjoy talking about themselves or expressing their thoughts and opinions. So ready yourself for events and gatherings by thinking ahead about questions you can ask.

However, be careful not to focus overmuch on people's jobs. The deplorable reality is that too many people don't really enjoy their work. Asking conversational partners questions mainly about their work may serve only to bring down the mood of a conversation.

Instead, try asking open-ended questions (that is, questions that can't simply be answered with a 'yes' or 'no') that allow people to talk about whatever topic they like. Of course, no list of questions can ever be considered comprehensive. And you will need to think about the relevance of different questions in various situations. But consider the following series of prompts to use or amend as you see fit:

- 'What do you like to do in your spare time?'
- 'What do you enjoy when it comes to entertainment?'
- 'Where do you like to go out?'
- 'What is your favourite thing to spend money on?'
- 'What would you do if you didn't have to work for a living?'
- 'What was the best part of your weekend/week?'

When the conversation is flowing, you could perhaps try some more whimsical questions, such as:

- 'What's your favourite guilty pleasure?'
- 'How do you find the world of social media/Facebook/ Twitter/Snapchat/etc.?'
- 'If you could go anywhere in the world, where would you go – and why?'
- 'What did you want to be when you grew up?'
- 'If you could have any superpower, what would it be?'
- 'What are you looking forward to doing this year?'

But please don't consider this anywhere near an exhaustive list of questions. Remember that the goal here is not simply to learn a list of questions off by heart. The point is merely to ask open-ended questions that allow people to express themselves. What questions would *you* feel comfortable asking at your next party, on a date, over lunch and so on?

Of course, people don't socialize purely for fun. Many people need to do it for professional purposes, too. If you're looking for a new job, it makes sense to network. If you're a small-business owner or would-be entrepreneur, you may do better by networking with customers and investors. If you're an executive wanting to make your organization more successful, you may gather insights through – you guessed it – networking, too.[3]

Many people don't like to network. They don't like the thought of having to interact with roomfuls of strangers at conferences or work-related social events. But, again, the most effective networkers don't spend most of the time talking about themselves – they spend more time getting the people around them to open up instead.

## Making the most of networking at work events

People are more likely to be useful to you and your career if they feel that there is at least a glimmer of rapport. So build that connection by asking questions that allow people to speak their minds.

The following are questions I've often heard being used to great effect:

- 'What brings you to this event today?'
- 'In your job, how do you spend most of your time?'
- 'What's the most interesting project you're working on right now?'
- 'What do you find most challenging in your work right now?'
- 'If you could change anything at work, what would it be?'
- 'What's the culture of your team/organization like?'
- 'How are advances in technology affecting your line of work?'
- 'As I move around this event, I'd be happy to send the right kind of people your way. What kind of people are you looking to meet in particular?'

Of course, please consider these questions prompts rather than a definitive list. You may find some of them facile or inappropriate for your line of work. But the point remains: in order to build worthwhile relationships, give your business contacts opportunities to talk about their working lives, their frustrations and ambitions.

## *Taking it in turns*

The previous study by Tamir and Mitchell found that people were even willing to give up money for the simple pleasure of expressing their thoughts and opinions. That finding may surprise a lot of people, but probably not you. Think about people you've encountered over the years and I'm sure that you can think of more than a few who can't seem to stop talking.

However, it's also worth looking at the result of that study another way: people did not relinquish *all* of the cash on offer in order to speak their minds. In other words, most human beings enjoy talking about themselves only to a degree. Few people relish having to do all of the talking.

And this points to a second underlying principle of good conversation. To illustrate it properly, consider a study overseen by Susan Sprecher, a distinguished professor of sociology at Illinois State University. In this experiment, Sprecher and her colleagues asked 156 undergraduates to take it in turns to disclose information about themselves.

The students were randomly paired up and given exactly 24 minutes to ask and answer questions about topics such as their favourite classes, their hobbies, whether they would like to be famous and their happiest childhood memories. But, as is commonplace in experiments, not all the pairings were given the same instructions.

Half of the pairs were asked to take it in turns disclosing. For example, suppose we have two participants called Timothy and Maya in one pairing. For the first question, Timothy might talk about his favourite class. Then Maya would give her response. Next, Timothy might talk about his hobbies before Maya talked about hers. Then it'd be back to Timothy to reveal his views on fame and then Maya to express her views on the topic. And so on.

The other half of the pairs were instructed to have one person do all the talking for the first 12 minutes. The other person was then required to speak for the second half of their time together. For instance, suppose we have two participants named Nassim and Beatrice in one of these pairings. Nassim spends the first half of the interaction asking questions while Beatrice does all the talking about her favourite class, her hobbies, her thoughts on fame and so on. During this time Nassim isn't allowed to express his opinions at all. Only when 12 minutes have passed do they swap to allow Nassim to share his views.

Which would you prefer? Would you rather take it in turns or have someone fire questions at you for 12 solid minutes?

The researchers found that the pairs who were instructed to take it in turns got on much better. They said that they liked each other more. They reported feeling closer to each other. They thought that they had more in common with each other. And they said that they enjoyed the interactions more, laughed more and had more fun, too.[4]

So being a good conversationalist is not just about asking questions and expecting the people around you to spend all their time talking. Being a good communicator is about give and take, give and take, give and take – that is, swapping roles of being listener and speaker over and over again.

> Being a good communicator is about give and take, give and take, give and take.

Again, preparing to talk about yourself isn't something that helps only in social settings. I have quite a few clients who feel that they aren't being taken seriously enough at work. They sometimes struggle to contribute to meetings and speak up there and then. So I have suggested on many occasions that such individuals should prepare – that they jot a few notes about projects they're working on or brainwaves that they have had. Sometimes they also write notes on questions they might like to ask or observations they might like to contribute, too.

That doesn't mean that they then recite everything on their lists whether it's relevant or not. But for people who wish they had more outward-social confidence, preparing and thinking about what they *might* say often helps them to take a more active role in proceedings.

## Learning to reciprocate

In the first section of this chapter, I suggested that you think about some open-ended questions that you could ask people on different occasions. Obviously, the questions you ask at a business conference may differ from the ones you may wish to use on a second date or at a friend's party. But asking questions and expecting others to speak can get you only so far.

Studies have consistently found that relationships – whether the slightly artificial interactions in a university laboratory or friendships in the real world – thrive best when people reciprocate when talking about themselves. The upshot: whatever questions other people answer, you should be happy to answer, too.

So take a look back at the questions that I suggested as prompts for enquiring about other people. How would you answer each of those? Think about responding in a way that's not merely factually correct but interesting or amusing as well. Share an anecdote or at least afford your conversational partners enough detail so that they could ask further questions about your thoughts or experiences if they wanted to.

For example, don't just answer factual questions too literally. If someone asks, 'What do you do for a living?' it may be technically correct to simply say, 'I'm a teacher.' But a better practice would be to say something more in order to extend the conversation – perhaps, 'I'm a teacher and my favourite thing about it is …' or 'I'm a teacher, but you wouldn't believe that …'

Likewise, in answer to a seemingly uncomplicated question such as 'Where do you live?', avoid saying simply, 'I live in Manchester.' Try something like 'I live in Manchester, which I love because …' or 'I live in Manchester, but I'm hoping to move because …'

## Focusing on similarities

As you question someone (in a genial, conversational fashion, of course) and they question you in turn and you discover more about each other, you may find that the two of you have certain things in common. You may both have once lived in the same city. Perhaps you both once had a good friend at school with the same name. Or you ascertain that the two of you share a love of the same book, film, TV show, holiday destination, type of food, clothing brand or charitable cause.

No matter how trivial the connection, it's worth highlighting it. 'Gosh, me too!'

Why?

Dozens of studies have shown that even the most seemingly inconsequential similarities tend to make people feel closer to one another. For example, a recent study by University of Chicago scholars Kaitlin Woolley and Ayelet Fishbach asked pairs of strangers to take part in an experimental game allegedly measuring trust in each other's investment skills. During the game each participant was allowed to choose a single snack out of four choices.

After the game had ended, the academics asked the pairs of participants to answer a handful of questions, including 'How close do you feel to your partner?' and 'How likeable was your partner?'

On analysing the results, the researchers found that partners who had chosen the same food said that they felt significantly closer to their partners than those who had chosen a different snack. Not only that, but in a further study, the researchers also found that people who consumed the same food said that they trusted each other more, too.[5]

If you think about it, there should be no rational reason for liking someone who chooses the same food as you. But then we humans are not always rational creatures.

I often say that people like people like them. But it's not just eating the same food that promotes liking and friendship. Other studies have found that people who believe they share the same birthday or even have a similar fingerprint also tend to respond more to each other. And the effect happens not only in real-life, face-to-face interactions but also online in social networks. For example, another group of investigators found that Facebook users were more likely to accept friend requests from total strangers when they received messages that mentioned at least one shared hobby or musical interest.[6]

> People like people like them.

## Harnessing the 'me too' effect

If you think about it, it's slightly ridiculous that two people who have been told that they share the same birthday or have very similar fingerprints should like each other more. But it happens, so the phenomenon of incidental similarity is a way to build rapport with the people you meet. Simply look out for genuine similarities – no matter how seemingly small – that you share with other people. And then mention them when you can.

If you're really keen on building that rapport, you could think about the food or drink that you order, too. And, of course, think about what to wear to an event or gathering as well. Clearly, people tend to feel more similar to people who are dressed in more or less the same clothing. If everyone else is wearing a suit but you're dressed casually – or vice versa – you may be giving up a small opportunity to appear more similar.

## *Presenting yourself in the right light*

When it comes to being a good conversationalist, there is a fine line between confidence and arrogance. But where is that line exactly?

A case in point: I worked not long ago with Marie, a young woman in her late twenties who smiled only rarely. She felt fairly confident at work, but less so in social situations. She felt uncomfortable meeting new people, especially when she found them in the least bit attractive. But it wasn't just romantic encounters that were worrying her. She reported often feeling like an outsider with her own friends, too.

But she was facing a conundrum. She worked as a junior doctor and had so far done stints in various branches of medicine including cardiology, oncology and dermatology. But to what extent should she talk about her work? For example, she had literally saved someone's life recently – helping to resuscitate an elderly woman who had had a sudden heart attack in the middle of the night. Should she talk about such events because it illustrated that she was doing something meaningful and exciting? Or should she steer away from such topics in case friends or prospective dates thought that she was trying to show off?

Of course, I could simply tell you the answer. But I think you'll be more likely to believe and therefore follow the advice if you understand the proof and where it came from.

So allow me to begin by asking you to take a guess at whether being positive about yourself or being more modest would create the better impression. Imagine you have been invited to take part in a psychological experiment with a complete stranger. You and a fellow participant will take it in turns to ask each other questions. But you will get a choice of acting in either a positive or a modest fashion. Which of the two following sets of instructions from the experimenter would you rather follow?

- 'I would like you to answer the questions in such a way so that you will present yourself in a very positive, outstanding fashion. I don't want you to lie or make up stories, but to draw upon your real experiences and slant them so you will appear positive and confident.'
- 'I would like you to answer the question in such a way that you will appear to be modest. I don't want you to lie or make yourself out to be a bad person, but to draw upon your real experiences and slant them to appear modest.'

Place your bets. Have a gamble before we move on. Do you reckon that the first, more self-enhancing instructions would help you to make a better impact? Or do you think that the second, more restrained instructions would be of more benefit?

Those precise instructions were used in a classic study conducted at Case Western Reserve University. Researcher Diane Tice and her colleagues invited experimental participants to interview each other using a specific set of questions. The questions asked the participants to rate themselves on a wide variety of topics, including their social prowess, their creativity, physical coordination and dexterity, work habits and career prospects. For each question, the participants were asked to score themselves on a 10-point scale, where a rating of 1 meant 'not at all good' to 10 for 'extremely good'.

These pairs of strangers dutifully interviewed each other. But half of the pairs were secretly given the first set of instructions to be positive and outstanding about themselves. The other half were told to be modest and self-effacing.

Immediately after the experiment all the participants were asked for their impressions of their partners. And you may not be surprised to find that the participants who had been more positive about themselves tended to be better remembered.

The implication: when you're meeting people you've never met before, you would be better off being positive about yourself. Don't be overly modest. But remember also the researchers' instructions not to lie or make up stories. This is not about pretending that you are something that you are not. I draw your attention to the instruction: 'Draw upon your real experiences and slant them so you will appear positive and confident.'

So be real. Tell the truth. But be upbeat, strong, spirited. When you meet anyone for the first time, be proud of who you are and what you have done.

> When you meet anyone for the first time, be proud of who you are and what you have done.

However, that's not the end of the experiment. Tice and her team also enticed pairs of actual friends to repeat the experiment. Again, half the participants were asked to be super-positive about themselves. The other half were told to be more humble.

This time, when the researchers asked the pairs of friends to recall the scores that their partners (i.e. their friends) had awarded themselves, they saw the results flipped around. Participants who had been more modest about themselves tended to be better remembered. Participants who had been told to be more confident with their friends actually ended up making themselves more forgettable.[7]

In other words, it may not pay off to try to be overly positive with established friends who already know the real you. If you want to make an impact with friends, don't try to 'present yourself in a very positive, outstanding fashion'. Instead, you may get a better result by thinking about a way in which you can 'draw upon your real experiences and slant them to appear modest'.

> It may not pay off to be overly positive with established friends who already know the real you.

To me, this set of findings is consistent with the modern way of thinking about confidence: that more confidence is not always better. The old-fashioned view of confidence mandated that it is advisable to act confidently at all times. But the newer, more nuanced psychology shows us that behaving in too confident a fashion with friends may actually backfire.

This doesn't mean that you should stop talking about yourself or downplay your achievements when you're with friends. By all means, share with your friends the thrilling, quirky, amusing or scary experiences you've had. Just don't feel that you need to adopt an excessively positive demeanour – unless you want to irritate or even alienate your friends.

I think this is a brilliant, insightful piece of research because it tells us that there is no single, supposedly best, way of making a strong impression. How you should behave in order to make a good impression hinges upon whom you're with. To summarize the ramifications of the study, I've put together a handy two-by-two matrix showing how different instructions (to be positive versus modest) may have disparate effects on strangers versus friends (Figure 7.1).

For example, an instruction to be positive coupled with an interaction with a stranger is likely to lead to a high impact on that stranger. On the other hand, an instruction to be positive when the interaction is to be with a friend may result in a lower impact on the friend.

**Instructions are to be ...**

|  | | Positive | Modest |
|---|---|---|---|
| **Interaction is with a ...** | Stranger | High impact on the stranger | Low impact on the stranger |
|  | Friend | Low impact on the friend | High impact on the friend |

FIGURE 7.1  Impact matrix showing the effects of different instructions on strangers versus friends

Hmm. But here's a thought. If being modest with our friends makes a more memorable impression than being positive, might it be even better to be somewhat negative – to put ourselves down a little bit?

In a word: no. Actually, three words: no, no, no.

Diane Tice and her colleagues wondered the same thing. So they ran a final experiment in which they asked friends or strangers to be somewhat negative about themselves. And being negative resulted in worse outcomes, whether it was with friends or strangers. Whether it's established friends or complete strangers doesn't matter. Being derogatory about yourself doesn't pay off. No one likes excessive negativity. So, if you want to make a good impression, don't put yourself down, reveal your insecurities or dwell for too long on your failings.

## Presenting different facets to different people

I've heard some supposed aficionados say that you should always strive to make a strong impression by being assertive and talking up your accomplishments. At the same time, I know more than a handful of both clients and friends who say that they would rather be more restrained in order to allow their achievements to speak for themselves.

However, the research suggests that neither camp is entirely correct. Or, putting it another way, *both* strategies need to be employed – only in different situations. In order to make a memorable impression on strangers, aim to be positive about yourself. When you're meeting people who don't know you, they can judge you only on what you say and do. So if you don't tell them about something you've done, they can't know about it. Your achievements cannot speak for themselves.

So be positive with strangers both at work and at play. When going for a job interview, think about how you will communicate your skills, achievements and most positive characteristics. When you're meeting potential customers or investors, don't volunteer your flops or personal failings. When meeting people at a party or going on a first date, be as upbeat as you can about your life without telling lies or making up stories.

With friends – people who know you well – a better tactic would be to err on the side of modesty. That doesn't mean hiding what you have been doing or pretending not to be pleased or excited about the things you have done. Just don't feel that you need to impress them. Be yourself and let the real you come through.

## Talking about others to reveal more about yourself

A thirty-something acquaintance I'll call Kieron is single and dating. His preferred method: his phone and a plethora of dating apps. He spends a lot of time swiping photos of women and tap-tap-tapping out messages from his phone.

He has a good job in finance. And, with his athletic frame and enviably square jaw, he gets lots of first dates. He manages to charm many of the women he meets into seeing him again, too. However, in the several years I've known him, all of these nascent relationships have fizzled out fairly quickly.

He said that Diana was needy and kept asking why he wasn't replying to her messages quickly enough. On the other hand, Shanice was too uninterested, taciturn and emotionless – as if she were constantly on the lookout for something better. Jemima was a bit too volatile and moody. He complained that Carla didn't seem to have any interests of her own or enough to say for herself. Agi had too much to say and had some opinions that Kieron found particularly grating. And so it went.

The thing is: more than one of Kieron's friends has started to wonder whether all these women were genuinely so flawed. After all, there was another common thread to all of these failed relationships: Kieron himself.

Psychologists have identified an effect that they have called *spontaneous trait transference*. Essentially, if we hear an individual describing someone else in a certain way, we often end up ascribing those characteristics to the individual, too.[8] So when Kieron complains that all his ex-girlfriends are needy or distant or screwed-up, we may subconsciously feel that Kieron is a tiny bit needy or distant or screwed-up as well.

> If we hear an individual describing someone else in a certain way, we often end up ascribing those characteristics to the individual, too.

The transference can also happen for positive traits – so if he were to consistently talk about the kindness and warmth of the women he met, we might ascribe a fraction of those qualities to him, too.

It's not a strong effect. But studies showing spontaneous trait transference at work suggest that it's often an inadvertent way in which people like Kieron unfortunately broadcast signals about their own personalities to others. As social scientists Bertram Gawronski of the University of Western Ontario and Eva Walther of the University of Trier say, 'the ones who dislike become the ones who are disliked'.[9] And *you* don't want to be disliked – do you?

## Choosing your revelations with care

Spontaneous trait transference can happen whenever you talk about the behaviour of any other person. Being negative about other people may reflect badly on you – and that's probably not a good thing when you want to make friends, find someone special or win over an interviewer. So bear that in mind, especially when you're meeting people for the first time and telling them about your friends, your family, your exes or the people you work with.

We saw in the previous section of this chapter that talking negatively about yourself isn't a good strategy for making a good impression. But the phenomenon of spontaneous trait transference tells us that talking negatively about *other people* isn't much good for you either. For example, you may still feel hurt by the way former friends, exes or former friends treated you. Or maybe you feel genuinely aggrieved by some of the clients or customers you've had to put up with. But be careful not to spend too much time talking about the failings of such individuals.

I'm not suggesting that you should lie about your former friends and acquaintances. However, it may be a good idea – in the initial stages of getting to know new people – to say less rather than too much about them. Or change the topic. Move the conversation on to your favourite people and talk about your funny, kind, ambitious, talented, smart and supportive friends, family members and workmates instead.

## Building rapport and attraction through word and deed

Would you like other people to think of you as desirable, hot and sexy? If you do, here's a straightforward technique that has been demonstrated to boost people's attractiveness when dating.

Academic Nicolas Guéguen at the University of South Brittany in France has spent several decades researching the psychology of interpersonal influence and persuasion as well as physical attraction. He's one of the world's leading authorities – if not *the* authority – when it comes to producing research-backed pointers on how to make a mesmerizing impression when socializing, dating and mating.

In one of his many experiments, Guéguen asked three female research assistants to mingle at a number of real speed-dating sessions. In total, the three women met 66 men over several days.

Half the time, the three women were told to behave normally. But for the other half of the time, the women were instructed to mimic both the verbal and nonverbal behaviour of the men they met. In terms of verbal mimicry, this meant repeating back exactly five phrases that the men used. For example, if a guy said, 'I work in marketing for a fashion business,' the research assistant might say something like 'Great, you work in marketing for a fashion business.' In terms of nonverbal mimicry, the women were told to copy physical movements or mannerisms five times – but only after a delay of between three to four seconds. So if a man crossed his arms or touched his face, the research assistant would pause for a few seconds before doing the same.

Immediately after the five-minute speed dates, the men were all asked to rate their dates. And there are no prizes for guessing that the research assistants were rated more highly when they mimicked the men: the women were rated as being significantly more sexually attractive. When they didn't mimic their dates, the women received average sexiness scores of 5.54 out of 9. When the same women mimicked the words and deeds of their dates, they received average sexiness scores of 6.39.[10]

That's a boost of 15 per cent! Not bad for a technique that took so little time to learn and mere seconds to put into practice.

Actually, mimicry pays off in lots of situations – not just dating. Other experiments have shown that subtly copying the mannerisms of other people helped participants to become more influential – for example when negotiating deals or trying to cajole people into donating money to charity.[11] In fact, so powerful is the effect of mimicry in interpersonal situations that some researchers have called it a form of 'social glue' in that it functions as an unconscious mechanism for 'binding people together and creating harmonious relationships'.[12]

> Mimicry pays off in lots of situations – not just dating.

So mimicry isn't purely about dating and appearing more attractive. It can be a surprisingly productive method for forging a social connection, whether your aim is business or pleasure.

## Using mimicry, not mockery

Mimicking the behaviour of someone you're talking to is a proven and potent technique. To put mimicry into practice, remember that you can mimic someone's words as well as actions.

In terms of words, look for a handful of opportunities to repeat back exactly some of the phrases or expressions that your conversational partner says. So if someone says, 'I'm so aggravated by her laziness', don't paraphrase by saying, 'Oh I'm sorry to hear you're really annoyed by her inaction.' Use the same words: 'Oh, I'm sorry to hear you're so aggravated by her laziness.'

When it comes to mimicking the physical movements and mannerisms of another person, try to copy the action in a similar but not identical fashion. And be sure to wait three or four seconds before doing so. Some authors use the term *mirroring* to refer to this technique, but I strongly prefer *mimicry*. I worry that 'mirroring' implies that you should copy another person's precise behaviour and do it more or less at the same time – as if you were watching your own reflection in a mirror. But mimicry should not be so exact – and should always be somewhat delayed.

It's vital that other people don't realize that you are trying to imitate their behaviour. They won't like it if they suss out that you are copying their words or actions – they tend to interpret it as a sign of mockery. So be careful. Don't mimic every phrase or gesture. Do it only sparingly.

Many people have heard of the power of mimicking body language. But, in my experience, fewer people realize that mimicry works for spoken language, too. In fact, I often harness the power of speech mimicry when working with individuals to resolve conflicts. When I am brought in to help two warring individuals – perhaps colleagues at work who need to collaborate but do not get on – I usually plead with them to engage in a very specific listening exercise.

In the week I began writing this particular chapter, I worked with Paula and Bertrand, two department heads in an advertising agency who had been clashing on and off for several years. To set them up for a more constructive conversation, I explained that I would be asking them to talk and then paraphrase in turn.

So, first, I gave Paula five minutes to say what was on her mind. She talked about her goals and the reasons she felt thwarted at work. When her time was up, I asked Bertrand to spend five minutes paraphrasing. So he had to spend five minutes talking only about what he had heard Paula saying. I encouraged him to start sentences off with phrases like 'I hear you saying that …' and 'I understand that you feel …' If he had talked about his own needs or frustrations during that time, I would have gently interrupted him and asked him to continue only with his paraphrasing. Because the goal here was to ensure that he had paid full attention to Paula's thoughts and concerns.

Only at the end of those five minutes did they switch. This time, I gave Bertrand five minutes to explain his side of their conflict. And then I asked Paula in turn to spend the same length of time repeating back what she had heard Bertrand saying.

I have often found this a remarkably powerful exercise. It encourages people to really listen to what's being said. By allocating specific time for each individual to repeat back what they think they heard, it gives me greater confidence that they have genuinely been listening as opposed to preparing their counter-arguments.

And perhaps one of the reasons for the technique's effectiveness is because it taps into the power of verbal mimicry. So I never ask people to copy each other's movements or gestures. But, in asking them to use the phrases and language that they hear, it conceivably helps people to move away from their entrenched positions and consider how to work more successfully together.

## Onwards and upwards

- Remember that you don't have to talk constantly to be considered a good conversationalist. Most people enjoy having the chance to talk about their hopes, dreams and lives – they take gratification from feeling that their thoughts and opinions are of interest. So ask a good number of open-ended questions to allow others to talk about themselves.

- However, consider that a bombardment of questions could feel more like an interrogation than a conversation. So be ready to answer any question that you ask of another person. If you find it difficult to talk about yourself, prepare beforehand by thinking about how you might recount some of the amusing, bewildering, exciting or interesting things that have happened to you.

- Be proud and positive when talking to strangers – whether at a party or in a work situation. The reality is that a little showing off and speaking about yourself in an optimistic fashion can be quite effective when meeting new people. However, feel free to be more modest with friends.

- As you discover more about other people, make an effort to highlight the things you genuinely have in common with them. Remember that even seemingly trivial similarities may help you to build real rapport with people.

- Consider that few people enjoy talking to others who are negative about themselves. So avoid putting yourself down or imparting too much about your troubles and woes. Similarly, remember also that talking about others in a negative fashion may lead listeners to judge you more harshly as well.

- Finally, think about using mimicry as a way to build rapport and even boost people's ratings of your attractiveness. But don't forget that mimicry needs to be subtle. You don't want people to think you are mocking them.

So many people find the prospect of dating immensely daunting. And sometimes there are questions that people feel they can only ask a psychologist.

One client asked me to sniff his breath – did he have bad breath? (Yes: I recommended that he seek further advice from his dentist.) Another said she had heard that she should laugh at least once every four minutes in an attempt to make men like her more – but did I think that she should be laughing more often? (No: it's true that laughter may help people to feel more connected, but probably not fake laughter.) Someone else asked if I could explain techniques such as fractionation or implanted commands. (No: they're pseudo-scientific nonsense terms frequently used by unscrupulous advisers to con folks into paying for guidance that probably won't work.)

Of course, I'm only one psychologist in one city in one country. So I suspect that there are probably millions of people all over the world who experience more than a hint of apprehension about meeting someone attractive and trying to come across well.

But it isn't just first dates or the process of dating that causes people to fret. Plenty of men and women also worry about losing the girlfriends and boyfriends or wives or husbands that they have. For these individuals, even being in long-term relationships lasting many years may not be enough to make them feel truly secure and confident about their relationships.

In this chapter, then, I'll share with you a handful of evidence-based tips for both early dating and long-term relationships. Whatever your relationship situation or age, I hope there will be something here that you can use.

## Augmenting your appeal

I'm sure you are well aware of what society considers attractive in men and women. Look at any advertisement in a magazine, on a billboard or on television. Men should be tall, broad-shouldered and square-jawed with firm pecs and hard abs. Women should be slender and curvaceous with pouting lips and long, flowing hair.

But have you ever noticed that some physically attractive people can be somehow less sexy than they should be? Conversely, other people may not have won the genetic lottery yet still manage to exude sexiness. How?

> Some physically attractive people can be somehow less sexy than they should be.

Research suggests that you can boost your attractiveness almost instantly by working on something called your postural expansiveness. For the evidence, we turn to a study published by Tanya Vacharkulksemsuk, a researcher at the University of California, Berkeley, who is a rising star in the field of research on interpersonal relationships. In a paper published in a top-notch journal, the *Proceedings of the National Academy of Sciences*, she and her colleagues discovered that speed daters who simply took up more physical space were judged to be more attractive than speed daters who took up less space. By observing 144 speed dates, the researchers found that speed daters who took up the most space were nearly twice as likely to get a 'yes' response from their speed-dating partners.

To me, that's a really tantalizing result, a really big deal. Just imagine nearly *doubling* your chances of meeting someone right when dating.

Postural expansiveness is simply a term describing how much literal space people take up with their bodies and limbs. For example, a man sitting with his feet planted widely and his knees apart would take up more space than a man sitting with feet together and knees touching. A woman talking while using her hands to gesture in the air around her body would take up more space than another woman holding her hands demurely in her lap or on a table.

Try it now for yourself. Clasp your hands behind your head with your elbows sticking out. If you're sitting down, straighten your legs and slide your heels away from you along the floor. Immediately, you can see that you simply occupy more physical space.

Gestures that take up more room are deemed as being posturally expansive. Gestures that require less occupied space are said to be posturally contractive. And it really is as simple as the fact that taking up more physical space through expansive postures tends to make people appear more attractive.

Taking up more physical space through expansive postures tends to make people appear more attractive.

Why? Looking at the data from not only her own team but also those of other research groups, Vacharkulksemsuk contends that the more spread-out postures seem to signal dominance. In an animalistic fashion, a bigger physical posture says, 'I'm bigger and scarier than you.' And even though we humans like to think that we are different from the rest of the animal world, that still equates to sending a subconscious signal to others that we are more powerful and therefore even attractive.

But the benefits of postural expansiveness are not limited to only when we're meeting people face to face. The research team also investigated the benefits of expansive postures when it came to photos on online dating profiles by putting together a dozen dating profiles and launching them on a real dating website.

Of course, there was a twist to the profiles. Six of the profiles contained photos of people adopting entirely expansive postures; the other six presented entirely contractive postures. As I'm sure you guessed, the expansive postures proved much more popular: those profiles got a lot more messages and requests for further interaction.[1] So the mere act of taking up more space gets more interest, both in person and online. And that's something that pretty much anyone should be able to do.

But should you? Again, a critic might protest that we should aim to be loved for who we are rather than how we appear. And yes, you may undertake to be yourself and look for someone who finds you lovable for your innate, perhaps quieter, characteristics. But I am only pointing out what you *could* do – I'm not telling you what you *should* or must do. It's entirely up to you whether you decide to exploit the proven psychology of postural expansiveness to make more of a splash when meeting people.

## *Appreciating the limitations of postural appeal*

Vacharkulksemsuk's team conducted their research in two ways. One part of their work looked at the natural postures of groups of speed daters. The second investigation examined the impact of either expansive or contractive postures in photographs on an online dating site. And, in both cases, they found that men as well as women who stretched out their torsos, spread out their limbs and took up more physical space tended to be judged as more attractive.

However, don't take these findings as a blanket endorsement that you should walk around, stand or sit down in expansive postures all of the time. No. It simply isn't appropriate to stick your limbs out in all directions in many situations. For starters, you've probably heard of the idea of personal space – that invisible volume of space that defines people's preferred distance from others. Get too close to people and they may feel uncomfortable or even intensely aggravated by you.

> Get too close to people and they may feel uncomfortable or even intensely aggravated by you.

But modern neuroscientific research has found that giving people their personal space really matters. An investigation headed by Daniel Kennedy, a social scientist at the California Institute of Technology, found that the amygdala becomes stimulated when people feel that their personal space has been violated.[2] Yes, that little component of the brain that acts as an early-warning system starts to tell the rest of the brain that a threat has been detected. And I can't imagine that people who feel threatened would want to date you.

My suggestion: by all means stretch out and take up more space if you're sitting opposite someone at, say, a table in a restaurant. Do allow your elbows and arms to move around you if you're, say, going for a walk with someone. But be careful not to push your arms or legs against someone else. Don't lean your face too close to people you don't know unless you want to be perceived not as appealing but menacing.

There may be another concern as well. I have a Japanese friend named Narumi who always sits with her knees together and her feet tucked under her chair. She covers her mouth when she laughs and I would describe her as quiet and demure in her manner. And I could never imagine her stretching her legs out, standing with her hands on her hips or sitting back with her hands clasped behind her head and elbows poking out.

Of course, that's just one individual, possibly not representative of a whole culture, but it led me to do some further digging into the science. And I found a study conducted in the 1980s by Hugh McGinley and his colleagues at the University of Wyoming. These researchers found that people in the United States rated a woman as most attractive when she smiled and adopted open body positions. However, viewers from Japan rated a woman as *least* attractive when she smiled and adopted open body positions; they liked her most when she smiled and adopted *closed* body positions.[3]

McGinley's study opens up a handful of possibilities. One is that the boost to attractiveness that men and women get for adopting open, expansive body postures may be a strictly Western phenomenon. Another is that, given that the study looked only at the body postures of women, it may be that only Eastern women are penalized for having open body postures. So it might be OK or even beneficial for Eastern men to adopt more powerful positions.

Unfortunately, without further research, we cannot know for certain. But taking all of these studies together suggests that expansive body postures may be more beneficial in Western than Eastern cultures.

## Projecting confidence through posture

Tanya Vacharkulksemsuk and co-workers wrote in their research paper that open, expansive postures are judged to be more attractive at 'zero-acquaintance'. In other words, adopting bigger postures, spreading out your limbs and unfurling your body may boost your attractiveness even when you're meeting someone for the very first time. In fact, you don't even have to meet someone in person for this to work. You will probably appear more attractive even in a photograph if you adopt expansive, as opposed to closed, postures.

So sit or stand upright. Avoid hunching over. Puff out your chest. Take up more space with your legs. If you don't feel comfortable sitting with your knees apart, at least stretch your legs out a bit by sliding your heels away from you on the floor. Keep your elbows away from your body and your hands apart. Feel free to make broader gestures with your hands, too.

So much of attractiveness is governed by your genes: your height, the structure of your face, the shape of your body and so on. But you can use postural expansiveness to give yourself a swift boost in the attractiveness stakes. Just remember not to invade other people's personal space, though.

Our body language can bolster our outward-social confidence in that it can help us to *appear* more charismatic and attractive. But some behavioural scientists believe that assuming an expansive posture may also enable us to *feel* more self-assured – it may also boost our inward-emotional confidence.

While many experts talk about expansive versus contractive postures, a team led by Columbia University's Dana Carney popularized a new term: the power pose. These investigators found that both men and women who adopted more open, expansive postures – the so-called power pose – for just two minutes said that they felt more powerful. The campaigning researchers also took saliva samples and discovered that people who held these expansive poses had more testosterone (a dominance hormone) and less cortisol (a stress hormone) circulating in their bodies.[4]

It was a finding that attracted a lot of press attention. A TED talk filmed in June 2012 by one of the researchers has garnered literally tens of millions of views. And many bloggers and journalists proclaimed the power pose a miracle technique. However, there has since been some controversy about the findings. A few writers in the popular press as well as certain academics have said that the so-dubbed power pose is a sham when it comes to changing how we feel. But allow me to walk you through the actual science so that we can see whether posture really can benefit us psychologically.

One notable, larger-scale experiment was run by an international team comprising Swiss, Swedish and American researchers led by Eva Ranehill at the University of Zurich. While Carney's group tested only 42 participants, Ranehill and her associates rallied together 200 subjects – nearly five times the size. This Swiss-led team did not observe either increased testosterone or reduced cortisol in participants instructed to pose in an expansive fashion. However, expansive postures did help participants to feel more powerful.[5] So there was a psychological benefit, at least.

However, an even more recent study, by University of Pennsylvania scientists Kristopher Smith and Coren Apicella, failed to find any benefits at all for participants who assumed powerful postures. If anything, participants who assumed powerful postures may even have experienced drops in testosterone. And these researchers tested an even larger sample of participants – 247 in total.[6]

The awful truth is that science is often messy and contradictory in this way. It happens not only in psychology but also in other fields, such as physics and medicine. Sometimes physicists claim to have discovered a new subatomic particle – only for later scientists to find an error in the earlier physicist's work. Or a group of medical researchers announce a promising next-generation treatment for a type of cancer but suffer subsequent disappointment when more rigorous drug trials find that it doesn't work so well after all.

It's likely, then, that Carney and her colleagues' initial finding about improved hormonal levels after adopting more expansive postures was a fluke – an uncommon but not entirely unknown anomaly. However, it's still possible that adopting strong postures may help us feel more powerful. I wish I could give you unequivocal advice. But to do so would be false advertising – and I imagine you would rather have the facts rather than a convenient but possibly misleading message.

But allow me to summarize the 2.0 state of affairs. We know that adopting an expansive posture at least boosts outward-social confidence by helping people to appear more certain and attractive to others. And, for this reason, I have included this technique in Part III, which is all about outward displays of confidence. Expansive postures *may* also benefit inward-emotional confidence by helping people to feel more powerful – but the evidence isn't clear on this. Arguably, the better advice is that, if you are looking for methods to banish anxiety and bolster your inward-emotional confidence, some of the tactics in Part II may prove the better bet.

## Developing winning body language

As a psychologist, I get asked about body language a lot. When I'm at parties and meeting people for the first time, I often hear the question: 'So, are you analysing my body language, then?' Sometimes the question is a joke. On other occasions, it's accompanied by a slightly nervous laugh, as if I might discern something unwelcome about them.

A lot has been written about the role of gestures, eye contact, smiling and other nonverbal behaviours when dating. But it's fairly straightforward, actually.

For definitive guidelines, we turn to research led by an award-winning professor in the field of human communication, Virginia Richmond from West Virginia University (yes, Virginia at West Virginia). She and her compatriots developed a questionnaire measuring something called nonverbal immediacy, or the extent to which people create a perception of closeness and likeability through their behaviour.[7] Subsequent studies – for example one by Marian Houser at Texas State University – have found that people who demonstrate higher levels of nonverbal immediacy tend to do better in dating situations.[8]

The thing is, I doubt that any of what follows will come as a surprise. Based on the questionnaire by Richmond and her colleagues, here is a summary of the main behaviours that lead to greater perceptions of immediacy, closeness and likeability:

- 'I gesture with my hands and arms while talking to people.'
- 'I touch others on the shoulder or arm while conversing with them.'

- 'I sit close or stand close to people while speaking to them.'
- 'I lean towards people when I talk to them.'
- 'I maintain eye contact with people when I speak to them.'
- 'I smile when I talk to people.'
- 'I have an animated face when I am speaking.'

And here are some behaviours that tend to reduce nonverbal immediacy:

- 'I look away from others or look over them while talking to them.'
- 'I sometimes move away from others when they touch me while we are talking.'
- 'I frown while speaking to people.'
- 'My voice is monotonous or dull when I chat to people.'

Duh. As I said, no surprises.

But remember that most people don't actually have very accurate ideas about their own skills. When discussing what I call the curse of confidence in Chapter 1, I explained that so many folks get it wrong: vast numbers of people suffer from a 'better-than-average effect' and overestimate themselves. At the same time, some people underestimate their skills.

So here's the point. You probably already know what you *should* be doing in terms of your body language. The better question is: to what extent are you actually doing it?

There's a big difference between understanding something and putting it into practice on a daily basis. Assume you're great or even just passably good enough at this nonverbal stuff and you could be heading for danger. When I first started running training workshops, one of my colleagues always used to repeat a popular adage to warn people about the dangers of overconfidence: 'Don't assume, because you will make an ASS out of U and ME.' You wouldn't want to be an ASS, would you?

The only way to find out how genuinely well you use body language is to ask the people in your life. Show your friends the 11 nonverbal immediacy statements and make an appeal to them for their genuinely honest opinions. Or, if you're still on friendly terms with your exes, perhaps ask them, too. Which behaviours are strengths for you? Which are relative weak spots?

> The only way to find out how well you use body language is to ask the people in your life.

So do consider inviting the people in your life to criticize you constructively. No matter your seniority at work or the experience you have accumulated in life, I'd be surprised if you did not learn something you could improve about yourself.

## Talking about your relationship history

If you're single and trying to get back into dating, how would you describe your relationship history? Or, to put it another way: whatever your age, how would you explain what happened in the past that has led to you currently being single?

Everyone has a relationship history. For example, I worked with Jonathan, a tax adviser in his fifties who started dating again for the first time in nearly 20 years. His wife had asked for a separation and then a divorce, which had led to several blisteringly adversarial years. On his initial post-divorce dates, he was told that he came across as quite bitter when talking about his ex-wife and the shattered fragments of their relationship.

In contrast, a 40-year-old friend I'll call Gabriella is finding it difficult to move on. She co-owns a house with her ex-partner and they still live together – although they sleep in separate bedrooms. They are financially tied to each other and also still somewhat emotionally attached. Their relationship has morphed into a benign companionship. Despite Gabriella's stated interest in meeting someone new, she has found that the men she has dated have been noticeably put off by her complicated situation.

Or consider Rudy, an erudite man in his mid-thirties who has only ever dated very sporadically. He has never been in a serious relationship. He was diagnosed in his late teens with a bowel condition that has needed extensive, recurrent treatment. And for many years he suffered from clinical levels of anxiety that needed medication and therapy. Unsurprisingly, he has been reluctant to bring up such matters even though they are the genuine reasons he has been single his whole life.

Your relationship history – or, rather, how you talk about it – matters because it is a frequent topic in many early dates. Elizabeth Stokoe is a psychologist and professor of social interaction at Loughborough University in the north of England. In one study, she gained the permission of men and women at a real speed-dating event to record all their discussions. The men and women were aged between 30 and 45. And the dates lasted between three and eight minutes.

The recordings were all transcribed, and when Stokoe forensically analysed the written transcripts, she discovered that there were 'surprisingly few compliments, flattery, or other potential flirting activities'. You might expect that people's conversations would be geared towards making their attraction known and pursuing some form of romantic connection. But that wasn't the case.

Instead, most of the conversations 'were more like interviews in which one party's attributes were assessed by the other, as a practical item on a list, including their romantic biographies'.[9] In other words, the daters seemed more interested in winnowing out inappropriate candidates than in flirting and having fun.

Perhaps that sounds somewhat abstract. To see how the so-called interview process has worked in practice, let's consider a couple of examples from Stokoe's analysis.

In one speed date, a woman asked a man whether he had children. He said that he had a daughter, but explained that she lived with his ex-wife. In other words, he was sending the unspoken message that he did not have full-time childcare responsibilities. He went on to say that he and his ex-wife had 'got a good relationship' – with the implication that he was not feeling bitter or in a tense battle with his ex-wife over their daughter. And he finished by sharing that he lived in his 'own house', which helped to distinguish him from divorced dads who might only be able to afford to live in meagre rented accommodation. In other words, much of what he said came across as a series of positioning statements. His answers were a way of assuaging concerns and making himself appear worthy of further, perhaps more serious, interest.

During another date, a woman talking about her relationship history revealed that she had never been married. However, she added that she had 'dated a guy for about five or six years' – perhaps implying that she was not incapable of having a longer relationship. She also added that she spent a lot of time 'travelling around Europe', which was not 'the best way to meet people'. Stokoe noticed that travel was often used as a reason for having never been married, suggesting that travel can make a person seem more worldly, experienced and sophisticated – as well as being a legitimate, circumstantial reason for being single (as opposed to being single because someone is an inherently difficult, unlovable person, for instance).

A third example was a man who seemed to be justifying why he was at a speed-dating event in the first place. He talked about his work being 'more or less a male-only establishment', so he 'didn't meet anyone through work' and that he lived 'in a village that's a bit restrictive'. By explaining his circumstances, he was indicating that it was lack of opportunity that was making it tough for him to meet a partner rather than anything intrinsically wrong with him.

Such examples clearly illustrate that people's relationship status and history are exceedingly likely topics of conversation. So don't be caught out by such questions. Be prepared to account for your relationship history in a way that presents you in a positive light.

> Be prepared to account for your relationship history in a way that presents you in a positive light.

## Giving a good account of your dating and relationship past

Preparing to talk about your relationship history is similar to preparing to talk about your employment history at a job interview. Imagine for a moment that you are a job hunter being interviewed for a job by someone you really want to work for.

Why did you leave one job for another? Did you experience any conflict or difficulty with previous bosses? Have you ever been fired? Have you ever been out of work for long periods of time?

Whether you have been single for most of your life or in just one lengthy relationship that ended recently, you are likely to have to talk about your relationship history. So don't be taken by surprise when someone asks you about it. Don't garble your words or overshare details that make you look bad. Think about how you would answer likely questions such as:

- 'Why are you currently single?'
- 'Why are you looking to date right now?'
- 'How many relationships have you had? Why did you split up on each occasion?'
- 'Are you on good, bad or indifferent terms with your exes?'
- 'Do you have children?'

When I coach job hunters, I gently insist that they should write notes on how they would answer likely interview questions. If you wish to prepare adequately for dates, you may want to consider writing down at least a few notes, too.

## Reconsidering your relationship

So far in this chapter I have talked about dating – the process of meeting someone new and potentially turning a one-off encounter into, first, a series of dates and then a relationship. If things go well, you may be meeting again and again over the course of weeks and then months. But what's next? When you've met someone who appears to be a good partner in life, how can you turn that relationship into something that will last years or even decades?

One of my clients has almost never been single. However, none of her relationships has lasted for more than a handful of years. Kristina is a vibrant, outwardly confident woman in her mid-thirties who has never stayed single for long. Never one to leave the house without immaculate make-up and a carefully chosen outfit, she gets offers of dates from men at work, men in her social life, even random men when she's shopping or working out at her health club. She gets offers whether she is single or in a relationship. So it's not difficult for her to go from one relationship to the next, almost without a break in between.

She would like to be in a monogamous, long-term relationship. However, she suffers from quite low inward-emotional confidence – something that people rarely suspect from meeting her at first. From almost the moment she enters into a relationship, she starts to worry. She worries about whether she is attractive enough. She worries about whether her partner really loves her. She worries that he might be being unfaithful. And so on.

Most of these concerns are completely unfounded. But her need for prolonged reassurance from a partner can be quite debilitating. For example, she once got into a series of squabbles with her then-boyfriend because she was insistent that he reply to her text messages almost immediately. When he wasn't able to reply, she accused him of losing interest or playing games with her. Rationally, she could see that there might be times when he couldn't reply straight away – when he was in a business meeting or working out at the gym or having a drink with his own friends. But she couldn't stop herself from feeling insecure and picking fights about it.

Many insecure individuals behave in ways that may ultimately drive their partner away. Researchers have long known that insecure individuals sometimes look for ways to distance themselves from their partner or even end relationships as a way of protecting themselves from heartbreak.[10] Although they may secretly long to deepen the relationship and seek greater security within it, they may even dump their partner rather than risk their partner ending the relationship first.

> Insecure individuals sometimes look for ways to distance themselves from their partner or even end relationships as a way of protecting themselves from heartbreak.

Insecure individuals – the many people who lack inward-emotional confidence – are often their own worst enemy. However, there is a brief intervention that may not only soothe the nagging self-doubts of such individuals but also help them to strengthen their relationships. It's a writing exercise that takes only minutes to complete. But, formulated by researchers at the University of Waterloo in Canada, it just might preserve or even save your relationship.

Denise Marigold, John Holmes and Michael Ross recruited a group of insecure people to recall a time they received a compliment from their partner. Specifically, the participants were told:

> Think of a time when your partner told you how much he/she liked something about you – for example, a personal quality or ability you have that he/she thinks very highly of, or something you did that really impressed him/her.

Half the participants were then asked to describe the details of the compliment:

> Describe exactly what your partner said to you. Include any details you can recall about where you two were at the time, what you were doing, what you were both wearing, etc.

The other half of the participants were asked to describe the implications of the compliment:

> Explain why your partner admired you. Describe what it meant to you and its significance for your relationship.

In other words, the instructions issued to the first half of the group focused on *what* the compliment was. The instructions given to the second half emphasized *why* the compliment mattered.

When the researchers then asked all the participants how they felt about themselves, they discovered a clear pattern. Participants who wrote about the ramifications of the compliment – why it was important – felt conspicuously more positive about themselves than those who wrote about the concrete details.

Even more impressively, the benefits of writing about the implications of the compliment were lasting. When the research team surveyed the participants two weeks later, they again found that the participants who had written about the implications of the flattering comment still felt better. Even though the researchers went to lengths *not* to mention the writing exercise, those participants who had a fortnight earlier written about the implications of a compliment continued to report feeling not only more contented with themselves but also more secure in their relationship.[11]

That study is good news because it suggests that writing about a compliment from a partner can augment our inward-emotional confidence for up to two weeks. But there's even better news.

Several years later the same research team led by Denise Marigold conducted a second series of experiments looking at whether the writing exercise could have an impact on the partners of insecure people, too. And the results here were amazingly positive as well. Specifically, when insecure people completed the writing exercise – that is, contemplating the implications of a compliment that they received – their partners actually noticed fewer negative, critical, moody behaviours from the insecure individuals as well.[12]

In other words, the exercise may not only affect your own feelings of security – boosting your inward-emotional confidence. It may also upgrade your outward-social confidence in the eyes of your partner, too, by allowing you to feel more positive about yourself and perhaps curtailing a few of your more critical or otherwise negative behaviours.

## Reframing the nature of your relationship

In Chapter 3 we saw that the technique of reappraisal can help people to reframe how they see a situation and reduce the anguish that they feel. In a similar way, it seems that choosing to write about the positive implications of a partner's compliment can help you to feel more loved and secure. As a result, your partner may notice a positive change in your behaviour, too.

Want to give it a go?

To try relationship reframing, simply think of a time when your partner told you how much he/she liked something about you. For example, it could be a personal quality or ability you have that he/she thinks highly of, or something you did that really impressed him/her.

Write down when it occurred. And then explain to yourself *why* your partner admired you. Again, in writing, describe what the compliment *meant* to you and its *significance* for your relationship.

## Avoiding the snare of silence in relationships

A few years ago some friends of mine – a couple named Peter and Tamara – split up. It came as a complete surprise, a devastating jolt to Peter.

Despite having been together only a handful of years, they had already stopped having sex: Tamara kept rebuffing his attempts for intimacy. Peter assumed that she simply had a low sex drive and, while he wasn't entirely happy with the situation, he loved her and decided to respect her wishes. Secretly, though, Tamara was dreadfully dissatisfied with their sex life and had sought out a number of affairs and even one-night stands. She eventually met a new partner with whom she could imagine having a more fulfilling life and she left Peter.

Tamara had been terribly unhappy. But Peter had made assumptions and felt unable to ask her further about the matter. What might have happened if they had simply communicated more frequently – and more honestly? Tamara had been terribly unhappy. Rather than discussing the issue, though, Peter had allowed the topic to remain unquestioned.

Communication matters in relationships. I'm almost certain that you've heard this message before. But the problem is that knowing what matters in theory and putting it into practice are often two separate things.

> Knowing what matters in theory and putting it into practice are often two separate things.

Think about all of the situations in life in which people know one thing but do another. Most people know that they should eat more healthily and perhaps lose a bit of weight – but it's often more enjoyable or just easier to eat junk food and stay overweight. Nearly everyone knows that smoking cigarettes is bad for them, but millions of people continue to smoke regardless.

So forgive me if I remind you here that communicating our wants and needs is essential in relationships. It can be dangerous to assume that we know how our partners feel. Sometimes, they don't feel that they can voice their opinions – unless we ask them the question and invite them to share their minds. Neither can we expect our partners to know how we are feeling unless we speak up. Our partners are not mind readers: they are not telepathic.

There's abundant research on the issue of communication, of course. For instance, a research conclave led by Lynne Smith at the University of Wollongong in Australia probed in depth the relationship between communication styles and satisfaction in cohabiting couples.

The researchers asked both partners in each of the relationships to assess not only their own but also their partner's communication skills. For example, let's say we have a couple named Jennifer and Ulrich. Jennifer completes a questionnaire first to assess her own communication prowess and then answers a second questionnaire to rate Ulrich's. Ulrich then does the same: evaluating first his personal communication skills before considering Jennifer's.

Unsurprisingly, couples who said that they avoided talking about their feelings reported feeling less satisfied than couples who communicated more openly. However, the researchers found a further predictor of relationship satisfaction. An individual's satisfaction with the relationship was predicted only by his or her own communication skills – and not those of his or her partner. Going back to Jennifer and Ulrich, that would mean Jennifer's happiness with their relationship is dependent only on Jennifer's rating of *her own* flair for communication. If she believes that she herself tends to dodge issues or withhold her true feelings, she is more likely to be dissatisfied with the relationship. Whether Ulrich is good or bad at communicating is not a significant predictor of Jennifer's feelings.[13]

That's quite an important result. In other words, it means that you have a significant responsibility for your own happiness in a relationship. Yes, it may be easy to blame your partner for his or her inadequacies and deficiencies when it comes to communicating. But this study suggests that *your* communication style is the bigger factor in determining your personal satisfaction with the relationship.

> You have a significant responsibility for your own happiness in a relationship.

If you tend to withhold your feelings or avoid conflict, you may make yourself unhappier. But if you express your feelings in too aggressive a fashion, you may end up feeling worse off as well. Effective communication requires a path between the two: if you can express your desires and frustrations openly but evenly, you can help yourself to be happier.

## Improving your communication style

Relationship therapists and marriage guidance counsellors often ask couples to think about various aspects of their communication styles. Based on one of the most frequently used questionnaires assessing communication quality, I'll present you with eight questions to assess how you express yourself and resolve issues.[14]

Here are four ways of communicating that are less than entirely constructive. Ideally, you want to do less of these where possible. To what extent do you …

- avoid discussing issues or problems?
- blame or accuse your partner?
- nag or make demands of your partner?
- become silent, withdraw or refuse to discuss matters further?

And here are four constructive communication behaviours. You may want to do more of these if you can. To what extent do you …

- express your affection and positive feelings to your partner?
- express your frustration and negative feelings to your partner in a sensitive fashion?
- suggest possible solutions?
- make compromises?

Thinking about how you communicate is a good start. That may help you to think about areas in which you are stronger or weaker. But remember from Chapter 1 that we tend to have fairly inaccurate pictures of our own true skills.

If you really want to make progress, how about asking your partner to work through the questions with you? It may make for an uncomfortable discussion, but it could end up being quite productive in the long run. So be brave. If you want to have a more fulfilling relationship, use the questions as a prompt for having a constructive conversation about how you each feel.

It is a cliché to say that communication matters. Who doesn't know that? But knowing on an intellectual level that communication matters is not the same as being able to communicate well.

> Knowing on an intellectual level that communication matters is not the same thing as being able to communicate well.

When I first introduced the five components of outward-social confidence back in Chapter 2, we established that one of the largest chunks was social interaction confidence, the ability to converse well with new people. One of the statements in the questionnaire was 'I can express disagreement or disapproval with people I do not know well.' But some people can find it easier to express how they feel to folks they don't know well than the people they know best.

Clients often approach me initially for help with professional issues and later find me a useful resource for their personal lives, too. The month before I started working on this chapter, for example, I worked with Winnie, an events manager in her early fifties. She initially wanted advice and coaching on starting her own business. In our second session together, a look of sadness descended on her face and she divulged that her mind was often in turmoil and that she was unable to focus on work because of her relationship.

Eighteen months earlier, she had entered into a relationship with a man who had just separated from his wife. He had moved out of the marital home but was still in frequent contact with his wife. They had children together and he was determined to retain the close relationship he had with their children. He hoped to maintain a courteous relationship with his wife as well.

Unfortunately, Winnie felt intensely jealous of the relationship he had with his wife. While he had said that he intended to initiate divorce proceedings, she felt that he was being too slow to act. Nearly two years later he was still technically married. She was not proud of how she felt. She wanted to be more supportive but knew that, deep down, she felt neglected and resentful. She decided that it would not be helpful to try to push him on the matter of the divorce. However, she could at least start a conversation with him and share the fact that she felt fragile and unloved.

Using the framework of the eight constructive and unconstructive communication behaviours as a loose set of guidelines for the discussion, she asked if they could have a proper sit-down chat. She admitted that she was becoming ever more accusatory, irritable and worrisome. However, she shared with him the observation that he tended to become silent and withdrawn. And she asked him if he could at least express his affection and feelings for her more often.

Soon after, she noticed a change in his demeanour. He began telling her more frequently how much he loved her and how important she was to him. He reassured her that his reluctance to initiate a divorce was because he did not want to upset the status quo with his children until they had passed a vital set of exams. In turn, this helped her to feel more confident about their future together, which greatly reduced her anxieties.

## Onwards and upwards

- Remember that you don't necessarily have to feel confident in order to appear confident. To afford yourself every advantage when dating, consider displaying more expansive body language. Simply occupy more physical space with your body and limbs and others will see you as more deserving of attention – and desirable, too.

- However, be careful not to invade other people's space with your expansive posture and gestures. Doing so may stimulate the amygdala in other people's brains, causing them to feel threatened by you.

- Consider that gestures, touch, facial expressions and other body language cues can help to forge a feeling of immediacy, closeness and likeability. But don't just trust that you're already good at this stuff; ask confidants to critique your performance.

- Bear in mind that early dates are not dissimilar to job interviews. Both men and women are often more interested in eliminating inappropriate partners than they may realize. So think about what you do and do not feel comfortable revealing about yourself.

- Write about a time you received a compliment from your partner. In particular, think about what the compliment meant to you and its significance for your relationship. This simple written exercise may upgrade not only your inward-emotional confidence but also your outward-social confidence by helping you to become less critical.

- Remember that your proficiency at communication predicts your relationship satisfaction more than the communication skills of your partner. So don't blame your partner's supposed communication shortcomings for causing you grief. The perhaps uncomfortable truth is that *your* communication deficiencies contribute most to your own unhappiness. To improve your relationship situation, it may be up to you to speak up and take charge a bit more.

# PART IV
# Cultivating lifelong confidence

About a year ago I met Daniel, a director at a small travel agency. I had just given a keynote speech on the topic of leadership at a conference. He sauntered up with a toothy smile and a strong handshake, telling me how much he had enjoyed my presentation. We chatted for a few minutes and he asked for my business card.

Over coffee several weeks later, he asked for my assistance. He explained that he was a confident salesperson. He could network reasonably well. And he felt perfectly comfortable talking in meetings to his employees. Now in his late thirties, he had over the last ten or so years helped to build up a business with nearly two dozen employees. But he hated, hated, hated the idea of having to give a proper presentation in front of an audience.

In recent months he had been invited to deliver presentations at several trade shows that would have involved addressing audiences of up to several hundred people, speaking for perhaps 45 minutes and taking questions for another ten or 15 minutes. But he did not feel that he could put himself in that situation. To him it was a simply awful prospect. So he had made excuses not to do them.

I told him that I could help him. But it would take time. There would be no magic wand that I could wave to make him feel instantly fearless. And he would need to practise giving presentations – tiny presentations at first, but presentations nonetheless. And, over time, we would nurture his confidence by improving his skills, step by step.

Fast-forward to the present and Daniel has become a solidly competent speaker. He still feels more nervous than he would like before delivering presentations. But he does them now. And he not only gets through them. He also receives unreservedly positive comments from the people in his audiences.

We have now moved into Part IV of this book, which is about longer-term strategies for cultivating lifelong confidence. But there's no big secret to gaining confidence at any skill. Yes, in Parts II and III, we looked at ways to give you a lift before a challenging situation – which could be a job interview, a date, a business meeting or an audition. But at some point you actually have to take action and test yourself in the real world. You must attend real job interviews and accept that it may take you more than a few attempts to get better at talking about your good qualities. You need to go on actual dates to hone your patter and become more practised at making conversation. Attend real client meetings. Go to proper auditions. You keep working and working and working at it to build your underlying competence and capability.

There's no miraculous method that will bring about results overnight. But there is a proven, structured approach to building your confidence. And that's what we shall delve into in this chapter.

## *Appreciating the perils of positive thinking*

Now some supposed experts have claimed that an important step in turning your goals into reality is to visualize your dreams fully: to invest time imagining in detail how you would like your desired future to look. Sometimes these gurus go on to suggest that you could collect together images and words that represent the future you want and assemble them to create a physical vision board.

It's a lovely idea. And you could end up with a pretty assemblage of pictures and inspirational phrases. But the thing is: wanting something doesn't mean that it will happen. Even wanting it massively, fervently, desperately isn't enough to translate dreams into reality.

In fact, a growing body of research in recent years suggests that spending too long imagining and longing for a more positive future may be worse than pointless: it may be actively harmful to us. So before I tell you how to build your confidence, let me explain what you definitely should not do.

> Imagining and longing for a more positive future may be worse than pointless: it may be actively harmful.

New York University researcher Gabriele Oettingen has headed the vanguard of research into goals and future-focused thinking for over a decade. Over the years her laboratory has been responsible for numerous studies showing the destructive power of thinking idealistically about the future. A recent, robust example comes in the form of a paper published by Oettingen along with Doris Mayer at the University of Hamburg and Sam Portnow from the University of Virginia. This international team conducted a series of four studies in which they tracked the progress of various groups of adults as well as school-age children over a number of months.

In the studies, Oettingen and her associates began by asking their participants to complete a battery of psychological tests. One of the tests measured their tendency to engage in positive future fantasies. Another of the tests measured psychological well-being. Across all four of the studies, Oettingen's group immediately noticed a pattern. The more people engaged in fantasizing about upbeat future scenarios, the more positive they reported feeling at that moment in time.

So that's good, right? Fantasizing and daydreaming can remove us from day-to-day hassles and worries. It can allow us to feel momentarily better. But the studies took a more sinister turn when the research investigators tracked their participants over time. In all instances, people who had engaged in more positive fantasies went on to feel worse – whether that was measured weeks or even months later.[1]

Why? The main reason seems to be that wishing and hoping for a positive future actually reduces people's motivations in the here and now. By spending time dreaming, they put less time and effort into actually improving their circumstances.

> Wishing and hoping for a positive future actually reduces people's motivations in the here and now.

So someone who spends a lot of time wishing she could be promoted may actually invest less time into doing the hard work that may earn her that promotion. A guy who spends his life dreaming of meeting the love of his life may not spend enough time in the real world actually trying to socialize and date.

That's not speculation, either. One of the studies by Oettingen and her colleagues found that university students who engaged in more positive fantasizing typically went on to achieve significantly worse grades than students who did less positive fantasizing.

The research team concluded their paper by writing: 'Indulging in positive future fantasies may be a risk factor for depression because it saps energy and reduces success.' Wow. To me, that is a pretty stout warning. Allow me to unpack that sentence because I think there are three crucial points within it.

First, Oettingen and Co. said that engaging in positive future fantasies may actually be a risk factor for depression. Not just a slight reduction in mood or some level of mere unhappiness but feelings of depression. The really dark feelings. And I strongly suspect that is not something you want to bring upon yourself.

Also, fantasizing sapped energy. Do you want to have less energy? Probably not. In your quest to become more confident, the last thing you need is to feel tired, drained and less motivated to do anything. But that's what fantasizing about the future may do.

Finally, how about reduced success? Again, I'm sure you don't want that, either. However, the research suggests that too much daydreaming and wishful thinking is more likely to reduce your chances of achieving anything tangible in life.

When I'm running confidence boot camps, I often use a short phrase to summarize the necessity of short-term pain for longer-term gain. I say: 'Feel good now, feel bad later; deal with bad now, feel good later.'

Fantasizing is a short-term tactic that can help people to 'feel good now' but, because it ends up reducing their actual success, may make them 'feel bad later' in the long term. In contrast, it's only when we actually tackle issues and problems head on ('deal with bad now') that we can make our lives better in the long run ('feel good later').

> It's only when we actually tackle issues and problems head on that we can make our lives better in the long run.

Now, you may be thinking that I endorsed several mental imagery and visualization techniques in Chapter 4. But those were entirely different. Some of them involved bringing to mind specific distressing images and then either pushing them away or mentally manipulating them to seem less credible, more ridiculous. Another method involved visualizing the actual steps you would go through in order to give a specific presentation, job interview or other kind of performance. Those techniques came with specific instructions on what images to conjure up and what to do with those images. It's only the kind of fuzzy and over-optimistic daydreaming associated with fantasizing that is likely to be detrimental to your chances of success.

## Climbing a ladder of confidence

So how can you build your confidence in the real world?

Let's pretend for a moment that you suffer from a distressingly strong fear of dogs. A long-established and effective way of overcoming such a fear is something that has been called *in vivo* exposure therapy. It essentially involves introducing someone to the feared object, animal or situation, but doing it in a gradual way. The *in vivo* bit means doing it for real – exposing you to a living, breathing, sniffing dog at some point in the treatment. There's robust evidence that it's a highly beneficial form of treatment that can make a significant difference to people's fears.[2]

So you could begin by asking a friend to put a photograph of a dog on one side of the room. You then come into the room and sit on the opposite side of the room. The photograph is about the size of your hand, but it's quite a long way away so the dog looks fairly tiny from where you're sitting. The idea is that you try to relax and get used to the presence of the photograph. So you may take slow, deep breaths. You may also slacken your muscles so that you aren't inadvertently tensing your shoulders or curling your toes.

If your fear is seriously strong, it may take you quite a long time to get used to looking at the photograph. But if you have only a moderate fear, it may take only a few minutes. It's difficult to say how long it will take, as people can be exceedingly different.

Once you are feeling utterly relaxed looking across the room at the photograph, you may edge your chair closer to the photograph so that the dog looms larger. This may make you feel a bit agitated, so, again, you make an effort to calm down. You breathe slowly. You relax your jaw. You unclench your fists. You focus on your breathing some more until you feel fairly comfortable looking at the photo.

Then you get even closer to the photograph and relax some more. And then you get closer again until you can pick the photograph up and stare at it.

Only then do you take things to the next level, perhaps by watching a video of a dog at play. And then you may ask a friend to bring a small dog into the room – although on the far side of the room. In stages, you may inch towards it, each time making sure that you can relax totally before you move closer. It may take you some time or even quite a few separate sessions, but eventually you may be able to stroke the dog briefly – so long as you can stay relaxed.

So that's *in vivo* exposure therapy. But I don't like that name for it. I think it's not very descriptive of what it actually involves. Instead, I usually talk about constructing a confidence hierarchy or climbing a confidence ladder.

The core idea is the same: put yourself into progressively challenging situations but ratchet up the intensity only when you feel you've mastered each stage. That challenge could be exposure to a feared animal, object or person (e.g. bees, cars or clowns). Or it could be a situation such as a presentation, a party or simply being in open spaces.

> Put yourself into progressively challenging situations but ratchet up the intensity only when you feel you've mastered each stage.

## Building your confidence through observation

Before we look at how you too can put yourself into increasingly challenging situations, allow me to present you with one more option. Here, we turn briefly to a classic study by one of the grandfathers of modern-day psychology, Stanford University's Albert Bandura, along with his junior collaborators Linda Reese and Nancy Adams.

This research trio mustered together a group of 14 participants who were not just a little afraid of spiders – they all reported having distressing ruminations and nightmares about spiders. For example, one of the participants confessed, 'Whenever I'd see a spider I'd picture myself being eaten by a spider.' Another participant said, 'I'd wake up three or four times a night to see if there was a spider on the ceiling. If there was, I'd get my step stool and spray and kill it. If it fell alive in the shag rug I would lie awake for hours to see if it began its climb up the wall.'

A lot of people don't like spiders. But these people were truly quite phobic about the little eight-legged creatures.

The researchers brought the participants in for treatment one by one with the hope of reducing their fears. But it would not involve them interacting with a spider in a gradual fashion – it would only entail observing someone else interacting with the spider. Could merely watching someone else do something bolster their confidence?

In a word: yes.

The spider phobic participants watched as a research assistant gently poked a live spider as it scuttled around inside a large plastic bowl. The assistant then removed the spider from its enclosure and allowed it to scurry over her hands. Over the course of several hours, the assistant even showed each terrified participant methods for catching spiders.

At no point did the participants actually touch the spider. The participants all sat at a distance and merely watched. But the researchers found that simply observing another person behaving fearlessly around a living spider was enough to augment their self-efficacy, their belief in their ability to master their fears. And when the researchers finally gave the participants a chance to actually get closer to a living spider, all the participants showed much greater confidence.[3]

Bandura and his colleagues originally called this technique modelling – in that it's about watching a role model perform the behaviours that you want to learn. Others call it learning through vicarious experience. But I simply call it building confidence through observation. And the point is this: you could get a boost to your own self-belief simply by watching others overcoming their fears and learning new skills.

> You could get a boost to your own self-belief
> simply by watching others overcoming their fears
> and learning new skills.

So, if you have a pressing need to hone your proficiency at public speaking, consider finding a buddy or two who also want to do the same. Watch them practising and you could help to bolster your self-belief, too. If you're aching to improve your tennis serve or golf swing, consider going to some kind of training camp to watch people working on their technique – or even just watch video tutorials where novices get taught how to be better.

And, of course, if you are scared of snakes, wasps, clowns or anything else, take heart from this research. Find a way to watch other people – either in person or online – overcoming their fears and you could help yourself as well.

Observing others may not be as potent a method for building your confidence as so-called enactive experience, or tackling your fears yourself. But, thankfully, you don't have to choose only one or the other. You can do both. You can marry the two methods to develop not only your self-belief but your skills and abilities, too.

## Constructing your own confidence ladder

Constructing a confidence ladder really isn't rocket science. It just requires a little bit of thinking at the beginning followed by a patient, methodical approach.

You probably already have a notion of the skill or part of your life in which you'd like to feel more self-assured. But if you're at all unsure, do consider the five facets of outward-social confidence that I outlined back in Chapter 2 to prompt your thinking. So, perhaps like Daniel, you want more public performance confidence, the ability to present or perform in front of audiences. Or maybe it's something else: being able to dine in public without discomfort or boosting your assertiveness, for example.

## Building self-belief with a confidence ladder

To build your self-efficacy – your self-belief – begin by writing your goal at the top of a sheet of paper. You may want to write something like 'Get better at networking at conferences' or 'Give the best man's speech at John's wedding next year', for example.

Next, write the numbers 1 to 10 up the side of a sheet of paper (i.e. 1 is at the bottom and 10 is towards the top). Imagine that this is a ladder that you will climb up over the days or weeks to come.

Now comes the more time-consuming bit. Write down a sequence of ten actions or activities that will challenge you bit by bit. A few of these may involve vicarious experience (i.e. observing others), but most should involve enactive experience (i.e. you directly working on your skill).

Each action should be slightly more challenging than the last, but in a manageable way. You want to increase the level of difficulty in small steps rather than supersized leaps.

Bear in mind that your confidence ladder will be specific and meaningful only to you. What works for you may be too daunting for someone else. Equally, it's possible that someone else's confidence ladder could feel overwhelming for you.

And don't worry if you only manage to work out the first few activities on your ladder. If you can figure out only the initial two or three actions, that's fine. What's more important is that you then put yourself into those situations one by one. Start at the bottom rung of your ladder and do that first activity. It's better to follow through on your first action than waste too much time trying to work out a perfect set of ten steps.

When you have done that activity, rate your level of confidence on a scale of between 1 and 10. So saying that you felt a 1 would mean that you felt stupendously uncomfortable and a 10 would mean that you felt really good.

If you rated your confidence at a 6 or higher, move on to the next rung of your confidence ladder. If your self-rated confidence is a lot lower, you may want to keep trying that activity until you feel more comfortable with it.

As you can imagine, it may take some time to climb up your ladder. You're always aiming to build up the level of confidence that you feel at each step before moving on.

But that's all there is to it. Gradually work your way up each rung of the ladder. Be patient. Accept that it will take time. Get comfortable with the activity at each rung before you move on to the next. And, over time, you should find yourself climbing your confidence ladder and conquering your fears.

Daniel, the travel agency executive, wrote the numbers 1 through 10 up the side of a sheet of paper. And he began to work out what he could do at each step.

Number 1, the first rung on his personal confidence ladder, was to write and then read out a three-minute speech at home. He wanted to video-record himself a handful of times until he felt that he both sounded and looked poised doing so.

The activity on his second rung was to search online for a local public-speaking group that he could join. By watching others give speeches, he hoped to build his belief that he could do the same, too.

Number 3 was to practise on his deputy manager, someone he thought of as kind and supportive by nature. Yes, he would enlist her assistance in turning him into a decent public speaker. He would keep rehearsing with her until she told him that he wasn't being completely rubbish.

The fourth rung on his ladder would involve him writing a five-minute presentation that he would deliver every Monday morning at work to update his team on what was happening in the coming week. He had been used to updating people by email, but he resolved to use email less in order to develop his speaking skills.

Number 5 would involve him giving a presentation to the 20 or so employees that made up the whole company. He had always written a paper to communicate the firm's strategic objectives. But this year he decided that it would be an opportunity for him to stand up and explain them in person.

At first, he couldn't think exactly what he would do for his sixth rung and beyond. He knew that there were some trade shows where he might be able to volunteer to give presentations to smaller audiences. Rather than being a keynote speaker, he could conceivably offer to run a satellite workshop or speak at a breakout session. So he pledged to research such events to find a shorter, more manageable session that he could run.

His inaugural public appearance was extremely short and to a low-key audience of fewer than a dozen people. And he felt flustered and nervous. But he plunged gamely on and survived. He even felt quite pleased with himself afterwards.

Then he found another opportunity. And a few more. And still more after that. As a result, he is getting better and better at giving presentations. He's still not where he wants to be. But he has come a long way.

So what about you? How might the first few rungs of your personal confidence ladder look?

Remember that your confidence ladder will be for you and you alone. So, even if you're wanting to work on your presentation skills like Daniel, you may decide that his ladder was either insufficiently daring or overly demanding. One person may determine that her first rung will involve giving just a 60-second speech to herself in front of a mirror; someone else may judge that he can deliver a ten-minute talk to his wife. There's no right or wrong answer here. It's all about what works for you.

> Your confidence ladder will be for you and you alone.

I believe that the principles of constructing and then climbing a confidence ladder are fairly uncomplicated. But you only get the benefit from thinking through what yours would look like and then putting yourself into those actual situations. So how about it? If you're serious about building your self-confidence in a proven, progressive manner, why not write down your goal and have a go at constructing the first few rungs right now?

Then take that first step, remembering that there are plenty of techniques from the chapters in Parts II and III that may help you to feel stronger and perform better. Try affect labelling, mental resizing or hemispheric activation. See if you can help yourself by using cognitive defusion, reappraisal or by writing out an aspirations and ambitions review. Use the methods that we've already used to help you to climb each rung of your very own confidence ladder.

Yes, you may currently feel either slightly daunted or even fairly frightened by the scale of the task ahead of you. But trust that psychology tells us that positive change is possible. With effort, you may find yourself going from 'I hate this' to 'Wow, I'm actually quite good at this!'

## Onwards and upwards

- While some writers endorse spending time on dreaming and conjuring up detailed images of what you'd like to accomplish in the future, consider what modern-day psychology has to say on the matter. The more time people spend on such thoughts, the *less* motivated they tend to become and the *less* they actually end up achieving. The research evidence on this matter is quite strong.

- To build your long-term confidence, seek out opportunities to challenge yourself in real-world situations. You will need to give more presentations, go on more dates, speak your mind more vigorously and so on. The more you can test yourself, the more self-assured you will eventually feel.

- Write out a confidence ladder so that you can tackle gradually more challenging situations in a way that allows you to feel safe. The idea is to grow your skill in small steps that feel comfortable and attainable rather than trying to make enormous jumps that could just set you up for failure.

- Begin by writing out the actions you could take for at least the first few rungs of your confidence ladder. Don't worry if you aren't sure what the uppermost rungs of your ladder should look like. When you have completed the activities on the lower rungs, you are likely to be in a much better position to judge what should come next.

- While most of your activities should involve you personally working on your skills, you can also often benefit from observing others vicariously. So seek out and watch people performing what you want to learn.

- Be patient in climbing your personal confidence ladder. Yes, of course everybody would love to build their self-confidence as quickly as possible. But this is about developing your skill in a properly sustainable manner. Insert yourself into the challenging activity at each rung of your ladder enough times until you are quite comfortable with it before moving on.

Penelope is a 43-year-old who often worries that her husband may be being unfaithful. He travels frequently for business, flying to destinations such as Dubai, Singapore and Los Angeles perhaps once or even twice a month, for up to four or five days at a time.

She agonizes over a lot of other things too: mistakes in her work, things she shouldn't have said or done, her ageing father's health, whether she's a good mother, political strife and the state of the world. But concerns about her husband are among the most persistent.

She can be at her desk at work and find herself zoning out and imagining her husband in bed with another woman. She can be at the gym or watching TV or reading a book and wondering with a grimace exactly where he might be. She sometimes can't sleep because of the thoughts and images whirling inside her head.

The bizarre thing is: Penelope has little reason to worry. She and her husband not only talk about important issues but banter about life's little ups and downs, too. He is an attentive partner who tells her that he loves her. And they still have what she believes to be a good sex life.

Rationally, Penelope understands that her husband has been a great partner for the nearly 20 years they have been together. But knowing that doesn't stop her from worrying.

Like Penelope, many people with lower inward-emotional confidence are harangued by bothersome thoughts or images of worst-case scenarios. The latest research suggests that many such individuals simply have brains that are more actively attuned to threats.[1] Their minds drag them to thinking about either past mistakes or future perils. Even when there may logically be nothing to fret about, they can't seem to help but worry. They simply think too much.

We looked at various techniques earlier in the book (in Part II) for combating troubling thoughts, images and feelings. Many of these methods, such as cognitive defusion and imagery rescripting, require you to spot what's going on within the inner workings of your mind: you need to think in a more rational, helpful way to defeat your mental demons. But one branch of psychological research takes almost the opposite approach: it recommends that we should perhaps think less.

One of the most popular techniques in recent years, it suggests that we should live less in our own minds and focus more on the actual world around us. We should simply observe rather than think. And we should practise the act and skill of mindfulness.

## Understanding mindfulness

Mindfulness is the act of bringing our full attention to the experiences happening to us at any given moment – but doing so in a non-judgemental or accepting way. I'll explain about the accepting bit later, but try to be mindful right now if you like.

Yes, here and now: give mindfulness a quick test drive. Push your awareness and attention outside of yourself to the world around you. If you're outdoors, perhaps notice the sensation of any breeze or the warmth or coldness on your skin. If you're sitting down, direct your concentration to the feel of the chair against your bottom or back. Now focus on what you can see: really notice the shapes, objects, people and details around you as you turn your head. Pay attention to any sounds that you can hear, too.

Now turn your attention internally to the experiences within you, to your state of mind. What are you thinking about right now? Have you been fully focused on this book and this mental exercise? Or has your mind been wandering? And how are you feeling – sad, ecstatic, aggravated, tired, curious or something else?

Mindfulness involves paying complete attention to your current experience, whether that experience is outside of you in the real world or only within the landscapes of your mind. When I'm running training workshops or coaching clients one-on-one, I customarily explain mindfulness by contrasting it with the autopilot mode of living that we can so easily fall into: that mindless mental state when we can commute to work without remembering our journeys or eat a pile of junk food without really savouring every mouthful. It's going through the motions – doing something without really focusing on it.

> Mindfulness involves paying complete attention to your current experiences, whether they are outside of you in the real world or only within the landscapes of your mind.

When it comes to your mental life, too, perhaps you have found your mind dredging up memories of things that happened long ago that you can't ever change, or worrying about something that might never actually happen. It's fine if you deliberately choose to focus on those issues, but the truth is that we often allow such scenarios to play out without our conscious permission. And that's the outright opposite of being mindful.

When I started writing on the topic of confidence more than a decade ago, the idea of mindfulness was still fairly new. One of the most influential research papers that arguably brought the topic of mindfulness to the attention of reputable scientists was only published, by superstar researchers Kirk Warren Brown and Richard Ryan of the University of Rochester, in 2003.[2]

The concept of mindfulness originally came from Eastern spiritual traditions; as such, some people initially found it a bit off-putting because they thought that it had the whiff of pseudo-science or even sorcery about it. But literally thousands of papers have been published by top-class researchers all over the world looking at the benefits of mindfulness since then. And the consensus view is remarkably positive.

So far, research has linked higher levels of mindfulness with better physical health. People who are more mindful seem to get more exercise, smoke less and eat more healthily. People who are mindful also tend to have lower blood pressure and better glucose regulation (which in turn may mean a lower risk of diabetes). People who are more mindful are less likely to be categorized as clinically obese, too.[3]

In terms of our inward-emotional confidence, mounting evidence suggests that practising mindfulness for just a few minutes as a one-off exercise may help to quell negative thoughts and feelings. For instance, a tidy little study led by scientist Michael Mrazek of the

University of California, Santa Barbara, found that as little as eight minutes of performing mindfulness produced psychological benefits that were greater than a similar length of time spent either reading or relaxing quietly.[4]

I consider that an incredibly heartening result. Mindfulness doesn't have to be an onerous, lifelong practice. You don't have to wait years, months or even weeks in order to get any benefit. Even if you've never done the mindfulness thing before and are doing it for the very first time, a mere eight minutes of it may be enough to give you a lift.

## *Beginning mindfulness one breath at a time*

OK, so we've established that this mindfulness stuff may be rather good for us. And it may only take mere minutes of it to be helpful. But enough of the theory. Let's put it into practice now by trying to be properly mindful for a little while.

### Learning to breathe mindfully

One of the easiest ways to practise mindfulness is by focusing on your breathing. People who have been practising mindfulness for months or years find that they can do it almost anywhere – even in a crowded office with ringing phones and chatting colleagues or a busy playground thronging with noisy children at play. But if you're new to mindfulness, you may want to pick a relatively quieter place to try this.

Begin by finding somewhere that you can sit undisturbed for several minutes. Sit in an upright position in which you feel comfortable but alert. Avoid slumping in a sofa or lying down on a bed, for example. Put both feet on the floor with the weight equally distributed between them. Relax your hands in your lap. Close your eyes, gaze into space or look ahead at a neutral object (i.e. one that does not evoke any strong thoughts or feelings within you – as opposed to, say, a photograph or book that may encourage you to think about past events or other topics).

When you are ready to start, simply focus your attention on the sensations of your breathing. For example, you may find your attention being drawn to the rise and fall of your belly or chest, or perhaps the air passing in and out of your nostrils. You don't need to breathe slowly or any differently. Don't change your rate of breathing. Just breathe normally.

Then begin to count your breaths. Continue to breathe normally but count each one until you get to ten. And that's it: you're done.

You may find your attention drifting perhaps to chores you have to do or topics that you're worrying about, but that's OK. Simply guide your focus back to your breathing when you can. If you lose count, simply pick up where you think you left off.

You may notice that your attention gets pulled away from your breathing to sounds, perhaps in the room with you or outside of it. It's also OK to listen to such sounds or noises for a while. But when you feel able to, gently usher your attention away from them and back to your breathing.

Breathing mindfully is simply about focusing as much of your attention as possible on your breathing. If you're fully focused, that's OK. But if you are quite distracted, that's OK too. Success is defined simply by counting ten breaths – it doesn't matter what goes on in your mind at the same time.

I would recommend that you listen to instructions as you try mindfulness rather than merely read how to do it. I have recorded a short audio track that you can listen to for free by visiting the website library.teachyourself.com or on the Teach Yourself Library app.

Quite a few studies have found that it's possible to detect significant psychological benefits after only around eight to ten minutes;[5] however, some people report that they need even less time to feel better. So the next time your mind is roiling with troublesome thoughts, images or feelings, do consider taking a few minutes to focus on breathing mindfully. Think of the time as a small respite, a cocoon of calm, a short break from whatever else you may be doing.

If you ever want to practise mindfulness for a certain length of time but don't want to have to break your focus by glancing at a clock, you could set a timer or alarm on your phone to alert you after so many minutes. But perhaps select a gentle ring tone or piece of music for attracting your attention rather than something that will jolt you back into the real world.

Or try a technique that I call the coin count. To begin, put a number of coins within easy reach of your right hand – so perhaps put them on a table in front of you, on the side of your chair or even in an outside jacket pocket.

Then begin counting your breaths until you get to ten. When you reach ten, take one of the coins and move it from your right to your left side.

Most people find that it takes between 30 to 60 seconds to count ten breaths. So if you're in a hurry and don't want to do more than five minutes of mindful breathing, you could start with, say, five coins on your right-hand side. Or use pebbles, paper clips, bottle tops or anything else you like.

There is no single method of breathing mindfully that is considered correct or more correct than others. Do whatever works for you. Just remember the two simple rules: focus on your breathing. And when any thoughts enter your head, notice them but gently focus your attention back on your breathing again.

> When any thoughts enter your head, notice them but gently focus your attention back on your breathing again.

## Training yourself to be more mindful over time

I think of a single session of mindful breathing as a method that people can use to take the edge off of how they are feeling. If they're feeling upset, it can be a way to impose a measure of calmness and a feeling of better control. So in one respect it's not entirely dissimilar from some of the other speedier techniques for boosting your inward-emotional confidence that I covered back in Part II.

But the greatest benefits of mindfulness come from practising it over time. That's why I put mindfulness into Part IV of this book. I consider it a strategy for developing a deeper, long-term confidence.

Thankfully, I'm not talking about years or even many months of practice. For example, a retinue of researchers led by Norman Farb at the University of Toronto found in a controlled experiment that a mere eight weeks of mindfulness training was enough to significantly reduce feelings of both anxiety and depression in participants.[6]

As a result of mindfulness training, people typically say that they feel more in control of their minds. They become better able to reflect on what to do in challenging situations rather than being buffeted by unruly thoughts and feelings. They feel calmer and more focused.

These changes aren't purely subjective, either. Mindfulness training actually seems to alter the structure of the human brain.

An example: a research team led by Britta Hölzel at Harvard Medical School assigned participants to either an eight-week mindfulness programme or a waiting list control group. Comparing the brains of participants in each group using magnetic resonance imaging (MRI) brain scanners, the researchers found clear differences. The mindfulness participants had increased grey matter concentration in multiple brain regions, specifically those involved in learning and memory, emotional regulation and perspective-taking.[7]

To put it incredibly simply, mindfulness training helped these participants to grow more brain. And in only eight weeks.

For me, that's a completely staggering result. When I was an undergraduate psychologist, I was taught that brain cells essentially started dying off by the time we enter our twenties or thirties and that mental decline was inevitable from then on. But Hölzel's neuroscientific investigation found that engaging in mindfulness for 45 minutes a day for just two months was sufficient to transform the physical structure of the brain.

Wow.

Many writers have compared the human brain to the inner workings of a computer. Adopting that metaphor, mindfulness does not purely upgrade the software of the human brain. Mindfulness seems able to alter the very hardware of the brain. That would be like owning a computer or mobile phone and finding that over the course of several months it has literally grown more RAM or a faster processor.

> Mindfulness seems able to alter the very hardware of the brain.

I said it before, but just give me a moment to say it again: wow! But we're still not done. There's even more good news, as mindfulness may also enhance outward-social confidence.

Cast your mind back to the five components of outward-social confidence that we came across way back in Chapter 2. One of these components was nonverbal performance confidence – people's ability to perform at their best in tests and exams.

We encountered brain scientist Michael Mrazek of the University of California, Santa Barbara earlier in this chapter. In a further study, he and his team found that a mere two weeks of mindfulness training was enough to improve university students' test scores. The students found that their minds tended to wander less, which enabled them to get significantly higher scores than other students who had not been trained in mindfulness.[8]

Again, that's a tremendous result. Only two weeks of mindfulness helped students to get better marks.

Taking all these studies together, I hope you can see that there's convincing evidence for a range of benefits from mindfulness training. But let me stop you in case you're getting too excited. Allow me to introduce a gentle note of caution here, too. Because I really don't want you to expect too much from mindfulness.

Mindfulness is not a cure-all. Simply weaving mindfulness into your life will *not* make everything miraculously better. Yes, there are benefits to inward-emotional confidence in that most people feel measurably better. Yes, it may boost aspects of outward-social confidence in terms of helping people to focus more in pressurized situations such as when taking tests. And yes, such benefits can be reaped fairly swiftly – within weeks or a couple of months. But mindfulness is still only one psychological technique.

I often say to clients that mindfulness is a bit like broccoli. I think broccoli is a sublime vegetable. It's high in fibre, packed with vitamin C and surprisingly calcium-rich. But simply adding lots of broccoli into your diet won't overhaul your body and health. You may need to cut back on pizzas or pastries. You may also need to stop adding so much salt to your food. Perhaps you may need to add in more protein and certain fats, vitamins and nutrients. There may be a bunch of things you need to do.

Along similar lines, I think that mindfulness is a remarkable psychological intervention. But simply adopting mindfulness on its own will not transform your confidence and your life. To put things in perspective, remember that this chapter on mindfulness is only one of 12 chapters in this book. And for a mentally healthy and appropriately courageous life, you will almost certainly need to deploy confidence-building technologies from those other chapters, too.

> Simply adopting mindfulness on its own will not transform your confidence and your life.

## Coming at mindfulness from a different angle

Psychological evidence tells us that mindfulness works. But how does it feel? If you ask people how they feel after performing mindfulness, they often reply that they feel 'calm', 'still', 'focused', 'peaceful' or similar adjectives. Some people say that they feel 'alert' or 'sharp'. Others report that they feel no differently at all. Not everybody feels the same way as a result of practising mindfulness.

Even if you feel as if nothing has changed, though, trust in the research by investigators such as Hölzel and her colleagues: your brain may be changing nonetheless. Your mind may be growing stronger and you may be becoming better able to manage your thoughts and feelings.

Not everyone responds to the simplest form of mindfulness, the breathing exercise, though. Thankfully, there's more than one way to perform mindfulness. If you like, try the other forms of mindfulness that are presented in this chapter to see which ones work best for you.

## Scanning your body

Here's an alternative way to be mindful. It's called the body scan. The idea is to focus your attention on the sensations you experience in different parts of your body.

You will need to find a location and time so that you won't be interrupted. Sit upright, perhaps in a hard-backed chair. You should feel comfortable but alert rather than so relaxed you could easily fall asleep. Some people find it helpful to loosen any tight clothing such as by undoing a top button, loosening a belt or taking off their shoes.

Plant both feet on the floor. Rest your hands in your lap. And either gaze into space or close your eyes.

When you are ready, simply focus on your breathing. If you notice thoughts, feelings or images entering your mind, gently draw your attention back to your breathing.

When you feel that you are calmly focused on your breathing, get ready to move on. Languidly move the focus of your attention to your left toes. No need to rush. Imagine that you have a mental spotlight that is shining on your toes. Notice the sensations that you may be feeling there – perhaps a sense of contact between your toes or your toes against a sock or against the ground, for example. Some people say they notice a tingling feeling. Others say that they notice how warm or cold their toes feel. A few say that they don't feel anything.

After several seconds, move on to the feeling of your entire left foot. Again, allow your attention to rest on your entire foot. Notice whether there may be any tension there. Whatever you feel, just gently notice it. Whatever you feel is whatever you feel – in the same way that some people like the taste of spicy food but others don't. There is no right or wrong answer, no better or worse feeling to experience.

After several more seconds, move your attention on to your ankle, then your calf, the knee and, finally, the thigh.

Next, repeat for the right leg. Begin at the toes and gradually scan each part of your right side.

Then move on to your left fingertips, then your entire hand, forearm, upper arm and, finally, the left shoulder. Then repeat on the right side.

When you have done all four limbs, focus on your trunk. Begin at the bottom: notice how your buttocks feel against the chair. Then move gently on to your pelvis, hips, abdomen, lower back. Keep scanning your attention to your belly button, chest, upper back. Keep moving up to your neck. Notice whether there is any tension in your jaw, then cheeks, forehead, the back of your head and, finally, the top of your head. And then you're done. Perhaps rest for a few seconds before you get up.

Most people find it easier to listen to such instructions rather than read them. You can get my audio track for free at library.teachyourself.com or on the Teach Yourself Library app.

I should add that the precise order of the body scan doesn't matter. Feel free to start with whichever section of your body you like. The idea is simply to scan your attention over the various parts of your body, noticing whatever you're feeling there. Take it at a leisurely pace.

If you try the body scan (or indeed any mindfulness exercise), it is almost inevitable that your mind will wander from time to time. That's entirely natural and you wouldn't be human if you didn't experience other thoughts or feelings at least occasionally. When you notice your focus roaming away from the body scan, there's no need to berate yourself. Simply shepherd your attention back to your body when you can.

If you find that your mind drifts a lot and that you can barely concentrate on your body scan or breathing, that's OK. Mindfulness is merely about engaging with whatever's going on with you.

If you're feeling sad or angry, inadequate or anything else, simply think of your time spent performing mindfulness as an investment in training your mind. You may not feel noticeably better immediately afterwards. Nonetheless, trust that you have spent time in recuperating and caring for yourself. And remember that it's not only an opportunity to take a time out and look after your longer-term well-being. You are helping your brain to strengthen itself through actual physical alterations, too.

> If you find that your mind drifts a lot and that you can barely concentrate on your body scan or breathing, that's OK.

## Developing day-to-day mindfulness

Both the mindful breathing and body scan exercises are mental workouts that require your full focus. The idea is to find a quiet time and place so that you can sit (or, less usually, lie down or even stand) silently to focus on your breath or physical sensations.

However, mindfulness is actually something that we can do at almost any time. In the last few years scholars have increasingly argued that the definition of mindfulness should be broadened to mean the practice of focusing our full attention on *any* activity. You could therefore be mindful in all sorts of situations: eating an apple, gazing out of a train window, exterminating weeds in your garden. Or walking the dog, contemplating art or even cleaning a toilet.

The aim of day-to-day mindfulness is simply to engage fully with an activity rather than doing it on autopilot. Importantly, science suggests that being more mindful and fully focused on such activities and tasks can be quite beneficial, too.

> The aim of day-to-day mindfulness is simply to engage fully with an activity rather than doing it on autopilot.

Consider an experiment run by Adam Hanley at Florida State University and his colleagues on the benefits of dishwashing in a mindful fashion. Bear with me. I know it sounds slightly ludicrous for university researchers to be investigating the value of washing dishes. But the results of the study make a valuable point.

The conclave of scientists posted advertisements online for volunteers to take part in a study entitled 'A bit of dishwashing'. The participants were told that they would complete a set of psychological questionnaires both before and after washing dishes in a sink of water.

Half the participants were given detailed written instructions on how to wash up. Their guidelines included commands to 'use the correct water temperature', 'wash the lightest soiled items first, usually including glasses, cups, and flatware' and 'don't forget to clean the bottoms of pans, as any oily residue will burn on to the bottom of the pan at the next cooking session'.

The other half of the participants were given a passage instructing them to wash the dishes in a more mindful fashion, specifically:

> While washing the dishes one should only be washing the dishes. This means that while washing the dishes one should be completely aware of the fact that one is washing the dishes.

The directions continued:

> The fact that I am standing there and washing is a wondrous reality. I'm being completely myself, following my breath, conscious of my presence, and conscious of my thoughts and actions.

The instructions for the mindfulness participants went on to warn:

> If while washing dishes, we think only of what we would rather do, hurrying to finish the dishes as if they were a nuisance, then we are not 'washing the dishes to wash the dishes.' What's more, we are not alive during the time we are washing the dishes. In fact, we are completely incapable of realizing the miracle of life while standing at the sink.

Participants in both groups spent the same length of time washing dishes – approximately six minutes. But there were measurable benefits for the participants who washed up in the deliberately more mindful fashion. These participants reported modest reductions in the extent to which they felt discomforting emotions; they also said that they felt small surges in their positive emotions. Further analyses of the participants' mood data determined that the mindful participants reported feeling detectably less nervous and significantly more inspired than the participants who had simply washed up according to the detailed instructions.[9]

More broadly, the study suggests that even a humdrum chore such as washing dishes can be made less tedious by making the conscious effort to do it more mindfully. Participants reported feeling less anxious and more fired up when they washed the dishes with the goal of simply washing the dishes rather than wanting to rush through it in order to do something else.

And remember that all the participants spent the same length of time washing the dishes. So it's not as if being less mindful helped participants to speed through the task any more quickly. Doing the job mindfully took no more time but had extra psychological benefits.

Granted, the gains were small. But if you have to do a task or duty that doesn't massively excite you, isn't *any* benefit better than none?

These small benefits may add up, too, according to psychological sleuths such as Kirk Warren Brown and Richard Ryan of the University of Rochester. These researchers have assembled a body of evidence showing that people who are more mindful on a day-to-day basis tend to experience greater overall psychological well-being.[10] And other research indicates that mindfulness reduces rumination, that pernicious, self-inflicted mode of negative thinking that we discussed in Chapter 5.[11]

So this isn't just about washing dishes more mindfully. This is about tackling more of your *life* in a mindful fashion to train your mind for the long term.

Over time, you may learn to make better decisions about what you focus on. Then, if you're feeling plagued by doubts or fears, you may become better able to escape them. You can simply decide to focus more intently on activities and events in the real world. With the flick of a mental switch, you may one day be able to choose to an extent when to stop worrying.

## Developing your dispositional mindfulness

Doing tasks in a more consciously focused, mindful way seems to deliver modest (but measurable) psychological benefits. You may sometimes hear people talk about mindfulness as the intention to be more present – in other words, to focus on what you're currently or presently doing as opposed to thinking back to past regrets or jumping ahead to worries about the future. But whether we call it practising mindfulness or being more present, the goal is the same: to focus fully on the single activity you're doing.

The ultimate aim here is not just to do a few tasks or activities in a more mindful fashion but to integrate mindfulness into more and more of your life. The more mindful you can be during your waking hours, the more sovereignty you may develop over your thoughts and emotions.

For example, think about the way you eat. Do you eat in a hurry – throwing food down your throat because you're rushing to work? Or do you perhaps watch TV or surf the Internet, barely noticing what you're eating? A more mindful approach would be to focus on the sensations of your food, to savour the textures and tastes.

Or if you commute to work, try to avoid seeing it as an annoyance. Aim to pay attention to the myriad details during the journey. Be curious about the sights and sounds and the people you encounter.

I find that most of my clients *understand* the benefits of mindfulness. They often just *forget* to be mindful.

However, research spearheaded by Peter Gollwitzer, originally a professor at the University of Konstanz in Germany and a rock star in the field of goal setting, suggests a way of translating good intentions into practice. Calling them implementation intentions, Gollwitzer discovered that people who write down their goals in a particular format are significantly more likely to achieve them.[12]

The phrasing has to be: *If situation X happens, then I will do Y.* In other words, if a certain cue (situation X) crops up, then you will take action (Y).

When it comes to weaving more mindfulness into your life, these would all be valid implementation intentions:

- If I wash the dishes, then I will do it mindfully.
- If I walk through a door, then I will bring my awareness to the environment around me.
- If I am getting ready for work in the mornings, then I will focus fully on what I am doing rather than what lies ahead at work.
- If I drink a coffee, then I will do it mindfully by focusing my full attention on the experience.
- If I am waiting in a queue, then I will practise mindfulness by focusing on my breathing.

I'm sure you get the gist.

To begin with, choose a handful of activities in which you will commit to becoming more mindful. When you have conquered those situations, then perhaps add a few more implementation intentions to your list. Then a few more. And still more, persisting with the process over time until you are mindful more and more of the time.

Most people begin working on mindfulness through formal practices such as the breathing exercise or the body scan. But the advantage of adding in periods of informal, day-to-day mindfulness is that it's highly portable: you can try to be more mindful while performing just about any task or activity. And, by melding both formal and informal practices, you should get the benefits that we've discussed, in terms of not only your feelings but also your performance in real-world situations.

## Being more mindful in difficult situations

So far, we've focused on mindfulness as either a formal discipline or an informal practice. But I shall end this chapter by explaining how it's something of an ongoing state of mind or attitude, too.

Mindfulness is sometimes classified as another technique within the school of treatment known as acceptance and commitment therapy (ACT), and I'd like to talk about the acceptance part. For me, mindfulness is about acceptance because the aim is to accept or acknowledge situations as they actually are rather than experiencing them through the filter of how we might wish them to be.

An example: I recently had coffee with a friend named Patrick who was feeling furious about something that had happened the week before. He had returned home to discover a series of dents and scratches along the side of his car. Someone had perhaps skidded and scraped the side of his car rather badly.

He had taken the car into the garage for repairs so he would now be without a car for a couple of weeks. And it was going to cost him a not insignificant sum of money, too. He was still incredibly hacked off about it. Speaking more loudly than usual and with a machine-gun pace, he kept saying things like 'The car driver should have left me a note' and 'People shouldn't just drive off like that.'

Yes, in an ideal world, the other driver would have left a note. Yes, it would be great if people didn't drive off after accidents like that. But, in reality, what actually happened was that the driver had not left a note. The driver had driven off. That was the situation that had actually transpired.

In other words, Patrick was ruminating on what he *wanted* to have happened. He was reliving the experience over and over again in a way that simply prolonged his anger and irritation. In a way, he was wishing he could change the past.

A more helpful approach would have been to accept or acknowledge the situation that had actually occurred – not to think about what people 'should' or 'shouldn't' do, but to accept that the accident had happened. He could have helped himself tremendously by dragging his mind away from reliving that past experience and to the real experiences that he could have been having instead.

Another example: a friend named Mariella was diagnosed with breast cancer a few years ago. She was only in her late thirties and she exercised, ate healthily and didn't smoke. Her diagnosis came as a monumental shock.

Now, she could easily have thought, 'This isn't fair' and 'This shouldn't be happening to me – I'm too young! I look after myself!'

She could have withdrawn from the world in bitterness and tears. But that would have been a path to rumination and experiencing the disease as she wished things would be.

Thankfully, she had the presence of mind to accept the diagnosis. That didn't mean that she intended to accept her fate and do nothing about it. She merely acknowledged that it had happened. She accepted that she couldn't modify the past – she could only focus on what to do next.

Indeed, she pursued multiple courses of chemotherapy and radiotherapy. Devastatingly, she had to undergo a mastectomy. She fought the cancer as aggressively as she could and her prognosis in recent months has been very good. But all the time, by experiencing her situation as it actually was – and not how she wished it might be – she helped to preserve her state of mind, her psychological well-being and mental health.

## Putting mindful acceptance into practice

Remember that mindful acceptance is only about accepting the fact that bad things happen. And, when bad things happen, you can't change the past. More than that, there's no point wishing what *should* or *shouldn't* have happened – dwelling on the unfairness or otherwise of whatever has befallen you.

I admit that this is one of the less straightforward aspects of mindfulness. But perhaps the following statements formulated by researchers led by Baljinder Sahdra at the University of California, Davis may be useful.[13] These investigators found that certain behaviours were linked to lower psychological distress. To help you cultivate an attitude of mindful acceptance, think about how you might put some of these behaviours into practice for yourself:

- 'I can let go of regrets and feelings of dissatisfaction about the past.'
- 'I view the problems that enter my life as things/issues to work on rather than reasons for becoming disheartened or demoralized.'

- 'Instead of avoiding or denying life's difficulties, I face up to them.'
- 'I find I can be happy almost regardless of what is going on in my life.'

Acceptance also means accepting our own flaws and failings. For example, when you've made a mistake, do you tend to beat yourself up about it? Perhaps. After all, many people do. But that kind of self-punishment is no different from wishing that you could alter the past. No matter how much you chastise yourself, you can't go back in time. A better strategy is to acknowledge that what happened is now past. And try to accept that we are all flawed individuals but that the best thing we can do is to endeavour to do better in future.

Allow me to say this one final time: mindful acceptance is only about accepting the situation as it is rather than wishing you could change the past. So yes, should you get fired from your job or should your home be destroyed in a fire, accept that no amount of wishing can revise what has transpired. If you make a humiliating blunder or offend someone by your actions, you cannot erase it from history. In such situations, allowing yourself to stay embarrassed or grouchy, depressed or otherwise tormented only hurts you further.

> Mindful acceptance is only about accepting the situation as it is rather than wishing you could change the past.

At the same time, though, acceptance does not mean giving in or allowing circumstances to paralyse you into doing nothing. You can accept what has brought you to a moment in time but still be hungry and determined to do something to change what happens next. In fact, I fully encourage you to make plans to tackle the situation and improve things. And that is precisely what we shall look at in the next chapter.

## Onwards and upwards

- Understand that mindfulness is simply the act of focusing your complete attention on what is happening to you or around you *and* doing it in a non-judgemental way. So that means accepting what is going on and noticing it rather than mentally critiquing it.
- If mindfulness is new to you, you may want to begin practising it by focusing on your breathing occasionally. Find a time and place where you can concentrate on your breathing for ten breaths. When you are ready to invest more time in developing your mindfulness, gradually lengthen the time you spend focusing on your breathing.
- Consider also the body scan exercise in which you focus attention on the separate parts of your body. Remember that there is no right or better order of body parts that you must follow. Find a sequence that works for you.
- To further develop your overall levels of mindfulness, find additional occasions throughout your day to incorporate mindfulness into whatever activities you're doing. Think of this as a better way of interacting with the world that you will gradually integrate into more and more parts of your life.
- Remember that a core principle of mindfulness is about accepting situations as they actually are and not how you might want them to be. When something bad has happened to you or you feel you've crashed and burned, avoid wasting energy wishing that things could be different. Accept what has happened and focus on the future instead.

Recently I ran a series of workshops aimed at developing a group of young managers in an Internet start-up. The company had grown incredibly swiftly over the previous year and all the managers attending the workshops were now managing teams of between three and 12 people for the very first time in their careers.

One of the managers, a late-twenty-something woman named Amelia, told me privately that her confidence was at an all-time low. Her team wasn't hitting its targets so she was working long hours to try to sort out their many problems. And she was grappling with an older engineer in her team named Dean who was extremely disgruntled and out to undermine her. With a break in her voice and glistening eyes, she confided that she was sometimes crying not only at home but occasionally in toilet cubicles at work, too.

I recommended several interventions, including the positive reminiscence exercise (from Chapter 6) and a key values audit (which we will encounter in Chapter 12). However, I told her that such psychological manoeuvres could confer only relatively modest boosts. The better solution was to sort out the issues she was facing.

So we spent a lot more time talking through options. Ultimately, Amelia wrote a loose script for a conversation to have with Dean. She had been avoiding having a confrontation with him. But, with some planning, she felt more emboldened broaching the issue with him; she thought about the actual words she would use to encourage him and harness his enthusiasm but at the same time dampen down his aggression. She also agreed to have a more honest conversation with her line manager to appeal for specific sources of support in tackling the team's wider issues.

My discussions with Amelia were more practical than psychological. And you may find that more than a few of the challenges and opportunities in your life require a practical rather than psychological approach, too. Or, as I often say when I'm running training workshops: sometimes it's not enough to change your mind; you also need to change your situation.

> Sometimes it's not enough to change your mind; you also need to change your situation.

For example, if your confidence is a shambles because you have money troubles, simply learning to worry less isn't going to be as useful as hatching a plan to reduce your spending and pay off your debts. If you're feeling lonely, something like mindfulness may strengthen your mind, but actually going out to join a book club or activity group may be more helpful. Or, if you feel put down or let down by a co-worker or spouse, the answer may be to speak up and ask for what you want.

But this isn't merely about tackling problems. It's about pursuing opportunities as well. You may be hankering to grasp that big promotion, set up your own business or renovate a dilapidated house, for example.

Plenty of research studies tell us that people who adopt certain methods and approaches tend to get better results in the real world. So in this chapter I will summarize the main steps that help people to tackle issues and achieve richer, more confident lives.

## Applying a process for both ordeals and opportunities

Allow me to warn you upfront that the ten steps in this chapter may at first seem obvious. But I am certain that you will come across at least several insights that you will never have encountered elsewhere.

There is also a gigantic difference between intellectually understanding something and actually doing it. When I'm running workshops, I often say that it's like the difference between grasping the theory of losing weight versus actually applying it. Many people understand the theory of weight loss: eat less and exercise more. Almost every adult appreciates that a burger with fries is more fattening than grilled chicken with steamed vegetables. However, merely having insight into the principles of weight loss on an intellectual level is not enough to get any benefit. It's the implementation – the enacting of that theory – that helps people to lose weight.

And it is exactly the same for tackling real-world impasses and opportunities. Comprehending the principles behind the ten steps is not enough. To get the benefit, you actually have to implement the steps by working through them.

OK. Lecture over!

A final word before we start: please consider these ten steps a rough guide rather than a strict set of rules. Sometimes, you may find that you need to work through only a handful of the different steps. At other times, you may find that they all have a role to play. The point is not to follow them slavishly but to apply them flexibly, depending on the nature of each situation. The tougher or more important the issue, the more steps you may want to follow.

Let's get started.

## 1. Identify your confidence gaps

Sometimes you may hear people – or yourself – saying things like:

- 'I'm just not happy.'
- 'Everything's such a mess.'
- 'I feel really depressed.'
- 'Life is incredibly difficult at the moment.'

The thing is, it's quite tricky to tackle such sweeping statements. So if you're not sure where to begin, consider that it really helps to identify more specific issues that you can concentrate on. For example, *what* in particular is making you depressed? *Which* areas of your life feel the most problematic? Are there certain individuals who are affecting you – *who* is the problem? Or *how* do you imagine you could realistically make yourself happier?

If you're feeling lost and need direction, begin by considering the different parts or domains of your life. Some people feel confident at work but may worry about socializing at parties or meeting new people. Many people feel in control about only some parts of their work – dealing with tasks but perhaps not with their bosses, for example. Others may be comfortable speaking their minds and asserting their rights but obsess about their weight or physical appearance. Others may be struggling with their finances, their sex lives or soul-destroying situations at home. Specify exactly what's bothering you and you help yourself to resolve it.

> Specify exactly what's bothering you and you help yourself to resolve it.

Or perhaps you need some more specific prompts. As a result of a series of studies, veteran researchers Gerhard Henrich and Peter Herschbach at the Technical University of Munich in Germany have identified that a rewarding, confident life typically requires a level of contentment across eight different domains of life:[1]

- Your friends and acquaintances
- Your leisure time and hobbies
- Your health
- Your financial resources and sense of financial security
- Your work
- Your home and living conditions
- Your family life (and children)
- Your relationship with your partner and your sexuality

If you want to identify the areas of your life that may need the most attention, consider pausing here to rate your confidence in each of those eight domains. You could rate each on a scale of 1 to 10, where a 1 indicates incredibly low confidence and a 10 indicates a deliriously high level of confidence.

So where are your lowest scores? Which are the handful of areas that are causing you the most heartache and frustration? Be really honest with yourself. What would most help you to feel more confident in life?

## 2. Write down both the facts and your feelings

Scoring your levels of confidence across the eight domains is a useful step if you're not sure where to start. But, once you've identified your priorities, focus on them one at a time.

Before we do that, though, allow me to take you on a minor detour. I'm going to ask you to multiply two numbers in your head. Here goes: what is 37 multiplied by 19?

That's incredibly difficult, right? But if you write it down, you'll find it a lot easier to get to the right answer. And the same is true for tackling real-world quandaries.

You may remember that I warned in Chapter 5 about the dangers of rumination – that pattern of excessive and often circular thinking and worrying. People who ruminate a lot may subconsciously believe that it is a useful activity. They may feel that it helps them to solve issues or prevent future disasters. But psychologists advise that worry – at least the kind that happens solely in your head – is actually rarely productive. However, if you capture your roiling thoughts on paper (or a computer screen), you may become far better equipped to disentangle real issues from perceived ones – and to plan what to do about them.

Actually, research suggests that you don't even have to follow through with the planning bit to benefit from writing down your thoughts and feelings. In a classic experimental inquiry, Carnegie Mellon University researcher Stephen Lepore asked a group of students to write down their deepest thoughts and feelings about an upcoming exam. The students were instructed to write 'about your thoughts and feelings regarding the exam itself, the effect of the exam on your life in the present, the exam's implications for your future goals, and alternative plans you may have. The crucial thing is that you dig down into your deepest emotions and explore them in your writing.' Another group of students was asked to write about an unrelated topic.

Cutting a long story short, the students who wrote about their thoughts and feelings reported feeling significantly less emotionally frazzled about the impending exam.[2] So the mere act of writing about your hopes, fears, thoughts and feelings may help you to feel better.

If you like, you could draw up a table with two columns. Scribble facts down in one column and your feelings in the other.

List all of the facts that you know about your predicament. For example, if you're feeling overwhelmed at work, it may be useful to itemize all of the individual tasks, projects and expectations that are causing you grief. Or, if you're feeling frustrated that you aren't getting the promotion you crave, you could list all of the different obstacles in your way.

Or say you're feeling rejected by your friends. Perhaps one friend has seemed particularly withdrawn. If that's the case, then write down, 'She has been withdrawn.'

But don't jump to conclusions. For example, you may be feeling that your friend 'hates me because I let her down last week'. But, unless she actually said to you, 'I hate you because you let me down last week,' then remember that it's only a feeling – something to go into the second column – a guess on your part for now.

As I said, research suggests that simply writing your thoughts and feelings down may already enable you to feel a little better. Furthermore, understanding your individual feelings and worries can help you to identify the most pernicious ones and allow you to neutralize them – perhaps through techniques such as cognitive defusion (as well as the other methods we covered in Part II). And seeing the facts of the situation laid bare will ultimately allow you to make better plans, too.

> Understanding your individual feelings and worries can help you to identify the most pernicious ones and allow you to neutralize them.

## 3. Write down multiple options

So now that you've noted the facts and your feelings around your situation, what next?

You've no doubt heard about brainstorming. As an aside, there's good research showing that group brainstorming – in which everybody tries to shout out ideas no matter how outlandish or unrealistic they may seem – doesn't work.[3] But one of the best ways of addressing a personal issue is to have a go at listing as many different ways you could tackle it as possible.

So get writing. Give yourself enough time to invest in some high-quality thinking. Capture whatever brainwaves come to mind, no matter how weird or impractical they may seem. The point is that even notions that at first seem impossible may spark further ideas that may actually work.

At this point, there can be a temptation to slip into wondering *why* the situation has arisen, for example with questions such as:

- 'Why has this happened to me?'
- 'Why don't they like me?'
- 'Why am I not more confident/successful/popular/etc.?'

Focusing on *why* questions may not be a good idea, though, according to researchers Ed Watkins and Simona Baracaia at the Institute of Psychiatry, part of King's College London (which was, incidentally, the place where I got my doctorate in psychology). They have found that people who focus on *why* questions tend to be conspicuously worse at problem solving than people who focus on *how* questions.[4] Speculating on the why – the reasons something may happen – is more associated with ruminating unhelpfully over problems rather than resolving them.

So take heed. Avoid *why* and focus on *how*. Rather than asking a question like 'Why has my boss not promoted me yet?' adjust the focus to 'How can I get my boss to promote me?' Don't wonder, 'Why do people talk over me?' Instead, ask yourself, 'How can I stop people from talking over me?' The same goes for your feelings. Rather than asking, 'Why do I feel this way?' reframe the question as 'How can I feel better? What techniques can I use to change my feelings?'

How can you solve the problem or improve your situation? How could you make more money or stand up to that bully or get people to notice you? How could you make new friends or get healthier or rebuild the level of intimacy with your partner?

Focusing on *how* rather than *why* may seem like an almost trivial difference. But that's part of the beauty of the science. The latest research is discovering that even seemingly tiny changes in how we think about the world can have actually quite measurable effects.

So remember, remember, remember to direct your attention to *how* actions rather than *why* reasons. And do give it some proper thought. Don't sit for one or two minutes and expect the perfect solution to pop into your head. If the issue is particularly tricky, you may want to set aside your list and return to it again later on – or even on multiple occasions as your thinking about the issues may evolve and mature over time.

> Remember to direct your attention to *how* actions rather than *why* reasons.

## 4. Weigh up the alternatives

Let's say you've come up with a list of four or five options for improving your situation. Often, the solution can be quite clear. One of the options may stand out above the others because it's the most sensible course of action. Sometimes, though, the path to take can be far less obvious. If that's the case, then spend some time assessing your options.

Back in Chapter 4, we looked at the technique of visualization. There, we discovered that visualization tends to work best when we adopt a first-person perspective – by immersing ourselves fully in our situations – rather than a third-person perspective as if we were an outside observer looking on. Could the same be true when it comes to problem solving?

This was the precise question explored by behavioural detectives Ethan Kross and Igor Grossmann of the University of Michigan, Ann Arbor. In one of their experiments, the researchers asked jobseekers to evaluate how the state of the economy might affect their job prospects. Half the jobseekers were asked to think about the events 'unfolding before your own eyes as if you were right there'. The other half were asked to take a different perspective and to consider events 'unfolding as if you were a distant observer'.

Ultimately, the job hunters who adopted the second, so-called distanced, perspective were judged by experts to have made smarter judgements.[5] So it may be a good idea to imagine that you are weighing up options for someone else. In other words, rather than weighing up how circumstances could affect you personally, pretend that you are advising a friend or colleague who is *like* you.

> Pretend that you are advising a friend or colleague who is like you.

Perspective matters. But remember that no one perspective is better all the time. For the best results, you may want to use the immersed, first-person perspective when engaging in visualization or mental rehearsal. However, you may be better off adopting the opposite, distanced, third-person perspective when evaluating options and trying to make smarter decisions for yourself.

In terms of weighing up your options, then, here are some questions that you could use as prompts. Remember that all of these are written as if you were considering someone else's life; so when a question mentions 'this person' or 'he or she', of course I actually mean *you*.

- How effective could this option be? Does this person have the right skills to do this well?
- What would be the benefits/advantages/pros of this course of action?
- What would be the costs/disadvantages/cons of this option? How much time and effort would be involved?
- How could this affect the important people (e.g. family, friends, business partners) in this person's life?
- What would the important people in this person's life say about the situation?
- How does he or she actually *feel* about this option?

Another way to encourage the so-called distanced perspective would be to answer such questions using your own name. For example, suppose I were to answer the last question on that list with regard to some project I was considering, I might write: 'Rob is feeling excited about the undertaking. But Rob is also feeling alarmed that he won't have the time to complete it.'

It can feel slightly surreal to write about yourself in the third person. But remember that there's evidence pointing to the value of doing it this way.

The half-dozen questions above are not designed to be comprehensive. Feel free to ignore my questions or make up your own set. And you may not need to evaluate the alternatives every time you have an issue to tackle. You may only need to be more considered in your approach when wrestling with the weightier problems or opportunities in life. Just be sure to adopt that distanced perspective: make believe that you're weighing up the options for someone else who happens to have a life a lot like yours.

## 5. Seek additional opinions

Remember back in Chapter 1 that I introduced what I call the curse of confidence: the fact that a multitude of people overestimate their own abilities without realizing it. Perhaps you don't think you're great at anything. But bear in mind that it's also possible to fall into the trap of thinking that you are average when you may in fact be quite weak at certain things. So please don't let this be you.

The best way (again, as I recommended in Chapter 1) to avoid the curse of confidence is to seek out the opinions of people who can be truly candid with you. Remember to grant people permission to be completely frank with you. Tell them that you genuinely want their most unflinchingly honest thoughts – that you would rather discover how best to tackle your situation than hear nice but unhelpful comments.

If you want to get the most out of whatever feedback you receive, you may need to be more precise in your questioning. In a research paper analysing the effectiveness of feedback across over 23,000 experimental participants, scientists Avraham Kluger of the Hebrew University of Jerusalem and Angelo DeNisi of Rutgers University found that feedback is generally most useful when it is about a task rather than a person.[6]

> Feedback is generally most useful when it is about a task rather than a person.

So ask about a particular assignment or skill area rather than asking broader questions. For example, you are likely to get more valuable insights from 'What do you think I need to do in order to give better presentations?' (i.e. you're asking about presentations in particular) than 'What do you think I need to do in order to be more charismatic?' (i.e. you're asking about how you communicate in general).

Or suppose you're dating. Ask specific questions such as 'What do you think I could do to make a better immediate impression on first dates?' or 'How would you suggest I rewrite my online dating profile?' Avoid untargeted questions such as 'Why do you think I'm single?'

As with several of these other steps, you may not need to seek advice every time. Sometimes, a course of action may be fairly clear-cut. But if you're tackling something trickier or more momentous in your life, you may want a second (or third or fourth or fifth, and so on) opinion, too.

## 6. Script and rehearse challenging conversations

Many less confident individuals feel that the most difficult part of sorting out their lives involves having to speak up and stand up for themselves. But sometimes that's precisely what is needed: being assertive and explaining politely but clearly what you want or don't want from the people around you.

Perhaps you're feeling that someone at home is not doing enough of the household chores. Maybe a colleague is acting in an overbearing fashion and snatching opportunities that should be yours. Or a friend is making jokes about you that are no longer funny but actually upsetting. Whatever the case, I frequently remind clients that they need to speak up because *other people are not telepathic.* You can't expect people to know how you feel unless you tell them.

> You can't expect people to know how you feel unless you tell them.

Recall from Chapter 1 that many people get ambushed by over-confidence. So perhaps the people in your life think that they do a brilliant job with chores around the house. They think that they are acting in a fair and impartial manner. They think that they are entertaining and amusing.

They may simply need a nudge that they're not so brilliant or fair and impartial or entertaining and amusing. You can't just hope that they will figure it out for themselves.

Other people are often more reasonable than you may at first think. Most of them are more than willing to change – or at least modify slightly – their behaviour. But they have to know that there's an issue. If you don't speak up, you cannot realistically expect them to intuit how you would like them to behave.

If you need to speak to your line manager or a colleague, a friend or a loved one, what would be the very first words to come out of your mouth? What would you actually say?

When I'm working with clients, I ask them to jot down some notes and then share them with me. We do a short role play as if I am the target of the conversation.

I recommend you do the same. Write down what you would like to say. Then rehearse your script.

One way to practise would be to engage in mental rehearsal or visualization. We looked at this technique back in Chapter 4. However, an even better way to practise would be to speak it out loud. Listen to how it sounds. If you don't like it, keep amending it until you have something you can see yourself saying to the person (or persons) involved.

You probably don't even need to consult anyone else about what to say. In a classic research study, Robert Schwartz from Indiana University and John Gottman of the University of Illinois asked 101 participants to complete a questionnaire called the Conflict Resolution Inventory. Based on their answers, the participants were categorized into three groups: low-assertive, moderate-assertive and high-assertive people.

The researchers then presented all the participants with hypothetical confrontations and asked them to write down what they thought would be the best response to each. Interestingly, the researchers found that all three groups produced nearly identical model answers.

In other words, the low-assertive people were categorically as good at writing polite yet effective refusals.[7]

Remember that. People who don't feel very assertive are categorically as good at figuring out the right thing to say as more assertive people. Your judgement is sound.

So trust yourself. You probably know what you need to say to the people who are causing you grief. You may just need to rehearse it a number of times until you feel comfortable enough to initiate that conversation.

## 7. Psych yourself up

OK, so perhaps you fancy asking your manager for a pay rise. Or you're getting ready to ask someone out. Or you've resolved to confront someone who has been making life miserable of late. If you've worked out what you want to say and do, *now* is the time to deploy one of the psychological sleights of mind that we covered earlier in Parts II and III of this book. That may be the visualization routine from Chapter 4, in which you create a positive mental movie depicting how you would like things to go. Or, if you're troubled by particular images of failure, it may be the mental resizing technique (also from Chapter 4) to send them away from you into the distance.

In the moments before your conversation or interview or presentation, you may want to give yourself a quick boost with a different tactic. That could be by reframing your panic by reminding yourself that how you feel is actually a form of physiological arousal, which is designed to help you to pay attention and perform better (from Chapter 3). Or perhaps it could be cognitive defusion or distraction from Chapter 5. And, of course, there were plenty of psychological boosts for your outward-social confidence in Chapter 6 as well: writing about your aspirations and ambitions or harnessing the power of positive reminiscence, to name but two.

The point isn't to do all of them. Be selective and endeavour to figure out what might be most useful in each particular situation. This step is simply a reminder to use a psychological tool to give yourself a proven lift.

## 8. Take action(s)

While many of the steps in this guide may be considered optional, this is the only step that must, must, must be taken. After all, writing down the facts and your feelings, generating multiple options, weighing them up and preparing would all be a waste of time if you didn't actually follow through.

In terms of tackling a problem or grasping an opportunity, there may be one clear action that stands out above all others. Maybe that's confronting the individual who is undermining you, starting that workout programme or pursuing whatever else you need to do.

Or there may be multiple actions you need to take. If you're feeling deluged at work, for instance, then you may want to have a discussion with your line manager to start with. You may also decide to pursue an online course to fine-tune your technical skills, ask a colleague for advice and adopt several psychological confidence-building techniques – all at the same time.

Whether you need to take one action or several, you can furnish yourself with the very best chance of success by writing them out as a series of implementation intentions. You may remember that I first mentioned these back in Chapter 9 (in a box entitled 'Developing your dispositional mindfulness').

Here's a brief reminder: help yourself to turn your intentions into reality by writing your actions out as 'If ... then ...' statements. In other words, when a particular situation arises, you are committing yourself to taking a specific action.

For example, someone trying to appear more gregarious in social situations may decide: 'If there is an awkward pause in the conversation, then I will ask, "So what is everyone up to this weekend?"' Or someone else who wants to stand up to an uppity colleague may resolve: 'If she puts me down again, then I will explain to her that I don't feel it's professional for her to make such cutting remarks.'

Writing your objectives down as a series of 'If ... then ...' implementation intention statements gives you a series of concrete aims. Then, when those situations arise, be sure to follow through. Or, as the sportswear company Nike always says, just do it.

> Writing your objectives down as a series of 'If ... then ...' implementation intention statements gives you a series of concrete aims.

## 9. Review the results

Sometimes, you will know pretty rapidly whether your action(s) worked. Maybe you asked your bank manager for a business loan and got turned down. Or you invited some friends out for dinner but you didn't enjoy the evening.

Even in situations when things don't turn out the way you wanted, you may still be getting stronger. Your self-efficacy – your self-belief – may have grown somewhat. And that may help to make things easier for you the next time.

At other times, though, accept that not a lot may change as an immediate result of your actions. For example, if your long-term problem is that you're overweight and lacking confidence in your body, you can't expect to see much of a difference after a single exercise session. Or, if you're trying to be more assertive at work, you can't anticipate that things will improve after a mere handful of attempts to speak up more.

Whatever the outcome, you can always look at how to make things better or easier the next time. So maybe you hadn't put in enough groundwork before asking your bank manager for the loan. Perhaps you exercised too hard that first time and need to do a bit less next time. Or you need to plan before meetings to make sure that you have something genuinely valuable to say.

By all means reflect on what happened. But remember to focus on *how* rather than *why* questions.

We already discussed this back in step 3. You'll recall that asking *why* questions (e.g. 'Why didn't my manager give me a rise?' or 'Why didn't I speak up more?') often leads to that circular, unhelpful pattern of thinking known as rumination. In contrast, asking *how* questions (e.g. 'How can I get my manager to give me a rise?' or 'How can I ensure that I speak up more?') tends to get better results.

Once you have identified how you could take action, be sure to translate these next steps into implementation intentions. So whatever your thoughts on the matter, consider tweaking your existing list of 'If ... then ...' statements – or even adding completely new ones.

## 10. Repeat and persist

The final step isn't really a distinct action so much as a reminder that the steps we've covered so far may need to be repeated over and over again until you get the outcome you want.

For example, if you're looking for a new job, it's unlikely that the first vacancy you apply for will be the one you get. You may need to take further actions – applying for further jobs, for instance (step 8). If you are invited to interviews, perhaps you may need to rewrite your answers to likely interview questions (step 6) and then psych yourself up for each fresh interview (step 7).

Every time you are rejected by an employer, you may need to review what happened (step 9). What would you continue doing? How would you behave differently and, you hope, better next time? And what does that mean for your 'If ... then ...' implementation intention plan?

Do you maybe need to seek further advice on finding more openings or honing your interview patter (step 5)? Or perhaps you need to be more strategic by looking again at your present situation (step 2) and considering any options that you may have missed the first time around (step 3).

The point is that you should apply whichever of these ten steps as and when you need them. Not every step may be necessary every time. As I said at the start of this chapter, these ten steps are more a set of potentially helpful guidelines rather than inflexible rules. If something works well or even a little bit, see how you can tweak it to get a better result. If something doesn't work, try to suss out what else may work better. Above and beyond these ten steps, I simply encourage you to keep trying and to keep reviewing the results so that you can learn as you go on.

## *Living a life without regret*

Of course, the voyage to a new and hopefully more confident you is not always going to go smoothly. You may encounter detours or even dead ends occasionally.

For example, I worked with a marketing executive soon after he lost his job. A 44-year-old with an easy grin and hands that buzzed about him in perpetual motion, Dylan had long had a dream of opening his own restaurant. However, he had no real experience of the hospitality industry as he had only ever worked in marketing roles for large organizations.

So together we strategized. He took action. As part of his plan, he got a job in a café with a view to learning about budgets, stocktaking, restaurant hygiene, profitability and everything else that he understood in theory but not practice.

Within a few months, though, he realized that he wasn't enjoying it. He didn't like the hours or the relative unpredictability of the job. And he discovered unexpectedly that he didn't like working directly with customers – he often found himself feeling irritable and drained.

He had liked the concept of running a restaurant. But he came to realize that the world of hospitality was not for him. So he quit. He went back to looking for another marketing job instead.

He did feel a bit annoyed with himself. But he didn't regret his attempted career change. He was glad to have explored his dream. Yes, he tried and failed. However, he went back to a marketing job fairly invigorated to know that corporate life was right for him.

Dylan's experience perfectly mirrors what research has to say on regret, too. Eminent psychologists Thomas Gilovich, Victoria Medvec and Daniel Kahneman concluded in a seminal paper that 'although action regrets are more intense than inaction regrets in the short term, the opposite is true in the long run'.[8]

Allow me to unpack that sentence so that we may consider it more fully. In the weeks and months after a bad experience, people do have action regrets – they feel annoyed or angry and regretful about the opportunities they pursued that didn't turn out well. But as the months turn into years and decades, people tend to be much more bothered by inaction regrets – they become more mournful about what they *didn't* do rather than what they did.

> People tend to be much more bothered by what they *didn't* do rather than what they did.

The team came from Cornell University, Northwestern University and Princeton University – three of the most prestigious centres of academic research in the world. So trust their judgement. In the short term, you may feel more stung by your seeming flops or failures. But, eventually, you may be more thankful that you at least tried – that you gave it a go and were able to move on.

So take a chance. Do something. Don't be that person who, in ten or 20 or 30 years' time, looks back and wonders 'What if?' or 'If only …'

## Onwards and upwards

- Bear in mind that, while psychological techniques can boost your confidence, you may also need to tackle the more direct causes of your unhappiness or low confidence. And that usually means facing up to real-world problems and opportunities.
- Rather than trying to tackle everything at once, aim to break things down into separate, smaller chunks. Tackle one issue at a time rather than trying to take on too much at once.
- Understand that you will probably get better results if you write things down. It's difficult to hold many competing ideas in mind at the same time. Writing things down – both the facts and your feelings as well as what you want to say or do – is most likely to give you the best chance of success.
- Resist the temptation to focus on *why* your situation has arisen, as such questioning may lead to that negative pattern of thinking called rumination. Instead, focus on *how* questions, which are more likely to generate concrete actions for actually improving your situation.
- Be flexible in your approach to obstacles and opportunities. Treat the ten-step method as a set of loose guidelines rather than strict rules. Do whatever makes sense for you in each different situation.
- Perhaps most importantly, do something. Inactivity and avoiding issues are sure-fire ways to keep feeling low in confidence. It's only through action that you can start to feel more positive and in control.

# 12
# Creating the life you want to live

'The principle of moving forward, as though you have the confidence to move forward, eventually gives you the confidence when you look back and see what you've done.'

*Robert Downey, Jr*

Not long ago, a client I'll call Charlotte asked for my support. On the cusp of turning 40, she was working in a demanding job as vice-president of human resources for an American bank. But she wanted to do something else. She was tired of the politics and what she saw as the meaningless nature of her work. However, she felt stuck. Having had a few conversations with recruiters, she was aware that moving into a different industry would probably mean a whopping pay cut.

To add to her difficulties, her teenage son had for several years been struggling with severe mental health issues. He had even tried to commit suicide on two occasions, although thankfully he had improved significantly since then.

As a result of all the turmoil in both her professional and personal life, she had gained a lot of weight. She was so full of shame that she had been avoiding her friends. She was certain that they would talk about her grotesque weight gain behind her back.

With downcast eyes and her mouth set in a hard line, she concluded that she felt terribly trapped. She had lost all confidence in her career, her parenting skills, her sex life, her social life. She wanted to change something, *anything*. But she couldn't seem to muster up the energy to do so.

Soon after hearing her story, I asked her, 'What's your life's purpose?'

Immediately, I told her that I didn't expect an answer straight away. I said that it would probably take her a few weeks of reflection and writing to come back with a proper response. And, even then, her answer would only begin a process of change and renewal, something that would take months. But I recommended the exercise as a starting point because I was genuinely convinced that it would aid her.

I'm always wary of hyperbole – both in articles written by other people as well as in my own writing. But I'm tempted to say that writing about your life's purpose may be one of the most powerful interventions in psychology. Dozens of research studies have shown this one odd exercise to have a surprisingly wide and long-lasting range of benefits.

> Writing about your life's purpose may be one of the most powerful interventions in psychology.

So have you ever thought about it? What is *your* life's purpose?

## *Learning to live a valuable life*

To be clear, I'm not asking you about the purpose of humanity's existence on earth. Instead, have a think for a moment: when you die (hopefully after you have lived for many decades to come), what would you like to be remembered for?

Do you want to be recognized for your professional achievements? Or maybe your personal achievements – your role in your family, your community or the part you played in your social circles? Perhaps you feel you have a gift that you would love to have shared with the world: you're a singer, an artist, a creator, an athlete. Or you yearn to be remembered for one of your traits: your humour, kindness, intelligence, determination, honesty or anything else.

All the chapters in Part IV of this book are focused squarely on the longer-term strategies that can make the biggest difference to your life. But it turns out that asking you about your life's purpose doesn't just have long-lasting repercussions. It can be incredibly handy when you need a speedy boost, too.

Researcher J. David Creswell is a luminary in the field of psycho-neuroimmunology, the study of how the mind and body interact in stressful circumstances. Some years ago, while at the University of California, Los Angeles, Creswell and his partners enrolled 80 men and women into an investigation designed to look at whether thinking about an important value could protect against stress.

The participants were told that they would have two tasks to perform. First, they were given only a few minutes to prepare for and then deliver a five-minute presentation to two experimenters. Second, the participants were then asked to spend a further five minutes counting backwards from 2,083 in jumps of 13. By the way, if you don't think that's tough, try it for yourself for just 60 seconds. And, to make the participants feel even tenser, the experimenters occasionally barked at them to 'go faster'.

If you're sensing that this whole set-up sounds familiar, you're right. We encountered this exact anxiety-inducing protocol in Chapter 3, when researchers Jeremy Jamieson, Matthew Nock and Wendy Berry Mendes discovered the benefits of reappraising fear as something that may actually help people to do better in exams and tests.

Anyway, back to the current study: Creswell and his associates asked each of the participants to rank five personal values in order of importance to that individual. The participants were then divided into two groups. One group was asked to answer a handful of questions about their most important value. The second, control group was asked to answer a handful of questions about their least important value.

Ultimately, participants in the experimental group who thought about their most important value reported feeling significantly less overwhelmed during the whole experiment. Also, when the researchers asked the participants for saliva samples, they found that the participants who had focused on their most important value had lower levels of the stress hormone cortisol in their saliva.[1]

In other words, writing about a value – or, more specifically, a relatively unimportant value – is fairly pointless. However, writing about your most cherished value in life may be yet another way of bolstering your inward-emotional confidence. It seems to reduce both psychological and physiological levels of stress.

That study alone points to the benefits of contemplating your most essential value. But there's more. Using a similar but not identical research design, investigators tested the effects of a modified values exercise on performance in a problem-solving test. This time, participants ranked 11 values. The researchers found that those participants who wrote about their first-ranked value exhibited better problem-solving abilities than those who wrote about their ninth-ranked (i.e. a fairly unimportant) value.[2]

We've seen on several occasions throughout the book that a small handful of techniques have been shown to benefit not only inward-emotional confidence but also outward-social confidence. But these studies together tell us that we can now add the values exercise to this list as well. Writing about your most important value in life may boost both your inward-emotional confidence and your outward-social confidence.

> Writing about an important value may be yet another way of boosting your inward-emotional confidence.

There are other, more lasting benefits from this exercise. And writing about what you value can also be the start of a longer process of working on yourself. But before we elaborate further on such matters, let's look at the core writing exercise first.

## Conducting a key values audit

The next time you want to not only reduce anxiety but also lift your performance (in a test, audition, exam, interview, presentation, etc.) consider writing about one of your values. This exercise has two parts. You can do the first part at any time, in advance of when you may need it. Then do the second part just before whatever stressful situation you're planning to experience.

**Part 1:** Look at the following 18 characteristics and values. Some of these may be important to you; others may be less critical or not at all important.

| Being creative | Excitement/ adventure | Friendships |
|---|---|---|
| Helping people/ animals | Love | Spirituality/ religion |
| Artistry/aesthetics | Relationships with family | Health |
| Serenity | Physical attractiveness | Personal growth |
| Sense of humour | Freedom | Career/ professional life |
| Fitness/athletic skills | Influence/status | Kindness |

Please rank the values in order from 1 to 18, with 1 being your most quintessentially important value and 18 being the least. And remember that this is a task for your own benefit;

so choose what you genuinely feel to be meaningful to you rather than what you think would be acceptable to the people in your life.

Some people find this relatively straightforward; others agonize over the list for some time. Take however much time you need in order to uncover the relative importance of the assorted values.

Part 2: When you need a boost, spend six minutes writing a few paragraphs about why your first-ranked value is so indispensable to you. Write whatever you genuinely feel on this topic.

## Taking a really honest look at yourself

I tell my clients that they don't have to share the results of their key values audits with me. But they often do. And I have seen their musings take many forms. Some have written page after page after page. Others have written just a few punchy paragraphs.

The only requirement is that you write about how you genuinely feel. Don't pick a value that you think *should* be important in your life. You won't ever need to share your reflections with anyone else. And it's when you can be truly honest with yourself that you'll get the most out of this.

The key values audit commonly points to small improvements that you can use to keep your life more strongly on course. Occasionally, though, it can lead to fairly eye-opening revelations.

Last autumn I coached someone named Bartholomew. The softly spoken 28-year-old initially came to me for coaching because he wanted to behave more intrepidly around his extremely outgoing friends. But when he completed a key values audit, it dawned on him that he had quite different values from most of them. They tended to be dramatic folks who sought to show off their achievements and victories; they constantly competed to outdo each other by telling extravagant stories about their work, their sexual encounters and relationship dramas, and their various ups and downs in life. But that wasn't what he really valued.

He gradually came to see that being around them wasn't much good for him. He was being fake or inauthentic. He had been trying to impress them by pretending to be something that he was not, by attempting to develop the showy, outward-social confidence that they seemed to have. But, deep down, he wanted to get to know people well enough that he could open up about his true hopes and fears, his regrets and frustrations.

Bartholomew wanted to be appreciated for his quieter but genuine qualities rather than have to turn his social life into a constant performance. So he decided that he would spend less time with them and instead try to nurture alternative friendships. Ultimately, his so-called friends would have to go.

Not everybody will have such powerful insights. But that's not crucial anyway. Whether the values exercise tells you something new about your deep-down beliefs or merely echoes what you already suspected, the research says that you will still benefit. Writing about your most profound value in life is a form of psychological self-defence. It can make you feel stronger in the face of adversity.

Hmm. Perhaps you're still not entirely convinced. And, if you're not, I don't blame you.

I agree that the idea of delving into your values can seem a bit obscure – more of a nice-to-have than a must-have. You may feel under too much pressure from your day-to-day life to think it worthwhile spending time wondering about stuff that you can't use straight away. But the research is quite conclusive: people who work through the values exercise experience a host of benefits.

> People who work through the values exercise experience a host of benefits.

In the short term, simply spending a few minutes writing about your most prized value may not only buffer you against imminent stress. It may enable you to perform at your best, too.

Now, you may be wondering how long those benefits last. Hours? A few days? A week or two feasibly?

Actually, the benefits may be quite long-lived indeed. And we know this because of a groundbreaking study led by University of Colorado's Geoffrey Cohen looking at the academic performance of several hundred high-school students. At the start of the investigation, half the students were asked to reflect on an important personal value, such as their musical interests or relationships with family and friends. The other half of the students acted as a control group and spent an equivalent amount of time writing about either their least important value or why their number-one ranked value might be important to someone else.

The researchers kept track of the students' academic progress over the course of two full years – and were astounded by the results. Participants in the experimental group that had written about their top value had better school grades not only for a few months or a year but for a full two years.[3]

Don't you think that's truly sensational?

People often think that they need weeks of coaching or months of therapy to revamp their lives. But, in this case, participants spent a mere ten minutes writing about their values. Doing just a brief, one-off exercise had truly lasting effects.

## Embedding your values more fully into your life

I think of the key values audit as a layered intervention. The topmost and most visible layer is that, like some of the techniques in Parts II and III of this book, it can boost both inward-emotional confidence and outward-social confidence in challenging situations. The next layer is that it can also lift motivation and people's level of achievement over the course of even many months – as demonstrated by Geoffrey Cohen's study of high-school students.

But dig deeper and there is a third layer. Writing about your values can also be used to start off a more involved and even more constructive process of change. So let's look at that now.

Many of the techniques and activities we've covered in this book could be described as forms of cognitive behavioural therapy (CBT). CBT is recognized as possibly the most effective form of psychological therapy for people with a range of issues, from clinical depression and anxiety to obsessive–compulsive behaviour and even eating disorders.

But there's a new kid on the block, a form of intervention that is increasingly being accepted as a powerful and equally valid method for improving people's mood, thinking patterns and quality of life. It's called behavioural activation – and it's about doing things that you personally find valuable in life.

Actually, it's not that new. One of the earliest experimental inquiries looking at behavioural activation was published in 1998 by a doctoral student named Eric Gortner under the supervision of Neil Jacobson, a psychology researcher at the University of Washington. The research team assigned 137 patients who had been diagnosed with clinical depression to one of three interventions.

One group was taught only cognitive skills, such as identifying and combating automatic negative thoughts (a proficiency that we covered back in Chapter 5). A second group was taught strategies based on behavioural activation. A third group was taught a mix of the two: a combination of both cognitive and behavioural skills.

The diligent researchers monitored the 137 patients over the course of two whole years, checking up on them at six-month intervals, that is, four times over the course of the study. When the researchers analysed the results of the three interventions, they found that all three forms of treatment had been equally effective.[4]

So what? Why does the study matter?

The vast majority of the methods we covered in Part II for upgrading your inward-emotional confidence could be described as cognitive in nature: they are exercises and tricks that you can do in your mind. But behavioural activation is pretty much its precise opposite: it's about behaviours that you must do in the real world. This is because sometimes it's good to get outside your own head to interact with physical tasks and projects, nature, architecture and buildings, objects, animals, and all the people and things that we can see and touch.

If CBT is about altering your thoughts to feel better, behavioural activation is about altering your behaviour in the real world to feel better. CBT is mainly focused on our internal, mental life; behavioural activation is mostly focused on our external, physical life.

For these reasons, some academics refer to CBT as an inside-out approach because it attempts to change what goes on inside your head in order to feel better. In contrast, behavioural activation is an outside-in method in terms of changing what you do in the outside world in order to feel better.

To me, this is the really crucial distinction: the key principle of behavioural activation is about doing things and taking action to change how you feel rather than only thinking the right things to change how you feel. So you can activate a better state of mind behaviourally (i.e. through your actions) and not just cognitively (i.e. through your thinking patterns).

Or, to do away with the technical language and to use plain English: you don't need to feel confident before you can start changing your life. You can start making changes right now – irrespective of whatever doubts and fears may be swirling around inside your head – and you will likely feel more confident.

> You can start making changes right now – irrespective of whatever doubts and fears may be swirling around inside your head – and you will likely feel more confident.

Mystifyingly, even though the study by Gortner and Jacobson was conducted two decades ago, it received relatively little interest from either academics or practising therapists at the time. Cognitive behavioural therapy continued to become more and more popular, to the extent that many people understand what the letters CBT mean (or at least that it's a form of psychological intervention). Yet ask people what BA stands for and they are probably more likely to name a major airline than a method for upgrading people's confidence and emotional well-being.

Behavioural activation still remained relatively neglected despite a further study on its effectiveness published in 2006. A small army of researchers led by Sona Dimidjian at the University of Washington found that clinically depressed patients who were treated with behavioural activation actually improved more than other patients who received cognitive therapy.

That alone is an exciting finding. But perhaps even more impressively, patients who received behavioural activation improved just as much as patients who were treated with antidepressant medication.[5]

That last comparison is worth thinking about a little more. Patients in the antidepressant medication group were given a drug called paroxetine. And up to a quarter of these patients reported side effects including diarrhoea, insomnia, decreased sex drive, excessive sweating and nausea. So bad were the side effects that 5 per cent of these patients dropped out of the study. Of course, medication may be necessary for some people. But for me personally, given the choice of two equally beneficial treatments – one of which could cause unpleasant side effects – I know which I would rather try first.

But the overarching point is that behavioural activation is a different yet unquestionably successful route to enhanced psychological well-being. By doing things in the real world – rather than trying to change things in your mental world – you may be able to activate a more confident you.

> By doing things in the real world – rather than trying to change things in your mental world – you may be able to activate a more confident you.

At the start of the chapter, I introduced the values exercise and here's where it all ties together. Behavioural activation isn't just about doing *anything*. It's about planning to do tasks, projects and behaviours that you *personally* find valuable.

Not everyone will get the same boost from doing the same things. For example, one of my good friends, Michaela, has decided to do a basic plumbing and house repair course at night school. She has been talking about it for some time and feels that it would help her to feel more independent and less reliant on her husband. For her, it will be a lift to her all-round confidence.

It's only 90 minutes every Monday evening for ten weeks. But I would personally find it a real drag. I can immediately think of at least a dozen ways I would rather develop myself, for example by spending the same amount of time reading about economics or politics, taking an online course on business analytics or raising money for an animal charity. I'd rather take tennis lessons, learn about design, pursue a course in creative writing or mentor underprivileged youths. The list goes on.

The point is that the plumbing course plays to Michaela's need for greater independence. But it does nothing for me.

So behavioural activation is not just about doing activities that *most* of society finds meaningful. It is about identifying the specific undertakings that *you* find meaningful or rewarding and that will give *you* the greatest upgrade to your confidence and quality of life.

## Creating your behavioural activation MARSH

There's more than one way to do behavioural activation. And sometimes you may see it referred to as activity scheduling. But the basic steps are pretty straightforward.

You start by monitoring what you do by keeping a record of the activities you've done each day. At the end of each day, you identify those that made you feel the happiest and most confident. Then you plan to do more of those activities over the coming weeks. And repeat.

I teach clients something that I call the MARSH method (Monitor, Assess, Review, Schedule, Hypothesize). Let's walk through the five steps in a little more detail.

### 1. Monitor your activities

We all do so much every day that it can be easy to lose track of the positive moments almost as soon as they have happened. So perhaps it's the enjoyment you got from sipping a proper espresso or the couple of minutes you spent chatting to a good friend. Maybe you got a little frisson from learning something new at work or you managed to read a few pages of an exceedingly engaging book.

The first step in the MARSH process is simply to keep some kind of diary, journal or log of what you did each day. Towards the end of each day, think back on everything even remotely enjoyable that you did in the last 24 hours. And write it down. Or, if you prefer, you could jot down notes throughout the day, perhaps on your smartphone or in a notebook.

> The first step in the MARSH process is simply to keep some kind of diary, journal or log of what you did each day.

Your notes don't have to be massively detailed. Just write enough so that it will make sense to you when you read your lists back in, say, a few weeks or months. If a few bullet points are enough for you to do that, then by all means keep it short.

That's all there is to the first step. It should take you only a few minutes each day. But it helps to do this every day or on as many days a week as you realistically can for at least a couple of weeks – but ideally a month or more.

## 2. Assess your activities

As you write your daily log, you don't need to note every single activity. Because what you're looking for in the second step of the MARSH method are activities that met at least one of five criteria: skills mastery, pleasure, autonomy, relatedness and key values (or SPARK). Yes, there are two acronyms here to remember: MARSH is the overall method and SPARK stands for five questions you need to ask yourself daily.

The original form of behavioural activation as devised by Jacobson and his colleagues focused only on two of those five outcomes: specifically skills mastery and pleasure. However, other research – particularly by superstar scientists Richard Ryan and Edward Deci of the University of Rochester – suggests that people typically feel good about life when they do activities in which they feel a sense of connection with other people (relatedness) as well as a sense of autonomy or freedom in their choices.[6] So that gets us to SPAR. And the final letter, the K in SPARK, refers back to your key values, which will already be familiar to you from the key values audit earlier in this chapter.

This probably sounds more complicated than it actually is in practice. As you're thinking back at the end of each day, ask yourself the following five questions:

- 'What did I do that gave me a sense of **skills mastery** – that I honed a skill, learned new knowledge, grew or improved myself in even a small way?'
- 'What activities or occurrences gave me **pleasure**?'
- 'What did I do that helped me to feel that I had **autonomy** – that I was in charge of my life and had freedom over my own actions?'
- 'What activities allowed me to feel a sense of **relatedness** or social connection with other people?'
- 'What did I do that enabled me to live my **key values**?'

The five SPARK questions are aimed at identifying the activities you did that helped you to feel more positive, alive or confident. And even though they may appear to tap into similar feelings, they are not exactly identical.

> The five SPARK questions are aimed at identifying the activities you did that helped you to feel more positive, alive or confident.

For example, we often get pleasure from spending time with friends – when we can laugh together or just feel that other people understand and care for us. In these instances, pleasure and relatedness often overlap.

In some situations, though, people can experience relatedness without pleasure. For example, many families get together only to argue. Siblings fight. Children disagree with their parents. Parents anguish over the choices that their errant children have made. Babies can scream and wail and put adults on edge. But if you were to ask people whether they find such time meaningful, the vast majority of them would say yes. In other words, they can value such occasions as opportunities to experience relatedness – even though there may be little pleasure to be had from such moments.

Or, to take a more extreme case, imagine that you are in hospital visiting a loved one who is dying. Your time by the bedside of someone who is seriously ailing is unlikely to be very pleasurable. However, experiencing a sense of relatedness – forming an emotional connection and feeling that you're there for someone – may be more important than whether you're having fun or not.

The same goes for all of the five SPARK criteria. Some activities may boost our feeling that we have mastered a skill – working through a problem at work, fixing something at home – even though we may have felt frustrated by the process (i.e. there was no pleasure to be had) or we may have done them alone (i.e. without relatedness).

The first four questions (skills mastery, pleasure, autonomy and relatedness) refer to things that the vast majority of people worldwide commonly find worthwhile. But you are also an individual. And you may have specific things that really, truly, deeply matter to you and maybe no one else.

If you completed the key values audit earlier in this chapter, you will already know what is important to you and you alone. If you skipped ahead, you may want to go back and complete that exercise now. Look now at your top handful of key values and see what further questions you could add into the mix. For example, if your religion is of central importance in your life, you may wish to ask yourself a question such as 'What did I do that allowed me to deepen my faith?'

If you identified 'helping others' as one of your top values, you could ask yourself something like 'What activities did I do that helped someone else?' Or if you value your fitness above everything else, perhaps ask yourself, 'In what ways did I spend my time that allowed me to feel fit and strong?'

Like the key values audit itself, there are no right or wrong answers here. This isn't about doing things that society or your family or friends would deem appropriate. This is about figuring out the activities that feel genuinely worthwhile to you – and therefore the questions to ask yourself during this assessment stage of the MARSH method. So remember: even if other people may deem an activity silly or meaningless, it's fine so long as it helps *you* to feel that you're feeling fulfilled.

## 3. Review your activities

Over a couple of weeks, see if you can pull together a list of activities and projects that you find interesting and valuable. Keep asking yourself the SPARK questions each day. And slowly you will see your list growing and growing.

It's worth doing this over at least a two-week period. For example, people often do different things on weekends than weekdays. So it's worth having at least two weekends' worth of data for you to look back on.

On your list, you will find that some of your activities are small things such as savouring your favourite chocolate bar occasionally or catching up on the latest news about your sports team. Other projects may be slightly more time-consuming, such as learning to cook a new recipe, perhaps educating yourself on world affairs or having a meaningful conversation with your best friend. A few of your undertakings may even be quite challenging: for example, you may have struggled to put together a business presentation, but then got some lovely comments for it afterwards. Or you spent two hours driving each way to visit an elderly relative or you finally painted your kitchen.

But remember that this is a list of activities that are meaningful or rewarding for you. These are things you *want* to do, not things you feel you *should* do.

Once you have a list of activities, try to rank them. Let's suppose that you have 17 activities. You could try ranking them from number 1 (being the hardest to do) to 17 (being the easiest to do).

Alternatively, you could divide your activities into three categories: easy to do, moderately difficult and hard to do. The only rule here, though, is that you must put roughly equal numbers of activities into each category. So, if you have a longer list of, say, 32, this would imply at least nine or ten activities in every category.

When you have completed this step, take a pause to congratulate yourself. Reviewing your activities will have taken you at least two weeks of writing about your life every evening or nearly every evening. Rest assured that you are well on track to improving your quality of life.

> Reviewing your activities will have taken you at least two works of regular writing for perhaps five or ten minutes every evening or nearly every evening.

## 4. Schedule in valued activities

I think of behavioural activation as an inherently optimistic method. The University of Washington's Neil Jacobson – one of the leaders in this field – argued that behavioural activation assumes that psychological distress is caused not by deficiencies in a person but in the activities and pursuits of that person.[7] In other words, there's nothing wrong with *you*. It's purely that you aren't spending your time in the right way yet.

The next step in the behavioural activation MARSH method is to incorporate one or more of your valued activities into your schedule for the coming week. So look at your list of activities and see which one or ones you feel you can add to your life. You probably do some of these activities or behaviours fairly frequently already. But, at this point, the aim is to introduce a few valued activities that you might not otherwise do, or to do them just a tad more regularly than you have been doing them.

If you're like many busy people, you may feel hassled and short of time. So you may only want to pick one or two of the quickest or easiest activities from the list you created. Or you may have a different approach. Perhaps you have spotted a couple of projects that are more time-consuming but so meaningful that you really want to integrate them into your life regardless of the effort involved. You know that the pay-off will be worth it.

A reserved but somewhat lonely client I worked with named Anna began with one activity that she wanted to schedule in more regularly. While she often went out for a drink after work with colleagues during the week, she often ended up with nothing to do at weekends because she had left it too late. So she resolved to spend a few minutes every Monday morning sending out emails and text messages to a select group of friends to see whether she could arrange something for the coming weekend. Then, on Wednesday lunchtime, she would review her plans and decide whether she needed to send out further messages to try to secure some form of socializing for her weekend.

Sometimes, you may identify activities or behaviours that may be personally meaningful even though other people may not see the point of them. For example, another one of my clients lived in five different countries when he was growing up (as a result of a father who was a career expatriate). He decided to dedicate around an hour a week to writing a blog and uploading photos to his Facebook profile. Some people may think it vapid to aim to spend time on social media. But, for him, it was both a psychological time-out and a means of feeling socially connected with his far-flung friends and family.

If you decide to try behavioural activation, carry on recording your activities and assessing the extent to which new projects or behaviours are valuable to you. Did they help you to SPARK? And then, whenever you feel ready (which may be after one week or many weeks), you can introduce further activities into your schedule for each week.

However, the key here is to introduce further activities only gradually. Some people make the mistake of trying to do too much at once. They decide to exercise three times a week, meet up with friends a couple of times a week, learn a new language, read something educational every day and so on. But aiming to do so much at once is often unrealistic – it may be setting you up for failure and disappointment.

If you want to introduce better habits and valuable activities that you'll stick with, it's a better idea to build up slowly. So take it a week at a time. Introduce perhaps just one activity in your first week. See how that goes. If you feel it went well and you did it easily, then think about introducing another one or two.

And aim for small – or even tiny – chunks of time on these new activities. Yes, in a perfect world you may wish to spend an hour painting, running, phoning friends or whatever other endeavour you choose. But that may be unfeasible – you may be too busy to spare the time. So perhaps aim for 15, ten or even five minutes of anything new – make it easy for yourself to succeed.

> Perhaps aim for 15, ten or even five minutes of anything new – make it easy for yourself to succeed.

Only when you feel that the new behaviour or activity feels comfortable and an established habit should you think about integrating more into your life. Take your time. This is about steadily shaping a more confident life – not trying to change things overnight.

In fact, incorporating new undertakings fully into your life is likely to take not just days or weeks but many weeks. Look online or read some of the more popular self-help books and you may come across an oft-repeated claim that it takes 21 days to form a habit. But research studies destroy that claim. Some years ago, University College London health psychologist Phillippa Lally and her colleagues tracked the progress of 82 volunteers as they tried to overhaul their eating, drinking or exercise habits. On average, it took the volunteers 66 days for their chosen activities to feel more like natural habits. More notably, though, there was a massive range in how long it took: from as little as 18 days to 254 days.[8]

I'm not trying to put you off. I want only to give you fair warning that weaving new activities into your life could take almost any length of time – and it may happen at a more gradual pace than you would wish.

But there is light at the end of the tunnel. Neuroscientists led by Gabriel Dichter at the University of North Carolina at Chapel Hill School of Medicine were able to detect changes in the brains of adults who went through a programme of behavioural activation over several months. Using functional magnetic resonance imaging (MRI) equipment, the scientists detected actual changes in their participants' brain structures in areas such as the paracingulate gyrus, the right caudate nucleus and the orbital frontal gyri.[9] So behavioural activation isn't just about changing how you feel – it may fundamentally revamp how your brain works, too.

## 5. Hypothesize about additional valued activities

So far, the first four steps of the MARSH method have focused on scrutinizing and then scheduling in valuable activities that you did in the recent past. But this fifth and final step is about hypothesizing or guessing what other acts may also prove meaningful.

To begin with, it may help here to think back over the entire span of your life to activities that may in the past have allowed you to feel alive or confident. For example, I used to read comics when I was growing up. I remember first reading *X-Men* and *Fantastic Four* comics when I was maybe nine years old – long before such heroes were turned into billion-dollar movie franchises. I continued reading them through my teenage years, then gave up when I went to university. But I realized just a few years ago (as a forty-something!) that I loved comics. So I gave myself permission to buy one comic a month. And when I got it home, I made myself savour it by reading it slowly and appreciating the art, the dynamism of each panel, the use of colour, the pithy dialogue. And that has now become a regular experience that can cocoon me from the world and lift my mood.

Another example: a client I recently worked with named Alexander realized that he had been neglecting his family duties. He had two older sisters who both had young families. One lived less than an hour away from his home, while the other lived more than a three-hour train ride away. While he did not relish the prospect of visiting them weekly, he made up his mind that he should visit one of his sisters once a month. So he would see each sister and her family six times a year rather than the once or twice that he had previously managed.

Hypothesizing is about completely new activities that could be good for you, too. What could fit one or more of the five SPARK criteria? Perhaps you have never taken a class in ballroom dancing but you think that it would be good for you in terms of skills mastery *and* pleasure *and* relatedness. Maybe you think that regularly seeking out a new podcast or documentary would be a way of expanding your mind. Or you think that buying a decent camera to take photographs of quirky buildings and breath-taking landscapes would be a great way to realize your artistic ambitions.

> Hypothesizing is about completely new activities that could be good for you, too.

When you have come up with a list of such hypothetically valuable activities, you may again want to rank them from easiest to do to hardest to do, or group them into easy, medium and hard categories.

And then start small and introduce just one of them into your next week and see how that goes.

My client Alexander had heard a few of his friends talking about meditation. But his friends meditated for 30 minutes every day and he wasn't sure that he could be that disciplined. So he decided that he would set himself a more realistic goal: to meditate for only ten minutes at a time and to begin with only two days of the week. Ideally, he wanted to meditate in the mornings, but he knew that sometimes he ended up getting up too late in the mornings. So, on those days, he would allow himself to be more flexible and do it in the evenings.

When you introduce these new activities into your life, keep reviewing them. Think of them as little experiments. Hopefully, you will find gratification, meaning or some element of SPARK from many of them. But a few may prove to be a bust. Occasionally, you'll find some things too bothersome, expensive or insufficiently rewarding to do again. And that's OK. At least you tried; you can rule it out and move on to a different activity.

## Crafting your more confident life over time

We began this chapter with the key values audit. And I explained that it could be used as a fairly immediate confidence booster before upcoming challenges. More notably, though, I made the case that the values exercise could more fruitfully be used as the start of a longer process. Not just as a one-off written assignment but something that feeds into the behavioural activation MARSH method, a way of identifying opportunities to feel better, stronger and more confident by actually pursuing meaningful acts in the real world.

A curmudgeon may argue that the steps of behavioural activation are facile, that the method doesn't really teach people anything new. But I disagree. Countless people get caught in the trap of living on automatic pilot. They unknowingly get stuck in the daily grind of going to work, looking after their families, doing household chores, and so on – of doing what they need to survive rather than thinking about what may allow them to thrive and flourish. As such, many clients have found that taking the time to identify valued activities provides them with a helpful reminder about what matters most to them in life.

> Countless people get caught in the trap of living on automatic pilot.

So yes, it's not rocket science. But such criticism is actually kind of redundant. Remember that behavioural activation isn't simply something that I conjured out of thin air. I'm not making an idle claim that it works. Study after study after study shows that behavioural activation is as effective for lifting mood and improving quality of life as cognitive behavioural treatment and even antidepressant medication.

Perhaps the most compelling evidence for the effectiveness of behavioural activation comes from a cutting-edge British investigation led by David Richards, a professor at the Medical School at the University of Exeter. The cavalcade of researchers spent nearly two years patiently tracking a large group of 440 people who regrettably had been diagnosed with clinical depression.

The majority of studies looking at the effectiveness of different therapeutic interventions only track people for a matter of weeks or months. It's fairly commonplace for participants to be observed for between eight to 12 weeks. So the lengthy 18-month timescale of the investigation by Richards and his colleagues alone is remarkable.

In addition, most of the other studies of this kind tend to monitor only a handful or several dozen participants. It's rare to get a study comprising over a hundred participants. Yet this particular investigation kept an eye on a comparatively massive group of 440 people.

Anyway, back to what the researchers did. As with most studies of this type, Richards' team assigned half the study participants to CBT and the other half to behavioural activation. Two years later there was thankfully improvement in both groups. But the researchers found that the two treatments were equally beneficial. Or, to put it another way, CBT was *not* more effective than behavioural activation.

But hidden within the paper was a perhaps even more important conclusion. The team observed that behavioural activation was 'a simpler psychological treatment than CBT' that 'can be delivered without the need for costly and highly trained professionals'.[10]

In the last decade or so CBT has typically been considered the gold standard of psychological intervention, the best tool that psychologists have for lifting people's mood and improving their quality of life. However, what Professor Richards and his retinue of researchers confirmed yet again was that behavioural activation was categorically as good – and simpler and cheaper, too. That's a win–win in my book.

My prediction is that you'll be hearing much more about behavioural activation in the coming years. CBT may have been the star. And I'm not saying that CBT doesn't work – it actually works eminently well. But there is another, equally powerful, option out there.

And it's such an uncomplicated method at heart. The core idea of behavioural activation is simple: make it a priority and set aside time to do more stuff that really matters to you. Don't allow work, family circumstances, societal pressures or the rigours of day-to-day life push you off course. Do more things that you genuinely want to do.

> The core idea of behavioural activation is simple: make it a priority and set aside time to do more stuff that really matters to you.

Do remember that any improvement in your outlook on life is likely to happen over the course of months rather than weeks. The studies I've mentioned in this chapter tracked people over the course of at least eight to 16 weeks, or even longer. Behavioural activation isn't going to transform you overnight.

But, by reflecting on what is meaningful and rewarding to you and making more deliberate choices about how to live your life, you can feel more in control. This is your opportunity to set a course and steer your life rather than be buffeted by everything around you. Do this and over time you may just find yourself achieving the more confident life that you want.

## Onwards and upwards

- While some (perhaps misinformed) people may dismiss personal values as intangible and therefore frivolous, consider that there's now formidable 2.0 evidence showing the benefits of identifying what is personally meaningful to you.

- Understand that the underlying principle of behavioural activation is that you can behave in different ways in order to activate a greater sense of confidence. Contrast that against the more cognitive techniques we covered earlier in the book, which often involved thinking in different ways in order to achieve greater feelings of confidence. Behavioural activation mostly involves changing your behaviour and introducing better habits into your life.

- Consider that behavioural activation can sometimes sound more complex than it really is. To use the behavioural activation MARSH method, begin by monitoring (i.e. writing down) most of the things you do each day. When you have captured enough data over, say, a couple of weeks, assess the activities to identify which ones made you feel good and confident. Then endeavour to do more of those activities. See? Not so complicated really.

- Experiment with various activities and behaviours. If an activity doesn't work out at first, perhaps try it again. But if it doesn't pay off after multiple attempts, accept that it may not be for you. Congratulate yourself for at least having tried; then give something else a go instead.

- Finally, remember that behavioural activation takes time. Aim to introduce only a couple of small, easily manageable behaviours into your schedule each week. Be patient. Set your sights on creating lasting habits that you can sustain for years to come rather than trying to fix everything at once.

I have profiles both on Twitter and Facebook. I write pieces advising on topics such as interview skills and job hunting, emotional intelligence, influence and persuasion, leadership and, of course, confidence. I like to point out good advice from other people as well.

If you too are a fan of social media, you've probably come across so-called clickbait headlines that lure you into clicking the link in order to read the article. So it's not uncommon to read clickbait headlines such as 'This is the one thing that all confident people do' or 'Here's the secret to successful dating' or 'This is what all millionaire entrepreneurs have in common.' Similarly, articles using phrases such as 'This weird trick will …' or 'This shocking method can …' promise that you can do anything from losing belly fat and spellbinding lovers to banishing anxiety and curing diabetes.

Such online articles claim that there is only *one thing* or *a secret* or *a single weird trick* that will allow you to triumph in life. They slyly imply that only one method or behaviour will solve all your problems.

I'm sorry, but I'm going to burst that bubble. There is no one single approach, technique or strategy that will sort out your entire life. Anyone who tells you otherwise probably does not have your best interests at heart. The truth is that successfully changing either your professional or personal life – or both – will require multiple methods as well as trial and error and a little patience. But research tells us that it can be done.

> Changing either your professional or personal life – or both – will require multiple methods as well as trial and error and a little patience.

As we have journeyed together through the 12 chapters of this book, I hope I have shown you that there really is a practical, helpful and achievable psychology of confidence. For example, we saw that many modern-day psychologists no longer deem high self-esteem an entirely desirable outcome. We also looked at arguments for distinguishing between inward-emotional confidence and outward-social confidence – and the fact that doing so could help you to prioritize better how to change yourself. We discovered that many techniques don't just change how you feel or behave – they may affect the hormones circulating within your body and neural activity within your very brain, too. As such, you can feel reassured that there are plenty of ways to build a stronger and profoundly more courageous life.

I hope you feel inspired to set out on your own voyage of self-discovery and change. And in the closing pages of this book, I would like to offer you three final pieces of advice to give you the very best shot at success.

## Creating your own confidence project

When I am running one-to-one coaching sessions, I always encourage clients to spend the last five or ten minutes of each session writing down what they are committing to do. When I am running workshops, I make sure to explain that understanding psychological principles is not enough to make a difference in life; you actually have to apply the principles over and over in real-world situations. The techniques only work if you use, use, use them.

> Understanding psychological principles is not enough to make a difference in life; you actually have to apply the principles over and over in real-world situations.

Forgive me for mentioning this a final time. But one day I genuinely want you to be able to look back and feel that this book truly changed your life. To set you up for success, my lasting wish and hope is that you will write down a set of 'If ... then ...' implementation intentions for what you will do.

If you don't write anything down, you're effectively saying that you're going to rely on your ability to memorize your goals and follow through on them faultlessly over the weeks and months to come. You're hoping your memory is so perfect and your motivation so superior that you couldn't possibly make a mistake or fail to turn your intentions into reality.

But doesn't that just smack a little of … overconfidence? We spent quite a long time in Chapter 1 looking at the perils of overconfidence. So don't fall into that trap. Get writing instead.

Your implementation intentions can be as specific or as broad as you like. Some of them may involve quicker techniques from Parts II and III. Others may draw from the longer-term methods that we covered in Part IV. To inspire you to craft your own, here are some examples:

- 'If it is 7.35 a.m. on a Monday, Wednesday or Friday morning, I will practise mindfulness for ten minutes.'
- 'If I am feeling terrified before a football game, I will reappraise my anxiety as something that's supposed to help me focus and play well.'
- 'If I am getting ready to go on a date, I will spend 15 minutes writing bullet points on what I've been doing recently so that I have something to talk about.'
- 'If it is 8 p.m. on a Thursday evening, I will review my confidence ladder and make a plan to do the activity on the next rung of the ladder.'
- 'If I am waiting for a job interview, I will label my thoughts as thoughts by telling myself, "Right now, I am having the thought that …"'
- 'If it is a Sunday morning, I will look through my MARSH behavioural activation notes and create my schedule for the coming week.'

Over to you, then. What will your first set of implementation intentions look like?

## Becoming a psychological scientist

I'm sure you noticed that I talked about study after study after study as we meandered through the chapters of *The Confidence Project*. Time and again, we looked at experiments in which researchers wanted to see whether a certain technique or intervention would augment the mood, confidence or performance of participants more than some control activity.

Of course, I've only told you about the studies that got positive results. But you can bet that there have been many thousands of experiments that failed: studies in which the scientists found that some technique or other actually didn't result in the benefits that they hoped it might.

You win some. You lose some.

And that's the attitude that I hope you will take.

As you apply the many tools and techniques from this book, consider yourself a psychological scientist. Experiment with different methods and see *what* works for you *when* personally.

> Experiment with different methods and see *what* works for you *when* personally.

Why? Let's take the practice of mindfulness as an example. You'll remember from Chapter 9 that mindfulness has been shown to have a host of benefits. Multiple studies have demonstrated its psychological effects.

But let's look at one final piece of research, this one conducted by Anthony Winning and Simon Boag at Macquarie University in Sydney, Australia. This pair of social scientists wanted to test the inkling that mindfulness training could boost a mental skill called cognitive empathy, which they defined as 'the ability to correctly recognize the emotional state of another, such as being able to identify that someone is angry or sad'.

The researchers gathered together several dozen participants and asked them to spend 15 minutes performing mindfulness. The participants listened to an audio recording, which instructed them on both the principles of mindfulness as well as how to do it in practice.

As expected, the participants were mostly judged to have experienced an increase in their cognitive empathy skills after having listened to the track. But the researchers were actually more interested in a specific question: *Who* benefited the most?

Just before listening to the mindfulness track, all the participants completed a short personality test. For example, they rated the extent to which they agreed or disagreed with statements such as 'I am the life of the party.' (As I'm sure you can spot, participants who agreed strongly with the statement were identified as more extraverted than their peers who disagreed with the statement.)

By analysing the participants' personality scores and the extent to which they got a boost in their cognitive empathy skills, the researchers were able to discern a statistical relationship between the two. Specifically, more introverted individuals got a bigger boost to their cognitive empathy than did the more extraverted folks.[1] In other words, not everyone benefited equally.

Now I'm not trying to argue that you should only practise mindfulness if you lean towards the more introverted side of things. This study looked only at the extent to which mindfulness improved this specific skill. I'm not aware of other studies looking at the extent to which mindfulness affects mood or the ability to focus or any other outcomes for different types of people.

The wider point I'm trying to make is that all the interventions in this book will likely benefit some people more than others. And you will need to treat yourself as an experimental participant to see which methods help you the most (and, by extension, which techniques or exercises are less helpful).

Some of the mental techniques may work better in particular situations, too. Maybe one tactic will work better when you're feeling overloaded with work. Another intervention may be more useful when you're feeling oppressed by your manager. A third method may be more effective when you're feeling overwhelmed by money troubles or family pressures.

I wish I could present you with a definitive manifesto of what to do: when situation X occurs, do Y. But to do so would be dishonest of me. After all, you wouldn't expect me to be able to tell you what books or films or foods you will for certain enjoy every single day for the rest of your life; in the same way, you will need to figure out which psychological techniques work best for you personally and when. Just because something works for someone else in a particular situation does not mean that it will necessarily work for you.

> You will need to figure out which psychological techniques work best for you personally and when.

## Studying yourself through trial and error

You may find certain techniques really helpful. You may discover others that are more moderately beneficial. But the reality of the science is that a few of the techniques may not resonate with you at all.

For example, you may find that you don't need to follow the ten-step problem-solving approach (from Chapter 10) but that the behavioural activation MARSH method is indispensable. Or it may be the other way around. Don't jettison new techniques too quickly, though. Most people find that it takes a handful of attempts to learn any new trick. You wouldn't expect to perfect *any* new skill (e.g. playing a computer game, cooking a soufflé, riding a unicycle) the first time you try it. So don't have that expectation for your confidence-building attempts, either.

Or you may find that certain manoeuvres work best in particular situations. For instance, cognitive defusion may not work when you're worrying about work situations, but perhaps it may aid you to realize that your concerns about your love life are overblown. Or you may discover that reminiscing about times you felt positive and happy helps you when you're getting ready to go out socially but less so for stressful work situations.

As you reach such insights, see if you can refine the set of guidelines that you establish for yourself. So perhaps you initially decided on an implementation intention that said: 'If I'm getting ready for a party or client meeting, I will write for five minutes about a positive reminiscence.' But, with time, you may decide to modify it to: 'If I'm getting ready for a party, I will write for five minutes about a positive reminiscence.' And you may decide to add a new implementation intention to try something different, such as: 'If I'm getting ready for a client meeting, I'll write a couple of power paragraphs.'

The only way to suss out what works for you personally and when is by running little experiments. Test the assorted techniques. Accept that it will be a process of trial and error. And reflect on what seems to work. Keep learning about what helps you to feel alive, capable and confident in the different situations and areas of your life.

## Having realistic but optimistic expectations

Change is possible. I am certain that the psychological techniques within these pages can have a lasting impact on your confidence and life. But how swiftly and how much can you expect to change?

> The psychological techniques within these pages can have a lasting impact on your confidence and life.

The methods in Part II were aimed mainly at your inward-emotional confidence; those in Part III were aimed squarely at your outward-social confidence. But remember that all of those techniques are likely to result in smaller, more short-term boosts to your state of mind or performance. I think of them as ways of granting you a psychological lift in much the same way a strong cup of coffee or a bar of chocolate may help to revive you when you're feeling tired.

To get greater, more enduring benefits, you will need to delve back into the chapters within Part IV. These four chapters looked at more lasting ways to build your confidence – either by changing your relationship with your own mind (through mindfulness) or by altering your actual circumstances in the real world. And all of those take time. Like going to the gym to get fitter or learning a foreign language, building up your strength of mind to a serious degree will likely take many weeks or months.

So that's why I encourage you to have realistic expectations. You can't simply read about various techniques and expect change to happen overnight. You have to *apply* them. You have to make plans and set aside time to follow through on them. You have to monitor your progress and keep looking for better ways to make things work for you. And you have to keep trying and trying, for week after week after week.

But there is so much cause to be optimistic, too. Remember that the methods within this book are based on the results of hundreds of experimental studies conducted by thousands of dedicated researchers on tens of thousands of participants all over the world. And if these techniques have been proven to work for all those other people, they will probably work for you, too.

## *Summarizing the summary*

Whether I'm running a workshop or giving a speech at a conference, I always summarize my final thoughts in a single slide (Figure 13.1). So here are my last words on the project ahead of you.

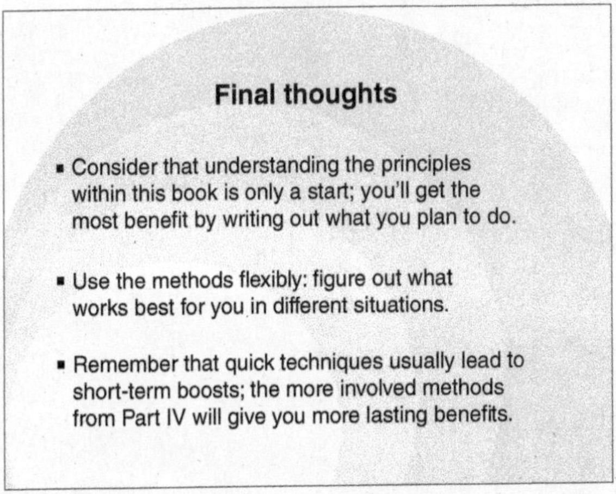

**Final thoughts**

- Consider that understanding the principles within this book is only a start; you'll get the most benefit by writing out what you plan to do.

- Use the methods flexibly: figure out what works best for you in different situations.

- Remember that quick techniques usually lead to short-term boosts; the more involved methods from Part IV will give you more lasting benefits.

FIGURE 13.1  How to use this book: the key points

I wish you the very best in your own confidence project. And if you enjoyed the book and want to read more on topics such as confidence, influence and persuasion, and achieving both personal and professional success, do consider following my musings online:

- www.robyeung.com
- www.facebook.com/drrobyeung
- www.twitter.com/robyeung

## *Onwards and upwards*

- To set yourself up for success in applying the techniques, write out what you plan to do in the form of 'If ... then ...' implementation intentions. If you haven't already done this, please, please, please consider doing it soon.
- Think of yourself as a psychological scientist. It's likely that not every tactic or strategy will work equally well for you. Try the different techniques from this book in a variety of situations. Over a period of weeks and months, work out which ones work best for *you* and *when*.
- By all means, use the confidence-boosting techniques from Parts II and III of this book. But remember that these easy-to-implement interventions will tend to give you more modest benefits. To make the biggest difference to your long-term confidence and life, be sure to invest time in the more intensive strategies from Part IV as well.
- Finally, trust that the techniques in *The Confidence Project* have been tested in experiments all over the world. The methods and manoeuvres within these pages have worked for many, many people. And, with a bit of effort on your part, they will almost certainly work for you, too.

# Glossary

**Acceptance and commitment therapy (ACT):** a branch of psychological therapy that has grown popular in the last decade or so. It gets its name from the ideas of accepting (rather than always challenging) how we feel and trying to commit to behaving in different ways. Cognitive defusion and mindfulness are both techniques linked to the ACT school of thought.

**Affect labelling:** a technique that involves paying conscious attention to your emotions in order to give what you are feeling a specific name. The very act of labelling your feelings by saying something like 'I am experiencing a feeling of …' has been shown to reduce both activation in the amygdala as well as levels of distress.

**Aspirations and ambitions review:** a written method aimed at boosting your outward-social confidence. It involves writing a handful of paragraphs about your aspirations and ambitions, i.e., the things you would *like* to achieve in life.

**Automatic negative thoughts:** the internal dialogue that we sometimes engage in with ourselves that is worrisome or self-critical.

**Behavioural activation:** a school of psychological therapy that advocates doing things and taking action in the real world in order to change how you feel. Research suggests that behavioural activation is equally as effective as cognitive behavioural therapy. The MARSH method is a form of behavioural activation.

**Body scan:** a specific mindfulness technique in which you focus your attention on the sensations within different parts of your body.

**Cognitive behavioural therapy (CBT):** a cluster of psychological techniques that mainly involve teaching people to identify and challenge distorted or otherwise unhelpful thoughts and feelings.

**Cognitive defusion:** a method of reminding yourself that your thoughts are often only your subjective interpretation of a situation and not an objective representation of reality. The so-called one-word cognitive defusion technique simply involves taking a distressing word and repeating it quickly for up to 30 seconds in order to reduce the hold that a negative thought may have over you. Another variant involves reminding yourself that your thoughts are only thoughts, for example by telling yourself, 'I am having the thought that …'

**Confidence ladder (or confidence hierarchy):** the set of ten steps that you construct when using the *in vivo* exposure technique.

**Disclosure:** the opportunity for a person to talk about him- or herself. Research suggests that most people actually enjoy the chance to talk about their own lives.

**Dispositional mindfulness:** the ongoing practice of focusing our attention on the experiences going on around us (as opposed to allowing our thoughts, worries, regrets and emotions to dominate our minds).

**Distanced perspective:** a point of view in which we imagine that events or a situation are happening to someone else. Research suggests that adopting this viewpoint may allow us to make more effective judgements and decisions than if we adopt the opposite, so-called immersed, perspective.

**Distraction:** the act of deliberately engaging in a diverting activity. Studies suggest that participating in activities that demand our attention can help to reduce the incidence of rumination and therefore reduce people's level of distress.

**Enactive experience:** merely a technical term used by some psychologists for situations in which you actually put yourself into a challenging situation in an attempt to build your self-efficacy or self-belief.

**Fantasizing:** the mental act of thinking about optimistic future scenarios. Research suggests that doing so can help us to feel better in the short term. However, people who engage in a lot of fantasizing may reduce not only their motivation but also their subsequent level of achievement compared with people who fantasize less.

**Hemispheric activation:** a method of activating the right hemisphere of the brain to allow better performance during high-pressure situations. Studies suggest that squeezing the left hand activates the right hemisphere of the brain, which may in turn encourage more automatic performance and less overthinking.

**Imagery rescripting:** a technique that involves taking distressing imagery and then methodically changing its upsetting elements so that it overall becomes nonsensical and less distressing. It often also helps to replace unlikely, harmful imagery with more realistic, more positive imagery.

**Implementation intentions:** a specific way of phrasing goals that has been shown to increase the chances that people will actually follow through with their intentions. These take the form of 'If situation X occurs, then I will do Y.'

**Incidental similarity:** a phenomenon in which people who believe they have something in common become more likely to bond with each other.

***In vivo* exposure therapy:** putting yourself into increasingly (but gradually) more challenging situations in order to build your confidence. The first stage is to construct a confidence ladder/hierarchy by working out ten gradually more challenging situations. The second stage then involves exposing yourself to those situations, moving from one situation to the next only when you feel quite comfortable and confident with each one.

**Inward-emotional confidence:** the extent to which we privately feel confident. People with less inward-emotional confidence may experience a great deal of doubt and worry; people with a lot of inward-emotional confidence tend to be calm and at peace with themselves.

**Key values audit:** an in-depth exercise aimed at identifying the key values that you personally find meaningful. The first step involves ranking different characteristics and values. The second step involves writing about why your top value is so important to you.

**MARSH method:** a form of behavioural activation which follows five steps: Monitor, Assess, Review, Schedule, Hypothesize. The assessment step involves evaluating activities against five criteria, which can be summarized by the acronym SPARK.

**Mental resizing:** picturing a distressing scene in your mind and deliberately reducing it in size as if it were receding away from you into the distance.

**Mimicry:** the act of reproducing either the words or behaviour of another person. Studies suggest that this repetition can build rapport when done surreptitiously.

**Mindfulness:** the act of bringing your attention in a non-judgemental way to your experience right now. This experience encompasses not only the events going on around you but also the thoughts and feelings that may be occurring in your mind.

**Nonverbal immediacy:** a psychological term for the extent to which people create a perception of closeness and likeability through their behaviour, e.g. gestures, touch, eye contact and facial expressions.

**Outward-social confidence:** the extent to which we appear confident in public settings. People with low outward-social confidence often come across as quiet and reserved; people with high outward-social confidence tend to be talkative and entertaining.

**Positive reminiscence:** a technique aimed at boosting your outward-social confidence, where you write about a time you felt happy and excited.

**Postural expansiveness:** the act of taking up more physical space with body and limbs. Expansive, spread-out postures are typically judged to be more powerful, attractive and indicative of more outward-social confidence than contractive postures.

**Power paragraphs:** a writing technique that has been shown to increase people's outward-social confidence. It involves spending a few minutes writing about an occasion you had influence or control over another person or persons.

**Power pose:** a colloquial term of reference for a bodily position that demonstrates postural expansiveness.

**Problem solving:** a series of steps aimed at tackling real-world problems and opportunities. The aim of problem solving is to change situations or our relationships with other people as opposed to merely changing how we view them.

**Reappraisal:** making a conscious effort to see either a situation or your physiological response in a different (e.g. neutral or even positive) light.

**Reflection:** the process of thinking about ourselves or events from a neutral, curious point of view. The aim may be to learn lessons about past successes as well as failures.

**Relationship reframing:** a written exercise that has been shown to improve people's relationships. It involves writing about a compliment your partner gave you and then explaining to yourself both what the comment meant to you and its significance for your relationship.

**Rumination:** a tendency to think about ourselves or events from an overly negative, unhelpful point of view. People who ruminate often blame or chastise themselves for their mistakes and failings. Replaying situations in this manner tends to result in distress rather than meaningful learning or problem solving.

**Self-efficacy:** a belief in your own ability to conquer particular challenges. You can develop your self-efficacy both by actually tackling challenging situations (in what are called enactive experiences) and by watching other people tackling such situations (which is called vicarious experience).

**Self-esteem:** your subjective evaluations of your value and worth as a human being. It used to be believed (up until the mid-2000s) that a high level of self-esteem was desirable. However, most modern-day psychologists now agree that high self-esteem can actually be associated with some negative consequences.

**Self-fulfilling prophecy:** having a belief about a future event that changes your behaviour and therefore makes that belief come true. Such beliefs can be either negative or positive. For example, if you think that people at a party are going to be unfriendly, you may end up behaving in an aloof fashion, which may then discourage other people from talking to you.

**SPARK:** an acronym used in the MARSH method of behavioural activation. The acronym stands for Skills mastery, Pleasure, Autonomy, Relatedness, Key values.

**Spontaneous trait transference:** a phenomenon in which an individual takes on the qualities or characteristics that he or she describes in others. Those qualities can be either positive or negative.

**Storytelling reappraisal:** a specific reappraisal technique that involves telling a story about what's going on in a way that focuses on possible benefits that may eventually come out of the situation.

**Thought suppression:** the act of trying to avoid, ignore or otherwise push out unpleasant thoughts or images. While people often do this because they feel it will help them to experience fewer unpleasant thoughts and feelings, research tells us that this style of thinking may in fact backfire and cause those thoughts or feelings to recur more frequently.

**Vicarious experience:** developing your self-efficacy or self-belief by watching others model or demonstrate whatever skill you want to improve.

**Visualization:** the act of mentally rehearsing a challenging (yet already familiar) situation so that you become more confident of the steps you need to take.

# Notes

## Chapter 1

1  The statement about Eleanor is false.
2  Kruger, J., & Dunning, D. (1999). 'Unskilled and unaware of it: How difficulties in recognizing one's own incompetence lead to inflated self-assessments'. *Journal of Personality and Social Psychology*, 77, 1121–34.
3  Ames, D. R., & Wazlawek, A. S. (2014). 'Pushing in the dark: Causes and consequences of limited self-awareness for interpersonal assertiveness'. *Personality and Social Psychology Bulletin*, 40, 775–90.
4  Zell, E., & Krizan, Z. (2014). 'Do people have insight into their abilities? A metasynthesis'. *Perspectives on Psychological Science*, 9, 111–25.
5  Pronin, E., Lin, D. Y., & Ross, L. (2002). 'The bias blind spot: Perceptions of bias in self versus others'. *Personality and Social Psychology Bulletin*, 28, 369–81.
6  Colvin, C. R., Block, J., & Funder, D. C. (1995). 'Overly positive self-evaluations and personality: Negative implications for mental health'. *Journal of Personality and Social Psychology*, 68, 1152–62.
7  Baumeister, R. F., Campbell, J. D., Krueger, J. I., & Vohs, K. D. (2003). 'Does high self-esteem cause better performance, interpersonal success, happiness, or healthier lifestyles?' *Psychological Science in the Public Interest*, 4, 1–44.

8  Poropat, A. E. (2009). 'A meta-analysis of the five-factor model of personality and academic performance'. *Psychological Bulletin*, *135*, 322–38.

9  Connelly, B. S., & Ones, D. S. (2010). 'An other perspective on personality: Meta-analytic integration of observers' accuracy and predictive validity'. *Psychological Bulletin*, *136*, 1092–122.

10  Jeffries, C. H., & Hornsey, M. J. (2012). 'Withholding negative feedback: Is it about protecting the self or protecting others?' *British Journal of Social Psychology*, *51*, 772–80.

11  Nissen-Lie, H. A., Rønnestad, M. H., Høglend, P. A., Havik, O. E., Solbakken, O. A., Stiles, T. C., & Monsen, J. T. (2015). 'Love yourself as a person, doubt yourself as a therapist?' *Clinical Psychology and Psychotherapy*, *22*, 317–27.

## Chapter 2

1  Judge, T. A., Erez, A., Bono, J. E., & Thoresen, C. J. (2003). 'The core self-evaluations scale: Development of a measure'. *Personnel Psychology*, *56*, 303–31.

2  Judge, T. A. (2009). 'Core self-evaluations and work success'. *Current Directions in Psychological Science*, *18*, 58–62.

3  Baker, S. L., Heinrichs, N., Kim, H.-J., & Hofmann, S. G. (2002). 'The Liebowitz social anxiety scale as a self-report instrument: A preliminary psychometric analysis'. *Behaviour Research and Therapy*, *40*, 701–15.

## Chapter 3

1  Holmes, T. H., & Rahe, R. H. (1967). 'The social readjustment rating scale'. *Journal of Psychosomatic Research*, *11*, 213–18.

2  Rahe, R. H., Mahan, J. L., & Arthur, R. J. (1970). 'Prediction of near-future health change from subjects' preceding life changes'. *Journal of Psychosomatic Research*, *14*, 401–6.

3  Rahe, R. H., & Arthur, R. J. (1978). 'Life change and illness studies: Past history and future directions'. *Journal of Human Stress*, *4*, 3–15.

4  Jamieson, J. P., Nock, M. K., & Mendes, W. B. (2012). 'Mind over matter: Reappraising arousal improves cardiovascular and cognitive responses to stress'. *Journal of Experimental Psychology: General*, *141*, 417–22.

5  Jamieson, J. P., Mendes, W. B., Blackstock, E., & Schmader, T. (2010). 'Turning the knots in your stomachs into bows: Reappraising arousal improves performance on the GRE'. *Journal of Experimental Social Psychology*, *46*, 208–12.

6  Troy, A. S., Wilhelm, F. H., Shallcross, A. J., & Mauss, I. B. (2010). 'Seeing the silver lining: Cognitive reappraisal moderates the relationship between stress and depressive symptoms'. *Emotion*, *10*, 783–95.

7  Drabant, E. M., McRae, K., Manuck, S. B., Hariri, A. R., and Gross, J. J., (2009). 'Individual differences in typical reappraisal use predict amygdala and prefrontal responses'. *Biological Psychiatry*, *65*, 367–73.

8  For a review on the topic of post-traumatic growth, see: Zoellner, T., & Maercker, A. (2006). 'Posttraumatic growth in clinical psychology: A critical review and introduction of a two component model'. *Clinical Psychology Review*, *26*, 626–53.

9  Lim, D., & DeSteno, D. (2016). 'Suffering and compassion: The links among adverse life experiences, empathy, compassion, and prosocial behavior'. *Emotion*, *16*, 175–82.

10  Luong, G., Wrzus, C., Wagner, G. G., & Riediger, M. (2015). 'When bad moods may not be so bad: Valuing negative affect is associated with weakened affect-health links'. *Emotion*, *16*, 387–401.

11  Burklund, L. J., Creswell, J. D., Irwin, M. R., & Lieberman, M. D. (2014). 'The common and distinct neural bases of affect labeling and reappraisal in healthy adults'. *Frontiers in Psychology*, *5*, 1–10.

## Chapter 4

1 Davis, J. I., Gross, J. J., & Oschsner, K. N. (2011). 'Psychological distance and emotional experience: What you see is what you get'. *Emotion, 11*, 438–44.

2 Knudstrup, M., Segrest, S. L., & Hurley, A. E. (2003). 'The use of mental imagery in the simulated employment interview situation'. *Journal of Managerial Psychology, 18*, 573–91.

3 Landers, D. M. (1983). 'The effects of mental practice on motor skill learning and performance: A meta-analysis'. *Journal of Sport Psychology, 5*, 25–57.

4 Yao, W., Ranganathan, V., Allexandre, D., Siemionow, V., & Yue, G. H. (2013). 'Kinesthetic imagery training of forceful muscle contractions increases brain signal and muscle strength'. *Frontiers in Human Neuroscience, 7*, 561.

5 Hunt, M., Bylsma, L., Brock, J., Fenton, M., Goldberg, A., Miller, R., Tran, T., & Urgelles, J. (2006). 'The role of imagery in the maintenance and treatment of snake fear'. *Journal of Behaviour Therapy and Experimental Psychiatry, 37*, 283–98.

6 Hunt, M., & Fenton, M. (2007). 'Imagery rescripting versus *in vivo* exposure in the treatment of snake fear'. *Journal of Behavior Therapy and Experimental Psychiatry, 38*, 329–44.

## Chapter 5

1 Titchener, E. B. (1916). *A Textbook of Psychology*. New York: MacMillan.

2 Masuda, A., Hayes, S. C., Sackett, C. F., & Twohig, M. P. (2004). 'Cognitive defusion and self-relevant negative thoughts: Examining the impact of a ninety-year-old technique'. *Behaviour Research and Therapy, 42*, 477–85.

3 Masuda, A., Hayes, S. C., Twohig, M. P., Drossel, C., Lillis, J., & Washio, Y. (2009). 'A parametric study of cognitive defusion and the believability and discomfort of negative self-relevant thoughts'. *Behavior Modification, 33*, 250–62.

4  Healy, H. A., Barnes-Holmes, Y., Barnes-Holmes, D., Keogh, C., Luciano, C., & Wilson, K. (2008). 'An experimental test of a cognitive defusion exercise: Coping with negative and positive self-statements'. *The Psychological Record*, *58*, 623–40.

5  Hooper, N., & McHugh, L. (2013). 'Cognitive defusion versus thought distraction in the mitigation of learned helplessness'. *The Psychological Record*, *63*, 1–10.

6  Trapnell, P., & Campbell, J. (1999). 'Private self-consciousness and the five-factor model of personality: Distinguishing rumination from reflection'. *Journal of Personality and Social Psychology*, *76*, 284–304.

7  Lyubomirsky, S., Layous, K., Chancellor, J., & Nelson, S. K. (2015). 'Thinking about rumination: The scholarly contributions and intellectual legacy of Susan Nolen-Hoeksema'. *Annual Review of Clinical Psychology*, *11*, 1–22.

8  Siegle, G. J., Moore, P. M., & Thase, M. E. (2004). 'Rumination: One construct, many features in healthy individuals, depressed individuals, and individuals with lupus'. *Cognitive Therapy and Research*, *28*, 645–68.

9  Yeung, R. R., & Hemsley, D. R. (1996). 'Effects of personality and acute exercise on mood states'. *Personality and Individual Differences*, *20*, 545–50.

10  Ekkekakis, P., Hall, E. E., VanLanduyt, L. M., & Petruzzello, S. J. (2000). 'Walking in (affective) circles: Can short walks enhance affect?' *Journal of Behavioral Medicine*, *23*, 245–75.

11  Lathia, N., Sandstrom, G. M., Mascolo, C., & Rentfrow, P. J. (2017). 'Happier people live more active lives: Using smartphones to link happiness and physical activity'. *PLoS ONE*, *12*, e0160589.

12  For an in-depth scientific discussion of why physical exercise may boost mood, see this review article: Yeung, R. R. (1996). 'The acute effects of exercise on mood state'. *Journal of Psychosomatic Research*, *40*, 123–41

13  Wegner, D. M., Schneider, D. J., Carter, S. R., & White, T. L. (1987). 'Paradoxical effects of thought suppression'. *Journal of Personality and Social Psychology*, *53*, 5–13.

14 Wenzlaff, R. M., & Bates, D. E. (1998). 'Unmasking a cognitive vulnerability to depression: How lapses in mental control reveal depressive thinking'. *Journal of Personality and Social Psychology*, *75*, 1559–71.

15 Butler, E. A., Egloff, B., Wilhelm, F. H., Smith, N. C., Erickson, E. A., & Gross, J. J. (2003). 'The social consequences of expressive suppression'. *Emotion*, *3*, 48–67.

16 For an example, see: Hofmann, S. G., Heering, S., Sawyer, A. T., & Asnaani, A. (2009). 'How to handle anxiety: The effects of reappraisal, acceptance, and suppression strategies on anxious arousal'. *Behaviour and Research Therapy*, *47*, 389–94.

# Chapter 6

1 Kilduff, G. J., & Galinsky, A. D. (2013). 'From the ephemeral to the enduring: How approach-oriented mindsets lead to greater status'. *Journal of Personality and Social Psychology*, *105*, 816–31.

2 Curtis, R. C., & Miller, K. (1986). 'Believing another likes or dislikes you: Behaviors making the beliefs come true'. *Journal of Personality and Social Psychology*, *51*, 284–90.

3 Beckmann, J., Gröpel, P., & Ehrlenspiel, F. (2013). 'Preventing motor skill failure through hemisphere-specific priming: Cases from choking under pressure'. *Journal of Experimental Psychology: General*, *142*, 679–91.

# Chapter 7

1 Cole, S. W., Hawkley, L. C., Arevalo, J. M., Sung, C. Y., Rose, R. M., & Cacioppo, J. T. (2007). 'Social regulation of gene expression in human leukocytes'. *Genome Biology*, *8*, R189.

2 Tamir, D. I., & Mitchell, J. P. (2012). 'Disclosing information about the self is intrinsically rewarding'. *Proceedings of the National Academy of Sciences of the United States of America*, *109*, 8038–43.

3 If you're interested in the business school research on networking and career success (as well as further advice on effective networking), you could take a look at my book: Yeung, R. (2014). *How to Win: The Argument, the Pitch, the Job, the Race*. Chichester: Capstone.

4 Sprecher, S., Treger, S., Wondra, J. D., Hilaire, N., & Wallpe, K. (2013). 'Taking turns: Reciprocal self-disclosure promotes liking in initial interactions'. *Journal of Experimental Social Psychology*, *49*, 860–66.

5 Woolley, K., & Fishbach, A. (2016). 'A recipe for friendship: Similar food consumption promotes liking and cooperation'. *Journal of Consumer Psychology*, *27*, 1–10.

6 Martin, A., Jacob, C., & Guéguen, N. (2013). 'Similarity facilitates relationships on social networks: A field experiment on Facebook'. *Psychological Reports: Relationships & Communications*, *113*, 217–20.

7 Tice, D. M., Butler, J. L., Muraven, M. B., & Stillwell, A. M. (1995). When modesty prevails: Differential favorability of self-presentation to friends and strangers. *Journal of Personality and Social Psychology*, *69*, 1120–38.

8 Crawford, M. T., Skowronski, J. J., & Stiff, C. (2007). 'Limiting the spread of spontaneous trait transference'. *Journal of Experimental Social Psychology*, *43*, 466–72.

9 Gawronski, B., & Walther, E. (2008). 'The TAR effect: When the ones who dislike become the ones who are disliked'. *Personality and Social Psychology Bulletin*, *34*, 1276–89.

10 Guéguen, N. (2009). 'Mimicry and seduction: An evaluation in a courtship context'. *Social Influence*, *4*, 249–55.

11 For a comprehensive review of the benefits of mimicry in other situations, see: Chartrand, T. L., & Lakin, J. L. (2013). 'The antecedents and consequences of human behavioral mimicry'. *Annual Review of Psychology*, *64*, 285–308.

12 Lakin, J. L., Jefferis, V. E., Cheng, C. M., & Chartrand, T. L. (2003). 'The chameleon effect as social glue: Evidence for the evolutionary significance of nonconscious mimicry'. *Journal of Nonverbal Behavior*, *27*, 145–62.

## Chapter 8

1 Vacharkulksemsuk, T., Reit, E., Khambatta, P., Eastwick, P. W., Finkel, E. J., & Carney, D. R. (2016). 'Dominant, open nonverbal displays are attractive at zero-acquaintance'. *Proceedings of the National Academy of Sciences*, *113*, 4009–13.

2 Kennedy, D. P., Gläscher, J., Tyszka, J. M., & Adolphs, R. (2009). 'Personal space regulation by the human amygdala'. *Nature Neuroscience*, *12*, 1226–7.

3 McGinley, H., Blau, G. L., & Takai, M. (1984). 'Attraction effects of smiling and body position: A cultural comparison'. *Perceptual and Motor Skills*, *58*, 915–22.

4 Carney, D. R., Cuddy, A. J. C., & Yapp, A. J. (2010). 'Power posing: Brief nonverbal displays affect neuroendocrine levels and risk tolerance'. *Psychological Science*, *21*, 1363–8.

5 Ranehill, E., Dreber, A., Johannesson, M., Leiberg, S., Sul, S., & Weber, R. A. (2015). 'Assessing the robustness of power posing: No effect on hormones and risk tolerance in a large sample of men and women'. *Psychological Science*, doi:10.1177/0956797614553946

6 Smith, K. M., & Apicella, C. L. (2017). 'Winners, losers, and posers: The effect of power poses on testosterone and risk-taking following competition'. *Hormones and Behavior*, *92*, 172–81.

7 Richmond, V. P., McCroskey, J. C., & Johnson, A. D. (2003). 'Development of the nonverbal immediacy scale (NIS): Measures of self-and other-perceived nonverbal immediacy'. *Communication Quarterly*, *51*, 504–17.

8 Houser, M. L., Horan, S. M., & Furler, L. A. (2008). 'Dating in the fast lane: How communication predicts speed-dating success'. *Journal of Social and Personal Relationships*, *25*, 749–68.

9 Stokoe, E. (2010). '"Have you been married, or…?": Eliciting and accounting for relationship histories in speed-dating interaction'. *Research on Language and Social Interaction*, *43*, 260–82.

10  Murray, S. L., Holmes, J. G., Griffin, D. W., Bellavia, G., & Rose, P. (2001). 'The mismeasure of love: How self-doubt contaminates relationship beliefs'. *Personality and Social Psychology Bulletin*, *27*, 423–36.

11  Marigold, D. C., Holmes, J. G., & Ross, M. (2007). 'More than words: Reframing compliments from romantic partners fosters security in low self-esteem individuals'. *Journal of Personality and Social Psychology*, *92*, 232–48.

12  Marigold, D. C., Holmes, J. G., & Ross, M. (2010). 'Fostering relationship resilience: An intervention for low self-esteem individuals'. *Journal of Experimental Social Psychology*, *46*, 624–30.

13  Smith, L., Heaven, P. C. L., & Ciarrochi, J. (2008). 'Trait emotional intelligence, conflict communication patterns, and relationship satisfaction'. *Personality and Individual Differences*, *44*, 1314–25.

14  The questions are based on the Communication Patterns Questionnaire-Short Form. See: Futris, T. G., Campbell, K., Nielsen, R. B., & Burwell, S. R. (2010). 'The Communication Patterns Questionnaire-Short Form: A review and assessment'. *The Family Journal*, *18*, 275–87.

## Chapter 9

1  Oettingen, G., Mayer, D., & Portnow, S. (2016). 'Pleasure now, pain later: Positive fantasies about the future predict symptoms of depression'. *Psychological Science*, *27*, 345–53.

2  For just one example of the evidence supporting exposure treatment for social phobia, see: Feske, U., & Chambless, D. L. (1995). 'Cognitive behavioral versus exposure only treatment for social phobia: A meta-analysis'. *Behavior Therapy*, *26*, 695–720.

3  Bandura, A., Reese, L., & Adams, N. E. (1982). 'Microanalysis of action and fear arousal as a function of differential levels of perceived self-efficacy'. *Journal of Personality and Social Psychology*, *43*, 5–21.

## Chapter 10

1 For a review on the topic of threat sensitivity, see: Perkins, A. M., Arnone, D., Smallwood, J., & Mobbs, D. (2015). 'Thinking too much: Self-generated thought as the engine of neuroticism'. *Trends in Cognitive Sciences*, *19*, 492–8.

2 Brown, K. W., & Ryan, R. M. (2003). 'The benefits of being present: Mindfulness and its role in psychological well-being'. *Journal of Personality and Social Psychology*, *84*, 822–48.

3 For a review of the relationships between mindfulness and physical health indicators, see: Loucks, E. B., Schuman-Olivier, Z., Britton, W. B., Fresco, D. M., Desbordes, G., Brewer, J. A., & Fulwiler, C. (2015). 'Mindfulness and cardiovascular disease risk: Status of the evidence, plausible mechanisms, and theoretical framework'. *Current Cardiology Reports*, *17*, 112.

4 Mrazek, M. D., Smallwood, J., & Schooler, J. W. (2012). 'Mindfulness and mind-wandering: Finding convergence through opposing constructs'. *Emotion*, *12*, 442-8.

5 For a further example, see: Gorman, T. E., & Green, C. S. (2016). 'Short-term mindfulness intervention reduces the negative attentional effects associated with heavy media multitasking'. *Scientific Reports*, *6*, 24542.

6 Farb, N. A. S., Anderson, A. K., Mayberg, H., Bean, J., McKeon, D., & Segal, Z. V. (2010). 'Minding one's emotions: Mindfulness training alters the neural expression of sadness'. *Emotion*, *10*, 25–33.

7 Hölzel, B. K., Carmody, J., Vangel, M., Congleton, C., Yerramsetti, S. M., Gard, T., & Lazar, S. W. (2011). 'Mindfulness practice leads to increases in regional brain gray matter density'. *Psychiatry Research*, *191*, 36–43.

8 Mrazek, M. D., Franklin, M. S., Phillips, D. T., Baird, B., & Schooler, J. W. (2013). 'Mindfulness training improves working memory capacity and GRE performance while reducing mind wandering'. *Psychological Science*, *24*, 776–81.

9   Hanley, A. W., Warner, A. R., Dehili, V. M., Canto, A. I., & Garland, E. L. (2015). 'Washing dishes to wash the dishes: Brief instruction in an informal mindfulness practice'. *Mindfulness*, *6*, 1095–103.

10  For a further review of the link between mindfulness and psychological well-being, see: Brown, K. W., & Ryan, R. M. (2003). 'The benefits of being present: Mindfulness and its role in psychological well-being'. *Journal of Personality and Social Psychology*, *84*, 822–48.

11  For another example study looking at how mindfulness training reduced rumination, see: Chambers, R., Lo, B. C. Y., & Allen, N. B. (2007). 'The impact of intensive mindfulness training on attentional control, cognitive style, and affect'. *Cognitive Therapy and Research*, *32*, 303–22.

12  Gollwitzer, P. M. (1999). 'Implementation intentions: Strong effects of simple plans'. *American Psychologist*, *54*, 493–503.

13  Sahdra, B. K., Shaver, P. R., & Brown, K. W. (2010). 'A scale to measure nonattachment: A Buddhist complement to Western research on attachment and adaptive functioning'. *Journal of Personality Assessment*, *92*, 116–27.

## Chapter 11

1   Henrich, G., & Herschbach, P. (2000). 'Questions on life satisfaction (FLZ$^M$): A short questionnaire for assessing subjective quality of life'. *European Journal of Psychological Assessment*, *16*, 155–9.

2   Lepore, S. J. (1997). 'Expressive writing moderates the relation between intrusive thoughts and depressive symptoms'. *Journal of Personality and Social Psychology*, *73*, 1030–37

3   If you're interested in the reasons why old-fashioned brainstorming does not work, see Chapter 1 of a book that I wrote: Yeung, R. (2012). *E is for Exceptional: The new science of success*. London: Pan Books.

4  Watkins, E., & Baracaia, S. (2002). 'Rumination and social problem-solving in depression'. *Behaviour Research and Therapy*, *40*, 1179–89.

5  Kross, E., & Grossmann, I. (2012). 'Boosting wisdom: Distance from the self enhances wise reasoning, attitudes, and behavior'. *Journal of Experimental Psychology: General*, *141*, 43–8.

6  Kluger, A. N., & DeNisi, A. (1996). 'The effects of feedback interventions on performance: A historical review, a meta-analysis, and a preliminary feedback intervention theory'. *Psychological Bulletin*, *119*, 254–84.

7  Schwartz, R. M., & Gottman, J. M. (1976). 'Toward a task analysis of assertive behavior'. *Journal of Consulting and Clinical Psychology*, *44*, 910–20.

8  Gilovich, T., Medvec, V. H., & Kahneman, D. (1998). 'Varieties of regret: A debate and partial resolution'. *Psychological Review*, *105*, 602–5.

## Chapter 12

1  Creswell, J. D., Welch, W. T., Taylor, S. E., Sherman, D. K., Gruenewald, T. L., & Mann, T. (2005). 'Affirmation of personal values buffers neuroendocrine and psychological stress responses'. *Psychological Science*, *16*, 846–51.

2  For just one example of a study showing the benefits of focusing on your values for problem-solving, see: Creswell, J. D., Dutcher, J. M., Klein, W. M. P., Harris, P. R., & Levine, J. M. (2012). 'Self-affirmation improves problem-solving under stress'. *PLoS ONE*, *8*, e62593.

3  Cohen, G. L., Garcia, J., Purdie-Vaughs, V., Apfel, N., & Brzustoski, P. (2009). 'Recursive processes in self-affirmation: Intervening to close the minority achievement gap'. *Science*, *324*, 400–403.

4  Gortner, E. T., Gollan, J. K., Dobson, K. S., & Jacobson, N. S. (1998). 'Cognitive-behavioral treatment for depression: Relapse prevention'. *Journal of Consulting and Clinical Psychology*, *66*, 377–84.

5  Dimidjian, S., Hollon, S. D., Dobson, K. S., Schmaling, K. B., Kohlenberg, R. J., Addis, M. E., …, Jacobson, N. S. (2006). 'Randomized trial of behavioural activation, cognitive therapy, and antidepressant medication in the acute treatment of adults with major depression'. *Journal of Consulting and Clinical Psychology*, *74*, 658–70.

6  For a primer on the psychological needs that help most people to feel inspired, curious and self-motivated, see: Ryan, R. M., & Deci, E. L. (2000). 'Self-determination theory and the facilitation of intrinsic motivation, social development, and well-being'. *American Psychologist*, *55*, 68–78.

7  Jacobson, N. S., Martell, C. R., & Dimidjian, S. (2001). 'Behavioral activation treatment for depression: Returning to contextual roots'. *Clinical Psychology Science and Practice*, *8*, 255–70.

8  Lally, P., van Jaarsveld, C. H. M., Potts, H. W. W., & Wardle, J. (2010). 'How are habits formed: Modelling habit formation in the real world'. *European Journal of Social Psychology*, *40*, 998–1009.

9  Dichter, G. S., Felder, J. N., Petty, C., Bizzell, J., Ernst, M., & Smoski, M. J. (2009). 'The effects of psychotherapy on neural responses to rewards in major depression'. *Biological Psychiatry*, *66*, 886–97.

10  Richards, D. A., Ekers, D., McMillan, D., Taylor, R. S., Byford, S., Warren, F. C., …, Finning, K. (2016). 'Cost and outcome of behavioural activation versus cognitive behavioural therapy for depression (COBRA): A randomised, controlled, non-inferiority trial'. *The Lancet*, *388*, 871–80.

## Conclusion

1  Winning, A. P., & Boag, S. (2015). 'Does brief mindfulness training increase empathy? The role of personality'. *Personality and Individual Differences*, *86*, 492–8.

# Index